ADVANCED FRACTAL
PROGRAMMING IN C

MW01012489

ADVANCED FRACTAL
PROGRAMMING IN C

Roger T. Stevens

 M&T Books
A Division of M&T Publishing, Inc.
501 Galveston Drive
Redwood City, CA 94063

Limits of Liability and Disclaimer of Warranty
The Author and Publisher of this book have used their best efforts in preparing the book and the programs contained in it. These efforts include the development, research, and testing of the theories and programs to determine their effectiveness.

The Author and Publisher make no warranty of any kind, expressed or implied, with regard to these programs or the documentation contained in this book. The Author and Publisher shall not be liable in any event for incidental or consequential damages in connection with, or arising out of, the furnishing, performance, or use of these programs.

Library of Congress Cataloging-in-Publication Data

Stevens, Roger, T., 1927-
    Advanced Fractal Programming in C/ Roger T. Stevens
       p.   cm.
    Includes index.
    ISBN 1-55851-097-4
    1. Fractals--Computer programs. 2. C (Computer program language)
I. Title.
QA614.86.S73   1990
514'.74--dc20   90-24306
                                         CIP

Trademarks:

All products, names, and services are trademarks or registered trademarks of their respective companies.

Cover Design: Lauren Smith Design

93 92 91 90   4 3 2 1

Contents

CHAPTER 4: THE MANDELBROT SET REVISITED

CHAPTER 5: THE CORE PROGRAM

CHAPTER 6: USING THE DISTANCE METHOD WITH THE MANDELBROT SET

CHAPTER 7: TRANSCENDENTAL FUNCTIONS

CHAPTER 8: ORTHOGONAL POLYNOMIALS

CHAPTER 9: SOME BARNSLEY FRACTALS

CHAPTER 13: ITERATED FUNCTION SYSTEMS

APPENDIX A: FORMAT FOR .PCX FILES

INDEX

Acknowledgments

All of the software in this book was written using Turbo C++ furnished by Borland International, 4835 Scotts Valley Drive, Scotts Valley, CA 95066.

Valuable technical information on the format of .PCX files and a copy of PC Paintbrush were supplied by Shannon of Z-Soft Corporation, 1950 Spectrum Circle, Marietta, GA 30067.

Software was developed and tested on computers using a Vega VGA card and a Vega VGA 1024i card both furnished by Headland Technology Inc., 46221 Landing Parkway, Fremont, CA 94538. Color pictures were viewed on a NEC Multisync Plus ColorMonitor furnished by NEC Home Electronics (U. S. A.) Inc.

I am indebted to Christopher D. Watkins for valuable insights into Z-buffer ray-tracing software techniques.

Why This Book Is For You

Readers who enjoyed producing fractal pictures with the programs included in *Fractal Programming in C* will be excited by the new fractals and detailed programs for fractal investigation contained in this book.

The book begins with a comprehensive program to generate pictures using the generic equation from which Mandelbrot and Julia sets and dragon curves are derived. You will be able to generate any of these curves and specify different color combinations which reveal the inherent beauty and mathematical characteristics of the curves, or set the coefficients of the equation to produce completely new curves that no one has ever seen before.

If you have a VGA, you will find programs to generate plasma clouds, as well as techniques for causing the colors of the display to vary continuously. Programs are included which allow you to generate exciting fractals using the 256 color display mode.

The book includes programs to create displays from the Newton method of solving an equation, allowing you to enter the coefficients for any equation up to the tenth order. Fractals using sine, cosine, hyperbolic sine, hyperbolic cosine, and natural logarithyms are also described.

There is a section of the book which describes a simple method to produce three dimensional effects such as 3-D mountains and Mandelbrot sets. Examples of new strange attractors are also included. Also included are 32 full color illustrations of fractals as well as numerous black and white illustrations.

All of the source code to generate the pictures in the book is available on disk in MS-DOS format. The programs require an IBM PC or compatible and a Turbo C, Quick C, or Microsoft C compiler. Some of the programs will run using an EGA card and color monitor; others require a VGA card and color monitor.

CHAPTER 1

Introduction

The first book in this series, *Fractal Programming in C*, provided an introduction to many different kinds of fractals and the C programs that generate them. Less than two years have passed since that book was published. In that time, developments in the field of fractals have exploded. The connections between fractals and the shapes and forms of natural objects have been further investigated (in particular, a beautiful book by Przemyslaw Prusinkiewicz called *The Algorithmic Beauty of Plants*), and dramatic developments have occurred in the use of fractals for image data compression. One thing hasn't changed, however. The person who wants to experiment with the newest developments in fractals will find many lovely pictures and equations in the literature, but few practical programs to run with minimum effort. This book corrects that situation by giving you many new tools and programs for working with fractals. However, since this an advanced book, you need some grounding in fractals and C programming to effectively use it. Furthermore, color is an important consideration if you investigate fractals, and it is assumed that you have an EGA or VGA graphics card and a color monitor. You just can't do justice to many fractal pictures with a monochrome monitor. A few black and white fractals are in this book, but they are the minority.

Hardware Considerations

I highly recommend that you get a VGA board and matching color monitor if you want to look at fractal displays. These boards are no longer prohibitively expensive; in fact a VGA display now costs just a little more than an EGA display. If you ever contemplate doing any ray tracing or other technique for producing highly realistic pictures, you need the VGA as a minimum. Many of the newer VGA boards have higher resolution modes than originally contemplated by IBM. Unfortunately, communicating to these high resolution modes seems to be different for each

3

manufacturer. I haven't included anything about higher resolution modes, but you will find them not too difficult to use. The plasma and color cycling effects described in Chapter 10 require a VGA system. Most of the other color fractal displays can be run with an EGA, but if you plan to modify the programs, you will find you can produce more exciting color effects with a VGA.

The other thing you'll find useful is a math coprocessor. Although a single integrated circuit chip is expensive, the increase in processing speed is dramatic and makes the price worthwhile. However, one of my computers is without the math coprocessor so I can make sure that all of the programs in this book will run on your machine in a reasonable amount of time even if it doesn't have a math coprocessor.

Using C++

If you have the opportunity to upgrade your present C compiler to include C++, you should definitely take advantage of it. The added capabilities of C++ are extraordinary, and you can use C++ immediately, expanding your knowledge at your own pace. In particular, all of the curves that are similar to the Mandelbrot and Julia sets involve the iteration of equations in complex numbers. Zortech's C++ version 2.1 and Turbo C++ both make use of the C++ capabilities to define complex numbers. Perhaps by the time you buy this book, Microsoft will have released a new version of C that includes C++ capabilities and complex numbers. The complex number operations include all of the mathematical operations, such as addition, subtraction, multiplication, division, and the transcendental functions. In the following chapters, we will primarily rely on complex numbers to perform our operations. However, you will be given some clues that make it possible to modify the programs for ordinary C. Although the programs are written using Turbo C++, some of the window and coloring commands used to produce a user friendly interface are different in Microsoft C version 6.0 and Zortech C++ version 2.1. These differences will be described so you can modify the programs accordingly. Chapter 2 describes the differences in C compilers in further detail and gives you the necessary clues to make the programs work with your own compiler. In addition, if you buy the disk, you will find compiled versions of all programs for immediate use, as well as source code, in case you want to modify it.

4

Complexity

As befits an advanced fractal book, the programs described in this book are a lot more complex than those in *Fractal Programming in C*. Unless you are very good at typing in a lot of code without errors, you would be well advised to buy the companion disk. This enables you to start with error-free code, but doesn't guarantee that you will not encounter problems in working out how to compile and run programs with your particular combination of compiler, system software, and hardware. On the other hand, typing in an entire program, although frustrating, is a very good way to understand how the program works and gain insight in how other people are using C and C++ to confront the programming problems facing them. I've tried to clarify what is being done at each stage in a program without getting down to a detailed explanation of each line of code. If you don't understand a particular operation, the source listing is there, and a little study plus reference to your C manuals can usually illuminate what is going on.

Useful Functions for Fractals

Chapter 3 describes some useful functions used repeatedly in the fractal programs throughout this book; a number of these are graphics programs. For example, there are programs to set the graphic mode, to change the palette colors and color registers, and to plot points and draw lines to the display in one or more graphics modes. Since there is no standardization of graphics terms in C from one compiler to another, creating a customized set of graphics tools makes the programs portable to different compilers. Also, some compilers, for some reason, seem to not include some of the graphics modes that we want to use. Another set of programs and functions in this chapter is involved with saving the generated displays to disk files and then restoring them to the screen. I've used the ZSoft (PC Paintbrush) .PCX file format to store color images, but the format is a little different because we need to store a lot of parameters particular to the fractal display. ZSoft encountered this problem when the 256 color graphic mode was introduced. They didn't have room in the header to store information on the 256 colors, so to maintain compatibility, they placed this information at the end of the file. Their method of determining whether this information was there was simply to count back the proper number of bytes and check for a unique character. If this character was in the proper position, the file was assumed to contain the additional color data. I've used this same method; since the quantity of data that I put at the end of the file is different from what ZSoft uses for the additional color data, the unique character is at a different location from the end of the file, so there is no danger of confusing the two formats.

In addition to functions for saving a display to a file and reading it back to the screen, there is a program to display a file and then print its code (this is handy when you have a beautiful picture but have forgotten what code you used to generate it), and a program to change the colors of an image if you aren't satisfied with the original.

The Mandelbrot Set Revisited

Chapter 4 looks into the Mandelbrot and Julia sets and the dragon curves in more detail than in *Fractal Programming in C*. First, with Mandelbrot and Julia sets and the dragon curves, one generic equation can be used to draw pictures of any of them. With this generic equation we can create many more interesting sets by modifying its parameters. We also look in some detail at several methods of assigning colors to the pixels that make up a display and see how dramatic differences in the display can result from different color assignment techniques. In addition, we will observe the important distortions in displays caused by changing the starting parameters of the iterated equation, and investigate the differences between Julia and Mandelbrot sets at high magnifications. All of these techniques are based upon a sophisticated Mandelbrot set program, which permits the user to customize a set through menu selections.

The Core Program

While the Mandelbrot set program described in Chapter 4 offers flexibility in specifying and generating different kinds of sets, there are cases in which we would like a simplified interface into which we can place a function designed to produce a specialized fractal display. Chapter 5 describes such a program and shows how it works with a simple Mandelbrot set-generating function. The same program is then used throughout the next few chapters to generate specialized sets and curves.

The Distance Method for Mandelbrot Sets

The method used to create Mandelbrot sets iterates the equation at every point on the display to determine pixel color. An alternate technique, that can be faster, is to make use of a distance estimate of how far a particular point is from the boundary of the Mandelbrot curve. In this way a number of points can be plotted after a single set of computations. Then a new distance estimate is computed and a new set of points plotted. The speed differential is not as important as the fact that it is possible to obtain the normal of the Mandelbrot set at every point using this technique. This is important information if we are going to illuminate three dimensional Mandelbrot sets.

Transcendental Functions

Transcendental functions, such as sine, cosine, tangent, and their equivalent hyperbolic functions, are represented as polynomials in a Taylor or Maclaurin series. If one truncates some of these series to the first couple of terms, they begin to look like the iterated equation of a Mandelbrot set. This suggests that the transcendental functions are good candidates for iterated equations investigated in Chapter 7. Programs are given to produce fractals and a number of color pictures.

Polynomials for Fractals

The generic iterated equation for Mandelbrot and Julia sets and dragon curves is a simple polynomial. One might think that a complicated polynomial will produce an unusual curve. Unfortunately, most of the polynomials that you create by assigning numbers to coefficients of various powers of a complex number do not give interesting fractal displays. In fact, in many cases, they produce nothing but a blank screen. So the problem of finding desirable polynomials to produce interesting displays is more complicated than it might at first appear. Fortunately, a number of well established polynomials found to be associated with the solution of differential equations, produce interesting fractals when iterated. These include the Tchebychev, the Legendre, Laguerre, and Hermite polynomials described in Chapter 8, together with the programs for generating these curves and tables of the coefficients. A number of color pictures generated from these functions are in the color section.

Some Barnsley Fractals

Chapter 9 describes fractals using special, iterated equations first discovered by Michael Barnsley. If you bought the accompanying disk, software for generating these pictures is provided.

Plasmas and Color Cycling

Plasmas are color displays produced by starting with randomly colored points at the four corners of the screen. The distance between each pair of points is divided by two. The resulting point is colored according to the colors of the two endpoints together with some rules on shading and an amount of random perturbation. The result is a captivating cloud-like image. A program for generating such displays is described in Chapter 10. Once a plasma display has been created, cycling the 256 VGA color register produces a constantly changing, hypnotic display. This program is also described in Chapter 10.

Three Dimensional Techniques

Chapter 11 describes simplified three-dimensional projection and coloring techniques for plasma display, Mandelbrot set or any other fractals. Two programs are included. The first renders a file of height data with a simplified z-buffer ray-tracing technique. The second processes the rendered data to produce a color display such as a realistic mountain scene.

The L-Systems Technique for Generating Fractals

The L-systems technique is a synthetic language appropriate to the specification and drawing of fractal curves such as the von Koch snowflake, the Hilbert curve, the Peano curve, etc. As with most languages, dialects may vary, and there is an interesting problem with the L-system definition exceeding the bounds of memory. Chapter 12 describes L-systems, the constraints to permit a recursion method with any size string definition, gives a program for L-systems, and provides tables of the parameters needed for generating various curves and pictures of the curves. The L-systems technique can also be used to draw trees and flowers. The additions to the L-Systems language needed for this, together with some sample sets of parameters and the resulting pictures are also given in Chapter 12.

8

Iterated Function Systems and their Encoding

Iterated function systems provide a technique for drawing a complex picture from only a few bytes of data. In *Fractal Programming in C*, an IFS program with some parameters yielded a fern leaf and a Sierpinski triangle. The IFS technique works by applying affine transformations (rotation, translation, and scaling) to a point and then plotting the point. Another of the set of transformations is then selected (randomly in accordance with a set of specified probabilities) and the latest point transformed accordingly and plotted. When a sufficient number of points have been plotted, the figure defined by the transformation data appears. When one wants to produce a display that represents an object, it is often not easy to determine what parameters are needed to define the IFS system. In fact, some objects are very difficult to duplicate with an IFS.

Recurrent, iterated function systems differ from ordinary iterated function systems in that the probabilities of any of the set of transformations occurring is dependent upon the transformation itself. This technique provides a rich variety of shapes and makes it possible to produce shapes that are difficult or impossible with ordinary iterated function systems. A program to reproduce such shapes, and typical result, is given in Chapter 13.

Onward and Upward

If you've been having fun generating fractals with *Fractal Programming in C*, or any of the numerous fractal programs that are commercially available or in the public domain, then here is new information that reflects the more recent work in fractals. Unlike many programs that let you create fractals without a basis of understanding, this book includes explanations and source code. There are no secrets. Try your luck at generating new fractals with the existing programs, or modify the software and create something completely new and exciting. Good luck!

CHAPTER 2

Painlessly Moving to C++

Chapters 6 through 9 are concerned with iterated equations that create fractal displays in the complex plane. To perform the necessary computations, it is necessary to manipulate complex numbers. It is possible to decompose the complex numbers into their real and imaginary parts, or special functions can be created to handle various mathematical and trigonometric operations on complex numbers. However, these are somewhat complex operations that could be simply handled if the C language accommodated complex numbers.

Fortunately, Turbo C++ and Zortech C++ version 2.1 include an implementation of all mathematical and trigonometric functions for complex numbers. This is a good reason for you to upgrade to C++, even if you don't have immediate plans to use of any of the other features of C++. The programs listed in the chapters mentioned above are all written in Turbo C++. However, they only use the complex number class of C++, so you don't have to learn anything exotic to compile and run them. In the sections below, we'll describe the changes you need to run programs with Zortech C++ version 2.1, an older version of Turbo C, or Microsoft C version 6.0. You'll find that having the class of complex numbers fully implemented as in the C++ compilers makes life easier, and this may inspire you to investigate some of the other unique features of C++. (For example, C++ has an improved method for commenting out a single line and an improved way of displaying data to the screen.) This is what is meant in the title of this chapter about painlessly moving to C++. Running the programs in this book will enable you to do something immediately with C++ that is simpler and more elegant than what you can do with C, but doesn't require any particular new learning on your part. If you can, switch to C++. You'll be glad you did, and within a few years, I believe you will find that all C compilers will include the C++ features.

How C++ Handles Complex Numbers

You don't need to know or understand the following information to be able to use the complex number features of C++. However, a little understanding of the underlying mechanisms will give you a flavor of how C++ works and more confidence in using the complex number features.

The C++ language has the capability to overload operators and functions. In the case of operators, this means that you, the programmer, can write a function which defines how the + or * or any other mathematical operator will work for a particular class of objects that you have defined. This function will override the normal definition of the operator when it is associated with a particular class similar to the way in which C works. However, the programmer has never before had the opportunity to get at the inner working of the compiler in this manner. Lets look at the + operator. In C, when you have a statement like:

```
c = a + b;
```
(Equation 2-1)

the C compiler first examines *a* and *b* to see what kind of numbers they are. If they are both integers, C performs an addition of the two. If they are both floating point numbers, it performs a floating point addition. If one is an integer and the other floating point, it converts the integer to floating point and then performs a floating point addition. Next the compiler looks at *c* to see what its type is and converts the result of the addition, if necessary, so that it is of the type specified for *c*. Now, suppose that we are working in C++ and have the above expression, where *a, b,* and *c* are all defined to be of the class *complex*. You can write a function to overload the + operator so that when the + operator is used with members of the complex class, this function is used instead of the ordinary adding methods. This function would perform ordinary addition of the real components and the imaginary components separately and transfer the real result to the real part of *c* and the imaginary result to the imaginary part of *c*. Similarly, the trigonometric functions can all be overloaded with new functions that perform the counterpart operations for complex numbers. It should now be obvious that you can define a vector or a quaternion or almost anything you can think of as a class and overload the mathematical operators and/ or functions appropriate to your new class. In the new version of C++ the complex class is already fully defined so all you have to do is use mathematical operators or trigonometric functions in an ordinary manner.

If You Don't Have C++

If you don't have C++, you can try to decompose your complex numbers and operate on their real and imaginary parts separately if your mathematical expressions aren't too complicated. If the expressions are complicated, you need to write functions for each operation. You begin by defining a complex type of structure as follows:

```
struct complex
{
    float real,
        imaginary;
};
```

Next, define whatever mathematical operations you are going to use. Figure 2-1 lists typical mathematical functions. With these as a basis, you ought to be able to define what you might need that is not given here. Note that while these functions make it possible to work with complex numbers, they do not allow you to write:

```
c = a + b;
```

where a, b, and c are complex numbers. Instead you must write:

```
/*
```

add() = Function to add two complex numbers

```
*/
```

```
struct complex add(struct complex a, struct complex b)
{
    struct complex c;
```

```
        c.real = a.real + b.real;
        c.imaginary = a.imaginary + b.imaginary;
        return c;
}
/*
```

```
        subtract() = Function to subtract one complex number from another
```

```
*/

struct complex subtract(struct complex a, struct complex b)
{
        c.real = a.real - b.real;
        c.imaginary = a.imaginary - b.imaginary;
        return c;
}


/*
```

```
        multiply() =Function to multiply two complex numbers
```

```
*/

struct complex multiply(struct complex a, struct complex b)
{
        struct complex c;

        c.real = a.real * b.real - a.imaginary * b. imaginary;
        c.imaginary = a.imaginary * b.real + a.real * b.imaginary;
        return c;
}


/*
```

```
        fmultiply() = Function to multiply a complex number by a real number
```

```
*/
struct complex fmultiply(struct complex a, float b)
{
```

```
      struct complex c;

      c.real = a.real * b;
      c.imaginary = a.imaginary * b;
      return c;
}
```

```
/*
```

┌───┐
│ ┌──┐ │
│ │ divide() = Function to divide one complex number by another   │ │
│ └──┘ │
└───┘

```
*/

struct complex divide(struct complex a, struct complex b)
{
      struct complex c;
      float denom;

      denom = b.real * b.real + b.imaginary * b.imaginary;
      c.real = (a.real * b.real + a.imaginary * b.imaginary) / denom;
      c.imaginary = (a.imaginary * b.real - a.real * b.imaginary) /denom;
      return c;
}
```

```
/*
```

┌───┐
│ ┌──┐ │
│ │ magnitude() = Function to find the magnitude of a complex number │ │
│ └──┘ │
└───┘

```
*/
float magnitude(struct complex a)
{
      float c;

      c = sqrt(a.real * a.real + a.imaginary * a.imaginary)
      return c;
}
```

```
/*
```

┌───┐
│ ┌──┐ │
│ │ normalize() = Function to normalize a complex number   │ │
│ └──┘ │
└───┘

```
*/

struct complex normalize (struct complex a)
{
    struct complex c;

    c.real = a.real / magnitude(a);
    c.imaginary = a.imaginary / magnitude(a);
    return c;
}
```
Figure 2-1. Complex Number Functions

```
c = add(a, b);
```

This isn't too much of a hardship, except that you must remember the proper order for the arguments passed in the function, which is a little more difficult than if you used mathematical operators directly as permitted by C++.

Window Functions for Zortech C++ or Microsoft C

Turbo C++ and the more recent versions of Turbo C have several functions to create, move around on, or clear a window on the screen. These functions have been used to generate user-friendly menus in some of the functions in this book. So if you are using a version of C or C++ which does not include such functions, you have to create and include them, where needed, in your programs. Figure 2-2 lists the functions needed for the window capability. Note first that there are some global variables that must be included at the beginning of your program. They are *wx1*, *wy1*, *wx2*, and *wy2*, which define the upper left and lower right corners of the window, and *xcolor*, which provides the color attribute for information displayed in the window.

The first function is the *window* function. This simply stores the coordinates of the upper left and lower right corners of the window in a set of global variables. Note that the row and column numbering scheme used by Borland in the Turbo C series of compilers differs from that used by IBM and Microsoft in DOS. Hence, to maintain compatibility, each variable needs to be reduced by one before being stored. The function then uses of a ROM BIOS call to position the cursor at the top left corner of the window.

Next is the function *gotoxy*. This function is used to position the cursor with respect to the window. It is the same as the ROM BIOS call used within the *window* function except that the column and row coordinates passed to it are added to the coordinates of the top left corner of the window before the cursor is positioned. Thus, if you specify the cursor to be positioned at coordinates (0,0), the cursor will appear at the top left corner of the window. If you specify (4,5), the cursor will appear four columns to the right and five rows down from the top left corner of the window (not from the top left corner of the screen, as occurs with many cursor positioning functions).

```
int wx1,wy1,wx2,wy2;
int xcolor;

/*
```

```
window() = Function to create a window on the screen
```

```
*/
void window(int x1, int y1, int x2, int y2)
{
    wx1 = x1 - 1;
    wx2 = x2 - 1;
    wy1 = y1 - 1;
    wy2 = y2 - 1;
    reg.x.ax = 0x0200;
    reg.h.dl = wx1;
    reg.h.dh = wy1;
    reg.h.bh = 0;
    int86 (0x10, &reg, &reg);
}

/*
```

```
gotoxy() = Function to position cursor within window
```

```
*/

void gotoxy(int x, int y)
```

```
{
    reg.x.ax = 0x0200;
    reg.h.dl = wx1 + x;
    reg.h.dh = wy1 + y;
    reg.h.bh = 0;
    int86 (0x10, &reg, &reg);
}
```

```
/*
```

```
    clrscr() = Function to clear window
```

```
*/
```

```
void clrscr(void)
{
    reg.x.ax = 0x0600;
    reg.h.bh = xcolor;
    reg.h.cl = wx1;
    reg.h.ch = wy1;
    reg.h.dl = wx2;
    reg.h.dh = wy2;
    int86 (0x10, &reg, &reg);
    reg.x.ax = 0x0200;
    reg.h.dl = wx1;
    reg.h.dh = wy1;
    reg.h.bh = 0;
    int86 (0x10, &reg, &reg);
}
```

```
/*
```

```
    textbackground() = Function to set window background color
```

```
*/
```

```
void textbackground(int color)
{
    xcolor = (xcolor & 0x8F) | ((color<<4) & 0x7F);
}
```

```
/*
```

┌───┐
│ ┌───┐ │
│ │ textcolor() = Function to set text color   │ │
│ └───┘ │
└───┘

```
*/
void textcolor(int color)
{
     xcolor = (xcolor & 0x70) | (color & 0x6F);
}
```

Figure 2-2. Functions to Provide Window Capability with Non-Turbo C Compilers

The next function is *clrscr*. This function makes use of the ROM BIOS video services to set up or scroll a window on the screen. The lower eight bits of register A represent the number of lines to be scrolled. When this is set to zero, as in this function, the entire window is filled with the background color. The function then positions the cursor at the top left hand corner of the window.

The function *textbackground* properly positions the background color information and uses it to replace the previous background color information in the global variable *xcolor* without disturbing the foreground color information. The function *textcolor* substitutes the foreground color information for that previously stored in *xcolor* without disturbing the background color information.

In the Turbo C series of compilers, the information stored by *textbackground* and *textcolor* functions is tied to the *cprintf* function so that when this function is used to display directly on the console, the foreground and background colors selected with the first two functions are used to display the text in the window. This is not true of other compilers (which do not even have the *cprintf* function), so we have to make use of a function *color_printf* which will properly use the color data. This function is listed in Figure 2-3. The function uses the capability of C compilers to pass a variable number of arguments in a function call. The first argument passed is a string containing format data and any text to be displayed, the same as for the *C printf* function. Then a color number is passed representing both foreground and background colors. Next a variable number of arguments may pass, each of which represents a value to be displayed. After setting up the variable parameter operations, the function uses the C function *vprintf* to produce an output exactly like *printf* would send to the display, but the output is sent instead to a character array called *string*. Then, the function begins a *while* loop which iterates for each character in *string* until a NULL indicates end of the string is encountered. If the character is an 0AH, indicating a carriage return, the function uses the appropriate ROM BIOS video service to reset the cursor position to the beginning of the next line. If any other character occurs, the appropriate ROM BIOS service is used to display the character on the screen at the current cursor location and in the specified colors. The function then reads the current cursor position and resets it incremented by one.

```
/*

    color_printf() = Performs functions of printf with display in a selected color

*/

void color_printf (char *msg,int color,...)
{
    union REGS reg;
    char ch, string[2000];
    int i = 0;
    va_list (ap);

    va_start (ap,msg);
    vsprintf(string,msg,ap);
    va_end(ap);
    while ((ch=string[i++]) != '\0')
    {
        if (ch == 0x0A)
        {
            reg.h.ah = 3;
            int86(0x10,&reg,&reg);
            reg.h.dl = 0;
            reg.h.dh++;
            reg.h.ah = 2;
            int86(0x10,&reg,&reg);
        }
        else
        {
```

```
                reg.h.ah = 9;
                reg.h.al = ch;
                reg.x.bx = color;
                reg.x.cx = 1;
                int86(0x10,&reg,&reg);
                reg.h.ah = 3;
                int86(0x10,&reg,&reg);
                reg.x.dx++;
                reg.h.ah = 2;
                int86(0x10,&reg,&reg);
            }
        }
    }
```

Figure 2-3. Function to Display Data in Selected Colors

CHAPTER 3

Useful Functions for Fractal Generation

Graphic functions of any particular C compiler are imcompatible with those of another compiler. Also, particular compilers ocassionally don't allow access to some of the standard graphics modes. Consequently, this chapter lists some graphics functions used throughout this book which are compatible with any brand of C compiler.

The *ftools.h* Header File

The first step in tying the fractal tools to your fractal program is to reference the header file ftools.h in an include statement at the beginning of your fractal program. This takes the form of:

```
#include "ftools.h"
```

This header file is listed in Figure 3-1.

```
/*

    ftools.h = Header file for use with fractal tools

*/

#include <stdio.h>
#include <math.h>
#include <dos.h>
#include <process.h>
```

```
#include <ctype.h>
#include <time.h>
#include <bios.h>
#include <conio.h>
#include <string.h>

void cls(int color);
void setMode(int mode);
void plot(int x, int y, int color);
void save_screen(int x1, int y1, int x2, int y2, char file_name[]);
unsigned char read_screen(unsigned long int address, int color_plane);
int restore_screen(char file_name[]);
void move_cursor(int type,int color,int min_col, int min_row);
int plot_point(int x, int y, int color);
void setEGApalette(int palette, int color);
void display(unsigned long int address, int color_plane, unsigned char ch);
int restore_parameters(char file_name[]);
void plot256(int x, int y, int color);
void setVGAreg(int reg_no, int red, int green, int blue);
void setVGApalette(unsigned char *buffer);
```
Figure 3-1. Header File ftools.h

The *ftools.cpp* Drawing Package

All of the tools used in fractal drawing are included in a file called *ftools.cpp*. There are several ways that you can use this file. It's your choice. First, and simplest, is to simply append the file (or whatever routines in it are needed in a particular program) to the end of the program. This makes each program a stand-alone unit. However, it increases the overall length of your fractal package, and it also means that if you decide to modify one of the functions in the package, you have to hunt up every occurrence of it and change it separately. The second is to make use of your compiler's ability to link separate files. In Turbo C or Turbo C++ you do this by creating a project file which includes the name of the *ftools.cpp* file and your main program file. If you have Zortech C++, when you issue a compile command from the integrated environment, the program will ask you for the names of additional files to be included and at this point, you should enter the *ftools.cpp* file name. If you are using Microsoft C, when you compile from the command line, you need to include the name of the *ftools.cpp* file. (For some compilers that do not have C++ capability you may have to change the file extension to .c for the program to compile correctly.) The problem with this approach is that you may spend a lot of time recompiling the *ftools.cpp* package, whenever you change the main program, even if you haven't made any changes in the package itself. One way to get around this is to make the package into a library, using the library-making capabilities that are a part of every compiler. You then use the procedures just described to include the library file in your compilation. The library is created from a package that is first compiled, so it never needs to be compiled again, thus saving both time and space. However, if you make a change in the package, you have to recompile and then update the library file. Finally, you can use the make capability that is a part of most compilers. By setting up a make file and compiling and linking from the command line, you can have the best of both worlds, since the compiler will check to see if your package exists in compiled form and if this compiled version is up-to-date, and if it is, will use it without recompiling. Whenever you make a change in the package, the compiler will automatically find that the source code version is of a later date than the object code version and will recompile the package. (For this to work properly, you need to be sure that your system clock is always running correctly with the right time and date.) The *ftools.cpp* package is listed in Figure 3-2. The individual functions in it are described in the paragraphs that follow.

```
/*
```

```
ftools.c = Functions for use in fractal generation

By Roger T. Stevens 10-14-90
```

```
*/
```

```
#include "ftools.h"

extern double XMax, XMin, YMax, YMin, Pval, Qval,
        a, b, c, d, e,   f, g, h,
        TXMax, TXMin, TYMax, TYMin, start_x, start_y;
extern int colors[15][3], max_iterations, color_option,
```

```
        CURSOR_X, CURSOR_Y;
extern unsigned char PALETTE[16];

union REGS reg;
struct SREGS inreg;

/*
```

```
    setMode() = Sets the video mode
```

```
*/

void setMode(int mode)
{
    reg.h.ah = 0;
    reg.h.al = mode;
    int86 (0x10,&reg,&reg);
}


/*
```

```
    setEGApalette() = Sets the color for an EGA palette number.
```

```
 */

extern unsigned char PALETTE[16];

void setEGApalette(int palette, int color)
{
    PALETTE[palette] = color;
    reg.h.ah = 0x10;
    reg.h.al = 0;
    reg.h.bh = color;
    reg.h.bl = palette;
    int86(0x10,&reg,&reg);
}
```

```
/*
```

```
    setVGAreg() = Function to set individual VGA color register.
```

```
*/
```

```c
void setVGAreg(int reg_no, int red, int green, int blue)
{
    reg.x.ax = 0x1010;
    reg.x.bx = reg_no;
    reg.h.ch = red;
    reg.h.cl = green;
    reg.h.dh = blue;
    int86(0x10,&reg,&reg);
}
```

```
/*
```

```
    setVGApalette() = Function to set all 256 color registers
```

```
*/
```

```c
void setVGApalette(unsigned char *buffer)
{
    reg.x.ax = 0x1012;
    segread(&inreg);
    inreg.es = inreg.ds;
    reg.x.bx = 0;
    reg.x.cx = 256;
    reg.x.dx = (int)&buffer[0];
    int86x(0x10,&reg,&reg,&inreg);
}
```

```
/*
```

```
    cls() = Clears the graphics screen
```

```
*/
```

```c
void cls(int color)
```

```
{
    reg.x.ax = 0x0600;
    reg.x.cx = 0;
    reg.x.dx = 0x184F;
    reg.h.bh = color;
    int86(0x10,&reg,&reg);
}
```

/*

```
plot() = Plots a point on the screen at designated system coordinates using
selected color.
```

*/

```
void plot(int x, int y, int color)
{
    #define seq_out(index,val) {outp(0x3C4,index);\outp(0x3C5,val);}
    #define graph_out(index,val) {outp(0x3CE,index);\outp(0x3CF,val);}

    unsigned int offset;
    int dummy,mask,page;
    char far * mem_address;

    offset = (long)y * 80L + ((long)x / 8L);
    mem_address = (char far *) 0xA0000000L + offset;
    mask = 0x80 >> (x % 8);
    graph_out(8,mask);
    seq_out(2,0x0F);
    dummy = *mem_address;
    *mem_address = 0;
    seq_out(2,color);
    *mem_address = 0xFF;
    seq_out(2,0x0F);
    graph_out(3,0);
    graph_out(8,0xFF);

}
```

```
/*
```

```
    plot_point() = Plots a point at (x,y) in color for EGA or VGA, using port output
                   functions and returns original point color.
```

```
*/
```

```c
int plot_point(int x, int y, int color)
{
    #define seq_out(index,val) {outp(0x3C4,index);\outp(0x3C5,val);}
    #define graph_out(index,val) {outp(0x3CE,index);\outp(0x3CF,val);}
    #define EGAaddress 0xA0000000L

    int index,old_color=0;
    unsigned char mask, dummy,exist_color;
    char far *mem_address;

    mem_address = (char far *) (EGAaddress +
        ((long)y * 80L + ((long)x / 8L)));
    mask = 0x80 >> (x % 8);
    for (index = 0; index<4; index++)
    {
        graph_out(4,index);
        graph_out(5,0);
        exist_color = *mem_address & mask;
        if (exist_color != 0)
            old_color |=(0x01<<index);
    }
    graph_out(8,mask);
    seq_out(2,0x0F);
    dummy = *mem_address;
    *mem_address = 0;
    seq_out(2,color);
    *mem_address = 0xFF;
    seq_out(2,0x0F);
    graph_out(3,0);
    graph_out(8,0xFF);
    return(old_color);
}
```

```
/*

    ┌─────────────────────────────────────────────────────────┐
    │ plot256() = Function to plot point on VGA 256 color screen. │
    └─────────────────────────────────────────────────────────┘
*/

void plot256(int x, int y, int color)
{
    unsigned int offset;
    char far *address;
    offset = 320 * y + x;
    address = (char far *)(0xA0000000L + offset);
    *address = color;
}


/*

    ┌─────────────────────────────────────────────────────────┐
    │ display() = Displays byte on the graphics screen           │
    └─────────────────────────────────────────────────────────┘
*/

void display(unsigned long int address, int color_plane, unsigned char ch)
{
    #define seq_out(index,val) {outp(0x3C4,index);\outp(0x3C5,val);}
    char far * mem_address;
    char dummy;

    mem_address = (char far *) 0xA0000000L + address;
    dummy = *mem_address;
    seq_out(2,(0x01 << color_plane));
    *mem_address = ch;
}


/*

    ┌─────────────────────────────────────────────────────────┐
    │ read_screen() = Reads a byte from the graphics screen      │
    └─────────────────────────────────────────────────────────┘
*/

unsigned char read_screen(unsigned long int address, int color_plane)
```

```
{

    char far * mem_address;
    unsigned char pixel_data;

    mem_address = (char far *) 0xA0000000L + address;
    graph_out(4,color_plane);
    graph_out(5,0);
    pixel_data = *mem_address;
    return (pixel_data);
}

/*
```

┌───┐
│ ┌──┐   │
│ │ save_screen() = Save a graphics screen to a disk file   │   │
│ └──┘   │
└───┘

```
*/

void save_screen(int x1, int y1, int x2, int y2, char file_name[])
{
    int i,j,k,add1,add2,number,num_out, line_length, end,
        start_line, end_line;
    unsigned char ch,ch1,old_ch,red,green,blue;
    FILE *fsave;

    sound (256);
    while (file_name[6] < 0x3A)
    {
        if ((fsave = fopen (file_name,"rb")) != NULL)
        {
            file_name[7]++;
            if (file_name[7] >= 0x3A)
            {
                file_name[7] = 0x30;
                file_name[6]++;
            }
            fclose(fsave);
        }
        else
        {
```

```
            fclose(fsave);
            fsave = fopen(file_name,"wb");
            fputc(0x0A,fsave);
            fputc(0x05,fsave);
            fputc(0x01,fsave);
            fputc(0x01,fsave);
            putw(x1,fsave);
            putw(y1,fsave);
            putw(x2,fsave);
            putw(y2,fsave);
            putw(640,fsave);
            putw(350,fsave);
            ch = 0x00;
            for (i=0; i<16; i++)
            {
                red = (((PALETTE[i] & 0x20) >> 5) |
                    ((PALETTE[i] & 0x04) >> 1)) * 85;
                green = (((PALETTE[i] & 0x10) >> 4) |
                    (PALETTE[i] & 0x02)) * 85;
                blue = (((PALETTE[i] & 0x08) >> 3) |
                    ((PALETTE[i] & 0x01) << 1)) * 85;
                fputc(red,fsave);
                fputc(green,fsave);
                fputc(blue,fsave);
            }
            fputc(0x00,fsave);
            fputc(0x04,fsave);
            start_line = x1/8;
            end_line = x2/8 + 1;
            line_length = end_line - start_line;
            end = start_line + line_length * 4 + 1;
            putw(line_length,fsave);
            putw(1,fsave);
            fwrite(&XMax,8,1,fsave);
            fwrite(&XMin,8,1,fsave);
            fwrite(&YMax,8,1,fsave);
            fwrite(&YMin,8,1,fsave);
            fwrite(&Pval,8,1,fsave);
            fwrite(&Qval,8,1,fsave);
            for (i=118; i<128; i++)
```

```
        fputc(' ',fsave);
    for (k=y1; k<y2; k++)
    {
        add1 = 80*k;
        number = 1;
        j = 0;
        add2 = (start_line);
        old_ch = read_screen(add1 + add2++,0);
        for (i=add2; i<end; i++)
        {
            if (i == end - 1)
                ch = old_ch - 1;
            else
            {
                if ((add2) == end_line)
                {
                    j++;
                    add2 = (start_line);
                }
                ch = read_screen(add1 + add2,
                    j);
            }
            if ((ch == old_ch) && number < 63)
                number++;
            else
            {
                num_out = ((unsigned char)
                    number | 0xC0);
                if ((number != 1) ||
                    ((old_ch & 0xC0) ==
                    0xC0))
                    fputc(num_out,fsave);
                fputc(old_ch,fsave);
                old_ch = ch;
                number = 1;
            }
            add2++;
        }
    }
    fputc(0x0C,fsave);
```

```
                    fwrite(&a,8,1,fsave);
                    fwrite(&b,8,1,fsave);
                    fwrite(&c,8,1,fsave);
                    fwrite(&d,8,1,fsave);
                    fwrite(&e,8,1,fsave);
                    fwrite(&f,8,1,fsave);
                    fwrite(colors,45,2,fsave);
                    fwrite(&max_iterations,2,1,fsave);
                    fwrite(&color_option,2,1,fsave);
                    fwrite(&start_x,4,1,fsave);
                    fwrite(&start_y,4,1,fsave);
                    fclose(fsave);
                    break;
              }
        }
        nosound();
}


/*
```

```
    restore_screen() = Displays the contents of a .PCX graphics disk file on the
                       screen.
```

```
*/

int restore_screen(char file_name[])
{
    #define graph_out(index,val) {outp(0x3CE,index);\
                                                outp(0x3CF,val);}
    FILE *fsave;
    unsigned char ch,ch1,red,green,blue,color,
        line_length,end;
    int line_end,i,j,k,m,pass,x1,y1,x2,y2;
    if ((fsave = fopen(file_name,"rb")) == NULL)
    {
        printf("\nCan't find %s.\n",file_name);
        return(0);
    }
    else
```

```
{
    ch = fgetc(fsave);
    if (ch != 0x0A)
    {
            printf("\n%s is not a valid ZSoft file.\n",
        file_name);
        fclose(fsave);
        return(0);
    }
}
setMode(16);
cls(0);

for (i=1; i<4; i++)
        ch = fgetc(fsave);
x1 = getw(fsave);
y1 = getw(fsave);
x2 = getw(fsave);
y2 = getw(fsave);
for (i=12; i<16; i++)
    ch = fgetc(fsave);
for (i=0; i<16; i++)
{
    red = fgetc(fsave)/85;
    green = fgetc(fsave)/85;
    blue = fgetc(fsave)/85;
    color = ((red & 0x01) << 5) | ((red & 0x02)
        << 1) | ((green & 0x01) << 4) | (green
        & 0x02) | ((blue & 0x01) << 3) | ((blue &
        0x02) >> 1);
    setEGApalette(i,color);
}

for (i=64; i<70; i++)
    ch = fgetc(fsave);
fread(&XMax,8,1,fsave);
fread(&XMin,8,1,fsave);
fread(&YMax,8,1,fsave);
fread(&YMin,8,1,fsave);
fread(&Pval,8,1,fsave);
```

```
fread(&Qval,8,1,fsave);
for (i=118; i<128; i++)
    ch = fgetc(fsave);
graph_out(8,0xFF);
graph_out(3,0x10);
for (k=y1; k<y2; k++)
{
    i = k*80 + (x1/8);
    line_end = k* 80 + (x2/8)+1;
    j = 0;
    while (j < 4)
    {
        ch1 = fgetc(fsave);
        if ((ch1 & 0xC0) != 0xC0)
        {
            display(i, j, ch1);
            i++;
            if (i >= line_end)
            {
                j++;
                i = k*80 + (x1/8);
            }
        }
        else
        {
            ch1 &= 0x3F;
            pass = ch1;
            ch = fgetc(fsave);
            for (m=0; m<pass; m++)
            {
                display(i, j, ch);
                i++;
                if (i >= line_end)
                {
                    j++;
                    i = k*80 + (x1/8);
                }
            }
        }
    }
}
```

```
        }
        graph_out(3,0);
        graph_out(8,0xFF);
        fclose(fsave);
        return(x2);
}


/*

    ┌─────────────────────────────────────────────────────────────┐
    │ restore_parameters() = Restore display parameters from disk file. │
    └─────────────────────────────────────────────────────────────┘

*/

int restore_parameters(char file_name[])
{
        FILE *f1;
        unsigned char ch;
        int i,j;

        if ((f1 = fopen(file_name,"rb")) == NULL)
        {
            printf("\ncan't find %s.\n",file_name);
            return(1);
        }
        else
        {
            ch = fgetc(f1);
            if (ch != 0x0A)
            {
                printf("\n%s is not a valid Zsoft file.\n",
                    file_name);
                fclose(f1);
                return(0);
            }
        }
        fseek(f1,-151L,SEEK_END);
        ch = fgetc(f1);
        if (ch != 0x0C)
        {
            printf ("\n%s is not Fractal file.\n",file_name);
```

```
        fclose(f1);
        return(0);
    }
    else
    {
        fread(&a,8,1,f1);
        fread(&b,8,1,f1);
        fread(&c,8,1,f1);
        fread(&d,8,1,f1);
        fread(&e,8,1,f1);
        fread(&f,8,1,f1);
        fread(colors,45,2,f1);
        fread(&max_iterations,2,1,f1);
        fread(&color_option,2,1,f1);
        fread(&start_x,4,1,f1);
        fread(&start_y,4,1,f1);
        fclose(f1);
        return(1);
    }
}


/*
```

```
move_cursor() = Moves cursor and saves position
          type 0 = cursor is top left corner
          type 1 = cursor is bottom right corner
          type 2 = cursor is arrow
```

```
*/

void move_cursor(int type,int color,int min_col, int min_row)
{
    #define LEFT_ARROW          19200
    #define RIGHT_ARROW         19712
    #define UP_ARROW            18432
    #define DOWN_ARROW          20480
    #define SHIFT_LEFT_ARROW    2047
    #define SHIFT_RIGHT_ARROW   2303
    #define SHIFT_UP_ARROW      1791
    #define SHIFT_DOWN_ARROW    2559
```

```
#define RETURN                7181

unsigned int mask;
int i,j,image,image_store[256],index,ch,temp,limit[7];
char far *base;

window(1,1,80,25);
limit[0] = 11;
limit[1] = 9;
limit[2] = 10;
limit[3] = 10;
limit[4] = 12;
limit[5] = 14;
limit[6] = 14;
do
{
    index = 0;
    switch(type)
    {
        case 0:
            for (i=0; i<16; i++)
                image_store[index++] = plot_point
                    (CURSOR_X+i,CURSOR_Y,
                    color);
            for (i=1; i<16; i++)
                image_store[index++] = plot_point
                    (CURSOR_X,CURSOR_Y+i,
                    color);
            break;
        case 1:
            for (i=0; i<16; i++)
                image_store[index++] = plot_point
                    (CURSOR_X+15,CURSOR_Y+i,
                    color);
            for (i=0; i<15; i++)
                image_store[index++] = plot_point
                    (CURSOR_X+i,CURSOR_Y+15,
                    color);
            break;
        case 2:
```

```
                for (j=0; j<7; j++)
                {
                        for(i=j; i<limit[j]; i++)
                        {
                            if((i==8) && (j ==5))
                                    i=10;
                            if((i==8) && (j ==6))
                                    i=12;
                            image_store[index++] = plot_point
                                    (CURSOR_X+j,CURSOR_Y+i,
                                    color);
                        }
                }
                image_store[index++] = plot_point(CURSOR_X+7,
                        CURSOR_Y+7,color);
        }
        ch = bioskey(0);
        if (ch != RETURN)
        {
            index = 0;
            switch(type)
            {
                case 0:
                    for (i=0; i<16; i++)
                        plot_point(CURSOR_X+i,CURSOR_Y,
                            image_store[index++]);
                    for (i=1; i<16; i++)
                        plot_point(CURSOR_X,CURSOR_Y+i,
                            image_store[index++]);
                    break;
                case 1:
                    for (i=0; i<16; i++)
                        plot_point(CURSOR_X+15,CURSOR_Y+i,
                            image_store[index++]);
                    for (i=0; i<15; i++)
                        plot_point(CURSOR_X+i,CURSOR_Y+15,
                            image_store[index++]);
                    break;
                case 2:
                    for (j=0; j<7; j++)
```

```
            {
                for(i=j; i<limit[j]; i++)
                {
                    if((i==8) && (j ==5))
                            i=10;
                    if((i==8) && (j ==6))
                            i=12;
                    plot(CURSOR_X+j,
                            CURSOR_Y+i,
                            image_store[index++]);
                }
            }
            plot(CURSOR_X+7,CURSOR_Y+7,
                image_store[index++]);
    }
    switch(ch)
    {
        case UP_ARROW:
            if (CURSOR_Y > min_row)
                CURSOR_Y -= 10;
            break;
        case LEFT_ARROW:
            if (CURSOR_X > min_col)
                CURSOR_X -= 10;
            break;
        case RIGHT_ARROW:
            if (CURSOR_X < 629)
                CURSOR_X += 10;
            break;
        case DOWN_ARROW:
            if (CURSOR_Y < 329)
                CURSOR_Y += 10;
            break;
        case SHIFT_RIGHT_ARROW:
        case 19766:
            if (CURSOR_X < 639)
                CURSOR_X++;
            break;
        case SHIFT_LEFT_ARROW:
        case 19252:
```

```
                    if (CURSOR_X > min_col)
                        CURSOR_X—;
                    break;
                case SHIFT_UP_ARROW:
                case 18488:
                    if (CURSOR_Y > min_row)
                        CURSOR_Y—;
                    break;
                case SHIFT_DOWN_ARROW:
                case 20530:
                    if (CURSOR_Y < 335)
                        CURSOR_Y++;
                        break;
            }
        }
        switch(type)
        {
            case 0:
                TXMin = XMin + (XMax - XMin)/
                    639*(CURSOR_X);
                TYMax = YMax - (YMax - YMin)/
                    349*CURSOR_Y;
                gotoxy(6,25);
                printf("XMin= %f YMax= %f",TXMin,TYMax);
                break;
            case 1:
                TXMax = XMin + (XMax - XMin)/
                    639*(CURSOR_X + 16);
                TYMin = YMax - (YMax - YMin)/
                    349*(CURSOR_Y + 16);
                gotoxy(42,25);
                printf(" XMax= %f YMin= %f",TXMax,TYMin);
                break;
            case 2:
                Pval = XMin + (XMax - XMin)/639*
                    CURSOR_X;
                Qval = YMax - (YMax - YMin)/
                    349*CURSOR_Y;
                gotoxy(6,25);
                printf(" P= %f Q= %f    ",Pval,Qval);
```

```
        }
    }
    while (ch != RETURN);
}
```

Figure 3-2. The ftools.cpp Package of Tools for Fractal Generation

Setting the Video Mode

Before any graphics can be displayed, the system must be set to the proper video mode. This function makes use of the ROM BIOS video services to perform that operation. It can also be used to reset to a text mode after the graphics operations are complete.

Setting the EGA Palette

In the EGA color modes, such as mode 16 which is used for most fractal generation throughout this book, the 16 colors are controlled by the contents of 16 palette registers. Each register may hold any one of 64 available colors. The function is passed a palette number from 0 to 15 and a color number from 0 to 63. The ROM BIOS video service is used to set the designated palette register to the designated color. The EGA board has no provision for reading the palette registers to determine what color settings they contain. This information is often necessary in the programs that we are generating. Hence, you need to include in your program a global variable named PALETTE, which contains an array of sixteen integers, which are initially set to the default colors of the sixteen palette registers. Each time the *setEGApalette* function is called, it not only changes the color in the appropriate palette register, but also changes this color number in the proper member of the PALETTE array so that this array always contains an up-to-date representation of the state of the palette registers. Note, however, that the global array PALETTE must exist in any program calling *setEGApalette*; otherwise a compiler error will occur and the program will not compile.

Setting a VGA Color Register

In the 256 color VGA mode, one doesn't try to mess with the palette registers, but instead sends information to one of 256 color registers that select the 256 colors which are to be presented on the screen from 256K possible color combinations. A color register is set by a ROM BIOS video service call, with the color register number specified in register *b* and the red, green, and blue components of the selected color (as a number from 0 to 63) specified in registers *ch*, *cl*, and *dh* respectively.

Setting 256 VGA Color Registers at Once

Sometimes it is desirable to update all 256 color registers of the VGA in one operation. There is a ROM BIOS video service which can perform this operation. The 256 new colors are stored in a character buffer, where each set of three characters comprises the red, green, and blue components of a color. The address of this buffer is then placed in the proper registers and the ROM BIOS service called. The service then transfers the buffer contents to the 256 color registers.

Clearing the Screen

The *cls* function makes use of the ROM BIOS video service scrolling function to clear the screen to a designated background color, when in graphics mode 16. The function requires that the upper left window coordinates are placed in *register c* and the lower right window coordinates in *register d*. The values used are those for a full screen window. When the lower eight bits of register a are set to zero, the function scrolls through the entire window setting the background color to that specified in *register b*. After the register values are set, the function performs an interrupt call to run the video service.

Plotting a Point to the Screen

Many of the EGA and VGA graphics modes are unusual in that a single memory address actually controls the contents of that address in four different memory planes. Unfortunately, it is not possible to address these memory planes directly; any changes must be made indirectly through inputs to the control and data registers of the EGA or VGA card. The plot function performs the operations necessary to plot a point on the graphics screen in mode 16, which is the 640 by 350 pixel by 16 color mode most often used for fractal generation. The function first uses the column and row coordinates that were passed to it to generate an offset from the base memory address, and then to come up with the actual memory address of the desired pixel. Note that this is the address of a byte containing eight pixels, so the parameter mask has to be used to single out the proper pixel to be manipulated. The function sets the contents of the required registers by port outputs and then does a dummy read of the desired memory address which places the contents of that memory location in the four memory planes into the proper registers. It then zeroes the memory location. Next a register operation sets the new colors into the registers and then sending an FFH to the memory address causes the register contents (containing the new color information) to be transferred to the four memory planes. The registers are then restored to their normal settings and the function terminates.

Plotting and Reading a Point

Consider the situation in which we generate a cursor with some shape, such as an arrow, and move it about on a screen. The very first display of the cursor is no problem; we simply plot the proper pattern of pixels to the screen in the desired cursor color. However, when we want to move the cursor to a new location, we not only have to plot the proper pixel pattern at the new location, but we also have to restore the original screen information at the old position of the cursor. If all we did originally is plot the cursor on the screen, we are in big trouble because the original screen information is gone forever. What we should have done is to read the original screen information and save it in an array so that we could write it back to the screen when we want to move the cursor. We'll discuss this further when we describe the *move_cursor* function. The *plot_point* function described here is the basic tool for the operation. It starts out by computing an offset, a memory address, and a mask, exactly like the plot function described above. It then enters a *for* loop which in turn reads the pixel color information from each color plane. This information is assembled into a variable *old_color*, which is returned by the function when it terminates. The rest of the function is just like the plot function in the way that it sends the new color information to the EGA or VGA memory. Incidentally, if you want to conserve on space, you could use this function for all of your plotting chores. It will run a little slower than the plot function, however, because of the additional memory accesses required to collect the old color information

Plotting a Point to the 256 Color Screen

As viewed from outside the VGA board, the technique for plotting a point to the screen seems much simpler for the 256 color mode than for the 16 color mode. Basically, one byte of the assigned memory is used to represent the color of each pixel. Consequently, the *plot256* function simply generates an offset from the base memory address at the rate of one byte per pixel, and then sends the color information to that memory address. It appears as if we are addressing memory directly, but this is not the case. Within the VGA board, all kinds of strange things are happening, apparently in order to allow the board to use the slowest possible memory chips. The VGA registers intercept the information being sent to video memory and rotate it through the four memory planes. The first byte goes to memory plane zero at the base address, the second byte to memory plane one at address *base + 1*, the third to memory plane 2 at address *base + 2*, the fourth to memory plane 3 at address *base + 3*, the fifth to memory plane zero at address *base + 4*, and so forth. Thus only one fourth of each memory plane is used. Fortunately, all of this manipulation is transparent to the programmer, who only needs to know about sending the information to the correct memory address.

Plotting a Byte to the Screen

If we are dealing with a single pixel, we have to use one of the functions given above to plot it to the screen. However, if we could know the value of eight pixels in adjacent columns of the same row (they have to begin at a memory byte boundary) we could plot the entire byte on one operation and generate our display a lot faster than we could by plotting individual pixels. Fortunately, this is the case when we are reading display information from a .PCX disk file and using it to restore a screen. The function display is used to send the byte to the screen, using the 640 by 350 pixel by 16 color mode. The function is set up to send a byte of color data to one color plane, so that to completely define the byte of color data, the function needs to be called four times. (Since, as will be seen below, the color data is stored on the disk as a complete row of color data from the first color plane, followed by the same line of color data for the next color plane, and so forth, this type of display function has the highest compatibility.) The input parameters to the function are an address representing the offset of the byte from the memory base address (this offset is computed within the plot function given above), an integer specifying the desired color plane, and an unsigned character giving the byte to be transferred. The address parameter is added to the base memory address and a dummy read of the data at that point is performed. The EGA/VGA sequence register is then set up to send data only to the desired color plane and the color character is then sent to the selected address. You can see that this function is much quicker than the plot function, not only because it handles a byte at a time, but also because the number of operations required is much smaller. This is true even considering that it must be called four times for a complete color operation.

Reading a Byte from the Screen

The paragraph above describes how to display a byte of color data on the screen. If we are working in the other direction, we want to read a byte from one of the color planes at a designated point on the display so that we can store it in a disk file. The function *read_screen* performs this operation. The two parameters transferred to it are the address (offset) and the number of the designated color plane. (This is the same as for the display function described above except that the color byte is not passed to the function, since it will be reading it from the screen.) As with the function above, the function first creates the actual memory address. It then sets up the graphics registers so that the color data for a single color plane (as selected) can be read. It then reads the memory address and returns the byte of data that was read.

Saving a Screen to Disk

Save_screen saves a function to a .PCX disk file. This format was developed by Zsoft and used with their PC Paintbrush and other drawing programs. This format is widely used. It permits your screens to be edited with PC Paintbrush and to be compatible with many other graphics programs. Zsoft is extremely cooperative in making information on this format available to those who want to write compatible software to use it. Shannon of their technical support group provided me with a pamphlet giving full technical details on the .PCX format. Details of this format are given in Appendix A. There is an excellent public domain program called 'ZS' which can be used to display any or all of your EGA .PCX files or run a slide show of them. This program is available on bulletin boards or may be obtained directly by sending $10.00 to :

Bob Montgomery

132 Parsons Rd.

Longwood, FL 32779

A number of parameters are saved in the file that are not a part of the original Zsoft program. These are included in an unused portion of the header and as an appendage to the end of the program, so hopefully they won't give you any trouble. In the header we save the limit values for a complex plane display and the constant for a Julia set, namely the double floating point numbers for *Xmax, Xmin, Ymax, Ymin, Pval* and *Qval*. Zsoft first designed the file format for displays having a maximum of 16 colors. When 256 color modes became available, they wanted the format to remain compatible, but found insufficient room in the header for the required color information. Consequently, they decided to append it to the end of the file, preceded by the hex character 0CH, which can never occur naturally in the file data. Their procedure for determining if 256 color data is present is to go to the end of the file and then back up the number of bytes that corresponds to the size of the color information. The character at that point is then read; if it is 0CH, the file is considered to contain 256 color information, otherwise it is assumed to be a 16 color file. I have used the same technique to append additional data needed for complex plane displays at the end of the file. Since all such displays are 16 color displays, there is no conflict with the added 256 color information. Since the length of the complex plane information is different from the 256 color information, when the function looks for an 0CH, it can never become confused between the two different applications. The data that is stored at the end of the file are: the *a, b, c, d, e,* and *f* double floating point parameters for the generic Mandelbrot/Julia/dragon equation; a 90 byte table of color ranges and the assigned colors; the maximum number of iterations for the iterated equation; the number of the coloring option selected; and the double floating point starting values for x and y in the equation.

The parameters passed to the *save_screen* function are the coordinates of the upper left corner of the window to be saved, the coordinates of the lower right corner, and the name of the file in which the screen data is to be stored. No protection is afforded for values that are outside the screen limits; the programmer must provide this in the calling program. Also, although any pixel location on the screen may be specified, the x value of each corner, as used by the program, is set up to be a byte boundary, which may be as much as seven pixels off from the specified value. Normally, this will not cause a problem. If it does, the programmer should assure that the x values are divisible by eight. The program assumes that the file name, which is passed to it as a parameter, consists of six letters, followed by two numbers. The program begins by trying to open the file, in the *read* mode, with the given file name. If the file can be opened (the file does indeed exist) the program assumes that the file already contains valuable data and therefore increments the two digit ending and tries again. The loop continues until a file name is generated which cannot be opened, indicating that the file does not exist. This file is then opened in the *write* mode to save the current screen. Note that if the two digits get to 99 without a non-existent file being found, the loop gives up. The file will then be written with the last two characters :0, and if this file already exists, it will be written over.

The function then continues by initiating a sound that continues until the function has completed its work of generating the screen file. Next, the appropriate header information is stored, including the palette information. To keep track of the colors, the function requires the global *PALETTE* array, which is initialized with the default palette values for the EGA. Whenever the *setEGApalette'* function is called, in addition to resetting the appropriate palette register, it also stores the information in a member of this array, so that it is available for transfer to the .PCX file. The double floating point x and y limits and P and Q values for Mandelbrot or other sets are also stored. This data is stored in a set of global coordinates.

The function initializes some address variables and then starts a loop that reiterates for every line of the display from the first one specified by $y1$, to the last one, specified by $y2$. At the beginning of this loop, the function gets the first byte of eight pixels from the first plane of the EGA screen. This is stored in *old_ch*. Next, another '*or*' loop is begun, which reads one byte at a time from the beginning to the end of the line for each of the four memory planes. After each read, action is taken based upon comparing the read character with the previous character, which was stored in *old_ch*. For the very last pass through the loop, instead of reading a byte (which wouldn't be there anyway, since we have already finished the line), we create an artificial character which is always different from *old_ch*, which forces a write out to the file of the previous data. On each pass through the loop, we check the value of the address variable *add2* (which is incremented at the end of each pass). If it is equal to the value representing the end of the line, we reset it to the starting value and also increment *j*, which determines which memory plane is read. After the character is read, we check it against the previous character value; if it is the same and if *number*, which stores the number of like characters so far encountered, is less than 63, we simply increment *number* and return for the next pass through the loop. If *number* had reached 63, or if the character read differs from the previous character, we write out to the file. If *number* is one, indicating that the previous character is unlike those on either side of it, and if the value in *old_ch* does not have its two most significant bits equal to one, we simply write this value out to the file. If the value in *old_ch* was repeated, or if it's two most significant bits are ones, we first write out the value of *number* with its two most significant bits set to one. We then write out the value in *old_ch*. We then reset number to one and are ready for another pass through the loop. When this loop and the display line loop have been completed, an 0CH is written to the disk file and then the additional specialized information is written. The disk file is then closed and the sound turned off.

Function to Restore a Display Screen

The *restore_screen* function restores the screen saved by the previous function. The function begins by attempting to open the file whose designation is passed through the parameter *file_name*. If the file does not exist, the function displays "Cannot find *file_name*," where *file_name* is the designated name, and then returns a value of 1. If the file does exist, the first character of the header is read. If it is not the password character *0AH* for .PCX files, the function displays "*file_name* is not a valid Zsoft file" and then returns a value of 1. If the file appears to be a valid one, the computer is set to EGA display mode 16 and the screen is cleared to a black background. The function then begins to read the header information. The window top left and bottom right coordinates are read and stored. The color data for each palette is read from each triple and converted to an IBM EGA format color word, which is sent to the appropriate palette. The display limits and P and Q values for Mandelbrot and similar sets are read. Dummy reads then take place to get to the end of the header block. The function then sends data to set up the registers of the EGA for reception of color data. Next, a *for* loop is begun for reading and displaying data for each line of the display from the top to the bottom of the window. Parameters are set up for the initial address of screen memory and for the address of the end of the current line. The parameter *j* is set to zero so that data will be sent to the first memory plane. The function then begins a *while* loop which reads data from the disk file, character by character. If the character does not have its two most significant bits set to one, it is simply sent to display memory and the memory address incremented. If the first two bits are one, these are stripped and the remainder of the byte is used as a counter. The next character is read from disk and repeatedly sent to display memory and the memory address incremented and the counter decremented each time until the counter reaches zero. After each incrementing of the memory address, the address is checked against the value for line end and if that value has been reached, the memory address is reset to the beginning of the line and the memory plane indicator is incremented. When this indicator reaches 4, all memory planes have been completed for the designated line, so the *while* loop is terminated. When all lines have been completed, the *for* loop terminates, the EGA registers are reset, the disk file is closed, and the function returns with a value of 0.

There are two important things to note. First, this function is not compatible with .PCX files written by the programs given in my books *Fractal Programming in C* and *Fractal Programming in Turbo Pascal*. This is because I felt that it was important to store the display parameters in double floating point numbers rather than ordinary ones. The double precision makes it possible to do large blow ups of the various sets and does not appear to significantly increase the processing time. If you really need to convert one of the previous version files, you will have to modify the functions appropriately. This should be a trivial operation. Second, this function does not read the appended data at the end of the file. This is done by a separate function, which is described below. Thus if you must work with a file that doesn't have the data appended, you can temporarily comment out the function that reads appended data and add your own code to initialize the appropriate parameters.

Function to Return Appended Display Data

The *restore_parameters* function reads the appended display data from a disk file into the proper parameters. The parameter passed to this function is the name of the disk file. If the function cannot open this file in the read mode, it displays an error message and returns to the calling function. If the file is opened successfully, the function reads the first file character. If it is not 0AH (which indicates a Zsoft .PCX file) the function displays an error message, closes the file, and returns. Otherwise, it goes to the location which is 151 bytes from the end of the file and reads the character there. If the character is not 0CH, the function displays the file name followed by "is not a Fractal file.", closes the file, and then returns. Otherwise, the function reads the appended data from the disk file. This requires the following global parameters: *a, b, c, d, e, f, colors*[15][3], *max_iterations, color_option, start_x*, and *start_y*. The function then closes the file and returns.

Moving the Cursor on the Graphics Display

The most complicated function in the *ftools.cpp* package is the *move_cursor* function which displays various shaped cursors and moves them about the screen. Before beginning the description of this function we have to point out some strange things about the function for using the ROM BIOS to read directly from the keyboard. We need to use this function because we want to make use of the shift-arrow key combinations to move the cursor one pixel per keystroke and the regular arrow keys to move the cursor ten pixels per keystroke. The function is called *bioskey* in Turbo C++. In Microsoft C version 6.0, the function is called *_bios_keybrd*. Zortech C++ can use either of these names for the same function. In the case of Turbo C++, a strange phenomena was found when using this function, namely that the values returned for the shift-arrow key combinations were different when running in the integrated environment than they were when the program had already been compiled and was run directly from DOS. Borland has acknowledged the problem, but there is no determination yet as to what causes it or how to correct it. In the meantime, the numerical values that were obtained for the different key combinations using bioskey were obtained by writing a small program which displayed the number returned from each keystroke and trying it for the desired keys in both the integrated environment and with a compiled program run from DOS. It is not clear what numbers may be returned when the corresponding function is used with other compilers; if you run into difficulty, you may have to do some experimentation with a test program as I did.

You will note that the function begins with a series of define statements that equate arrow key names with the numbers they return. These statements are applicable to the integrated environment of Turbo C++ and are used to make the cases in the switch statement used below to control cursor movement more understandable to the programmer. Under some of the cases, you will see a second case with another number; this number applies when the compiled function is run directly from DOS.

The function begins by setting up some initial values for limit and then enters a *do* loop which comprises the whole function. The loop reiterates until the character returned from the keyboard is that of the Enter key. When this character is encountered, the loop terminates and the function returns to the calling program. The first thing that happens within the loop is that the function sets the parameter index to zero. It then enters a switch statement which uses the *plot_point* function to draw the cursor on the screen at the coordinates specified by the global variables *CURSOR_X* and *CURSOR_Y*, with the cursor shape depending upon the type parameter passed to the *move_cursor* function. At the same time, the display information that is written over by the cursor is saved for restoration when the cursor is moved. The first two cursor types are the top left corner and the bottom right corner. These are easily drawn with two straight lines of pixels. The third cursor type is an arrow. To draw this figure, we make use of two *for* loops and a couple of *if* statements. The method may seem a little obscure, but if you follow through the loops, plotting each point on a piece of paper, you will see that a nice arrow is produced.

Next, the function reads an input from the keyboard using the *bioskey* function. The index is reset to zero and a switch statement is entered which does exactly what the *switch* statement above did, except that it displays the original display information where the cursor was. Then another *switch* statement is entered which changes the value of the global variables defining cursor position if any of the arrow or shift-arrow keys were struck. The function then enters another *switch* statement, which converts the new cursor position in pixels to the appropriate values in the complex plane for the current display and then displays these values at the bottom of the screen.

This process of moving the cursor and displaying values is repeated until the Enter key is hit. The function then terminates, leaving the appropriate display parameters in the appropriate two of the global parameters *TXMax*, *TXMin*, *TYMax*, *TYMin*, *Pval*, and *Qval*. These values can then be used by the calling program to determine the parameters of the next display to be generated.

The bounds Program

The *bounds* program is not part of the *ftools.cpp* package. It is a separate program designed to allow you to look at a .PCX file containing a display that has been generated and see what all of the parameters of the display are. This is important because it is easy to forget just what parameters were used, and while the file stores these for use in generating expanded displays, etc. they are not ordinarily available to the user. The bounds program is listed in Figure 3-3. It should be fairly self-evident how it works. First, the program asks for the name of the desired file and then restores it as a graphics screen. This is done so that you can make sure that you have the right display. Then the program reads the various parameters from the file and displays them superimposed on the graphics display.

```
/*

    bounds = Program to get saved screen parameters

*/

#include <stdio.h>
```

USEFUL FUNCTIONS FOR FRACTAL GENERATION

```
#include <stdlib.h>
#include <math.h>
#include <dos.h>
#include <process.h>
#include "ftools.h"

double XMax, XMin, YMax, YMin, TXMax, TXMin, TYMax, TYMin,
    Pval, Qval, a, b, c, d, e, f, start_x, start_y;
int CURSOR_X, CURSOR_Y, colors[15][3], error, max_iterations,
    color_option, i;
unsigned char PALETTE[16]={0,1,2,3,4,5,20,7,56,57,58,59,60,61,62,63};
char file_name[13];

main()
{
    setMode(3);
    printf("Enter file name: ");
    scanf("%s",file_name);
    error = restore_screen(file_name);
    if (error == 0)
    {
        printf("\nCannot find %s. Hit any key to"
            " exit",file_name);
        getch();
        exit(0);
    }
    else
    {
        error = restore_parameters(file_name);
        if (error == 0)
            exit(0);
        else
        {
            for (i=0; i<16; i++)
                printf("Palette #%d = %d\n",i,PALETTE[i]);
            printf("XMax = %lf\n",XMax);
            printf("XMin = %lf\n",XMin);
            printf("YMax = %lf\n",YMax);
            printf("YMin = %lf\n",YMin);
            printf("P = %lf\n",Pval);
```

```
printf("Q = %lf\n",Qval);
printf("max iterations: %d\n",max_iterations);
printf("color option: %d\n",color_option);
for (i=1; i<15; i++)
{
    gotoxy(40,i);
    printf("Start: %d        Stop: %d          Color: %d",
    colors[i][0], colors[i][1], colors[i][2]);
}
gotoxy(40,16);
printf("a: %lf",a);
gotoxy(40,17);
printf("b: %lf",b);
gotoxy(40,18);
printf("c: %lf",c);
gotoxy(40,19);
printf("d: %lf",d);
gotoxy(40,20);
printf("e: %lf",e);
gotoxy(40,21);
printf("f: %lf",f);
gotoxy(40,22);
printf("start_x: %lf",start_x);
gotoxy(40,23);
printf("start_y: %lf",start_y);
getch();
            }
        }
    }
```

Figure 3-3. Listing of bounds Program

CHAPTER 4

The Mandelbrot Set Revisited

Everyone has seen the Mandelbrot set. It is the granddaddy of all fractal curves. In my book, *Fractal Programming in C*, I described a bare bones Mandelbrot set program and a more sophisticated one that enabled the user to move around on the Mandelbrot set display and select an area for expansion. Programs were also included for Julia sets and dragon curves. For any one of these sets, it is possible to generate an infinite variety of interesting pictures by choosing different parameter values and different magnifications. In this chapter, we are going to look at these sets in a lot more detail. To do that, we need a program that is quite sophisticated and fairly user friendly. We shall describe such a program and the show how to use it to obtain some interesting results.

Basics of Mandelbrot and Julia Sets and Dragons

The Mandelbrot and Julia sets are obtained by iterating the following equation:

$$z_n = z_{n-1}^2 + c \qquad \text{(Equation 4-1)}$$

where both z and c are complex numbers. For the Mandelbrot set, our display represents the values of c in the complex plane. For each pixel of the display, we begin by solving the equation for z_1, where c is the value represented by the pixel. Note that for the same result, you have the choice of setting z_0 equal to either 0 or c. The only difference is that if you start with 0 you have to iterate one more time. (Beginning with 0 we have c after one iteration). Now we iterate the equation until it either blows up (approaches infinity) or reaches a maximum number of iterations without blowing up. We now represent the result of this set of iterations by the color that we assign to the pixel. There are a number of techniques that we can use to assign the color. We will go into these in more detail later. However, the most common one is to assign black to all points that don't blow up, and to cycle through the other available colors, depending upon the number of iterations before blow up, for other pixels. Thus color pixels represent, in a sense, how fast that point blows up.

For the Julia set, we make use of the same equation. In this case, our display, instead of representing c in the complex plane, represents the initial value of z in the complex plane. We iterate and assign colors in the same manner, except that we begin each set of iterations by assigning to z_0 the value represented by the pixel, and assigning to c a predetermined value that is unique for the Julia set that we are going to plot.

Relationship Between Mandelbrot and Julia Sets

You have probably read that the Mandelbrot set is a one-page dictionary of Julia sets. It is so called because if you enlarge the Mandelbrot set sufficiently at any given point you obtain something that looks very much like the Julia set at that point. Let's see what that means mathematically. Suppose we have a Julia set for which we set the value of c to be w. Consider the point of the Julia set at which z_0 is also w. We then have:

$$z_0 = w \qquad\qquad \text{(Equation 4-2)}$$

$$z_1 = w^2 + w \qquad\qquad \text{(Equation 4-3)}$$

Now suppose we look at the Mandelbrot set at the point where c is w. We have:

$$z_0 = w \qquad\qquad \text{(Equation 4-4)}$$

$$z_1 = w^2 + w \qquad\qquad \text{(Equation 4-5)}$$

Thus, the result of iterating is the same for both the Julia and Mandelbrot sets at this particular point. Now suppose we move from this point by a distance d (where d is also a complex number). For the Julia set, we then have:

$$z_0 = w + d \qquad \text{(Equation 4-6)}$$

$$z_1 = (w + d)^2 + w \qquad \text{(Equation 4-7)}$$

and for the Mandelbrot set:

$$z_0 = w + d \qquad \text{(Equation 4-8)}$$

$$z_1 = (w + d)^2 + w + d \qquad \text{(Equation 4-9)}$$

We see that if d is very very small, the result of iterating will again be the same for the two sets, but as d increases, the results diverge more and more. Furthermore, d can be varied so that the result $w + d$ represents, in turn, every point on the screen. We then observe that at every point on the screen, the iteration begins in the same way for both sets, but diverges more and more as the distance d increases. Hence, for very large magnifications, the pictures of the Mandelbrot and Julia sets should be the same. Plates 1 and 2 are pictures of the Mandelbrot and Julia sets respectively having the following parameters:

$$z_{min} = -0.108382 + i0.909756 \qquad \text{(Equation 4-10)}$$
$$z_{max} = -0.105624 + i0.915431$$

and for the Julia set

$$c = -0.107042 + i0.911175 \qquad \text{(Equation 4-11)}$$

This makes the value of c correspond to the center of the display for both sets. You can see that the two pictures look very much alike. Next, we are going to use the core program, which will be described in the next chapter, to compute the points for both sets simultaneously and display for each pixel a color that represents the difference in the number of iterations for which each point blows up. The part of the program that actually does the fractal computation is listed in Figure 4-1. You will note that the function begins in the middle of the screen, and with *x* and *y* values that correspond to the real and imaginary parts of the fixed Julia set parameter c.

```
/*
```

```
fractal() = Computes and displays the difference between the Julia and
            Mandelbrot sets.
```

```
*/
```

```
void fractal(void)
{
    double p1, p2, q1, q2, xsq, ysq;
    int iter1, iter2, color;

    deltaP = (XMax - XMin)/640;
    deltaQ = (YMax - YMin)/350;
    for (col=0; col<320; col++)
    {
        p1 = Pval + col * deltaP;
        p2 = Pval - col * deltaP;
        if (kbhit() != 0)
        {
            save_screen(0,0,col,maxrow,filename);
            exit(0);
        }
        for (row=0; row<175; row++)
        {
            q1 = Qval + row * deltaQ;
            q2 = Qval - row * deltaQ;
            x = p1;
            y = q1;
            xsq = x*x;
            ysq = y*y;
            iter1 = 0;
            while ((iter1 < max_iterations) && (xsq + ysq <
            max_size))
            {
```

```
        y = 2*x*y + q1;
        x = xsq -ysq + p1;
        xsq = x*x;
        ysq = y*y;
        iter1++;
}
x = p1;
y = q1;
xsq = x*x;
ysq = y*y;
iter2 = 0;
while ((iter2 < max_iterations) && (xsq + ysq <
max_size))
{
        y = 2*x*y + Qval;
        x = xsq -ysq + Pval;
        xsq = x*x;
        ysq = y*y;
        iter2++;
}
color = abs(iter1 - iter2);
if (color > 15)
        color = color%15 + 1;
plot (319+col,174+row,color);
x = p2;
y = q1;
xsq = x*x;
ysq = y*y;
iter1 = 0;
while ((iter1 < max_iterations) && (xsq + ysq <
max_size))
{
        y = 2*x*y + q1;
        x = xsq -ysq + p2;
        xsq = x*x;
        ysq = y*y;
        iter1++;
}
x = p2;
y = q1;
```

```
xsq = x*x;
ysq = y*y;
iter2 = 0;
while ((iter2 < max_iterations) && (xsq + ysq <
max_size))
{
    y = 2*x*y + Qval;
    x = xsq -ysq + Pval;
    xsq = x*x;
    ysq = y*y;
    iter2++;
}
color = abs(iter1 - iter2);
if (color > 15)
    color = color%15 + 1;
plot (319-col,174+row,color);
x = p1;
y = q2;
xsq = x*x;
ysq = y*y;
iter1 = 0;
while ((iter1 < max_iterations) && (xsq + ysq <
max_size))
{
    y = 2*x*y + q2;
    x = xsq -ysq + p1;
    xsq = x*x;
    ysq = y*y;
    iter1++;
}
x = p1;
y = q2;
xsq = x*x;
ysq = y*y;
iter2 = 0;
while ((iter2 < max_iterations) && (xsq + ysq <
max_size))
{
    y = 2*x*y + Qval;
    x = xsq -ysq + Pval;
```

```
        xsq = x*x;
        ysq = y*y;
        iter2++;
}
color = abs(iter1 - iter2);
if (color > 15)
        color = color%15 + 1;
plot (319+col,174-row,color);
x = p2;
y = q2;
xsq = x*x;
ysq = y*y;
iter1 = 0;
while ((iter1 < max_iterations) && (xsq + ysq <
max_size))
{
        y = 2*x*y + q2;
        x = xsq -ysq + p2;
        xsq = x*x;
        ysq = y*y;
        iter1++;
}
x = p2;
y = q2;
xsq = x*x;
ysq = y*y;
iter2 = 0;
while ((iter2 < max_iterations) && (xsq + ysq <
max_size))
{
        y = 2*x*y + Qval;
        x = xsq -ysq + Pval;
        xsq = x*x;
        ysq = y*y;
        iter2++;
}
color = abs(iter1 - iter2);
if (color > 15)
        color = color%15 + 1;
plot (319-col,174-row,color);
```

```
            }
        }
    }
```

Figure 4-1. Function to Produce the Difference between the Mandelbrot and Julia Sets

The function uses *while* loops to perform the iteration process for the Mandelbrot and Julia sets for this point and then colors the pixel to represent the difference in the number of iterations (which is black, for zero). It then performs the same computations for these sets at one pixel above and below the starting point. Next it moves one additional pixel above and one below and computes the data for these points. When the line is complete, it goes back to the center and computes values for the pixels to the right and left of center, then for these columns and one up and one down, and so forth until the display is complete. The resulting display is shown in Plate 3. The black areas are those where the results from the two sets are identical and the other colors represent the amount of the divergence at each point. If you were to expand each set by reducing the limiting boundaries, you would get a display that was all within the black area and would thus be totally black. This wouldn't be very interesting, but would indicate that within that range, the two sets were exactly alike (at least to the limits of precision of our computer).

Dragon Curves

The dragon curve is similar to the Julia set, but is obtained using the following iterated equation:

$$z_n = c(1-z_n)^2 \qquad\qquad \text{(Equation 4-12)}$$

The characteristics are similar to the Julia and Mandelbrot sets, including the way that computations occur, the existence of a dragon correspondence to the Mandelbrot set, and the identity of the two sets at high magnifications.

Contents of an Advanced Set Generation Program

First, let's consider the following iterated equation:

$$z_n = (a + ib)z_{n-1}^2 + (c + id)z_{n-1} + e + if \qquad \text{(Equation 4-13)}$$

Note that by properly selecting the parameters, this equation will generate any Mandelbrot/Julia set or dragon curve or many other curves that have not yet been investigated. We are going to look at a program for generating all sort sets and curves using this equation. It's a pretty complicated program. If you plan to type it into the computer yourself, rather than buying the disk, or if you plan to modify it, you need some experience in using the C language. We'll give a listing of the program and describe it a little later, but first we'll describe how to use the program to create fractal displays. Once you understand how the program is used and what kinds of control you have over the display parameters, it will be easier to understand the actual functioning of the code.

Using the Advanced Set Generation Program

The program begins with a window that asks you to "Make your choice with the up and down arrows." Next is the following list:

Generate a New Set
Expand a Section of an Existing Set
Complete an Unfinished Set
Quit

Initially the first of these lines is in a contrasting color. As you touch the up and down arrow keys, the contrasting line will move up and down so that you may select the desired option. Once you have chosen the option that you want, you can proceed by hitting the Enter key. Let's begin at the beginning.

Generating a New Set

Suppose you select, "Generate a New Set". The program then opens a new window which says the following:

Make your choice with the up and down arrows:
Mandelbrot Set
Julia Set
Mandelbrot-like Set for Dragons
Dragon Curve
Select Parameters for curve

By moving the cursor arrows, you can select one of the options and then hit the Enter key to proceed. If you selected, "Mandelbrot Set", or Mandelbrot-like Set for Dragons, the program will next ask you for the starting value of x and after you enter that and hit the Enter key it will ask you for the starting value of y.

Initial Values for Iteration

It has become so well established that the starting value for the Mandelbrot set is either 0 or c that we scarcely give it a thought anymore. Mathematically, however, there is no reason why some other value couldn't be used instead. When we do this, a distorted version of the Mandelbrot set is produced which looks quite unlike the one we are used to. Now, we have to give some thought to the dragon curve. If you'll look at Equation 4-13, you'll see that for the dragon equivalent of the Mandelbrot set, if we were to start with a value of zero, the resulting value would always be zero, no matter how many times we iterate. Obviously, the resulting curve would not be very interesting. So we must consider just what is a normal starting value. We've already pointed out that the Mandelbrot set can be used as a road map for selecting Julia sets. The various cusps of the Mandelbrot set are good places to select for the parameters of a Julia set that will be interesting. For the distorted Mandelbrot sets that are created by using different initial values, this is no longer true. It can be shown that the Mandelbrot-like sets that make good maps for their Julia-like counterparts, the initial starting value should be such that the derivative of the function is zero. For the case of the dragon counterpart of the Mandelbrot set, this value is 0.5 for the real part and zero for the imaginary part. If you use the program to generate some of your own unique sets, you need to take the derivative of the function to determine the starting value that will give you the best mapping set. The program is set up to give you complete flexibility as to the starting values, so the next window that appears on the screen allows you to enter starting values for x and y (and also indicates what the normal values are for the Mandelbrot set and its dragon counterpart).

Plate 5 is the conventional Mandelbrot set, produced by the program, using 512 iterations. Plate 4 shows the distortion that occurs when the starting values x and y are both set to 0.3.

Number of Iterations

Once you have entered both starting values and hit the Enter key again, a new window will appear which says:

Enter number of iterations desired (16-512):

Take a look at plate 4, which is a distorted Mandelbrot set generated with cycling colors and 512 iterations. The outer edge of the display is a blue border, which indicates that the function blew up on the first iteration. Just inward from this is a green area indicating that in this region the function blows up at the second iteration. You can proceed toward the black area which represents the area where the function does not blow up and count the number of color cycles to see how many iterations are required to produce all of the available detail at any point on the display. (You may need a magnifying glass.) You will observe that the required number of iterations to get the fine detail differs widely at different places on the display. By carefully observing this display, you will be able to determine just where detail will be lost when you reduce the number of iterations. The program has been set up so that regardless of what you type in, the lower limit is 16 iterations and the upper limit is 512. You are probably asking, "Why would one want to change the number of iterations, anyway?" The answer is that the more iterations you specify, the longer the program takes to run. Therefore, for each display that you create, you need to make a compromise between how long you want the program to run and how much detail you want in the display. You may want to use the minimum number of iterations at first to make a quick pass and determine what the display looks like and then use a larger number of iterations later to create a more detailed display for preservation.

Selecting the Coloring Technique

After you have selected the desired number of iterations and hit the Enter key, the color selection window appears on the screen in the following form:

Make your choice with the up and down arrows:
Select colors and ranges of iterations
Cycle through colors as iterations or values change
Cycle colors for closed solution values

As previously mentioned, one simple way to assign colors is to assign black to all points that don't blow up and cycle through the available colors for points that do blow up, with the various colors indicating how quickly the point blows up. This is the technique that is used if you select the middle option, "Cycle through colors as iterations or values change". (Our criteria is that any time the magnitude of the iterated equation reaches two, the equation will ultimately blow up to infinity. This can be shown to be true mathematically.) If you use this technique, you will note a blue area around the outer perimeter of the set, which represents all points that have exceeded the blow up criteria on the very first iteration. Within this is a green area representing all points that meet the blow up criteria after two iterations. This color cycling continues until one reaches the edge of the Mandelbrot curve. In many areas, this happens after just a few color cycles, but there are some areas where there are as many color cycles as the maximum number of iterations that you permit. Note that this method of specifying colors gives the maximum amount of detail. Whenever there is a change of just one in the number of iterations required to exceed the threshold, the color changes.

Although this color assignment technique gives the maximum amount of detail, there are times when we learn more about the nature of the curve when we assign a single color to a group of iterations. For example, points that blow up after 1 to 5 iterations might be assigned to red, points that blow up after 5 to 15 iterations might be assigned yellow, and so forth. This is the technique that is used when you select the first option, "Select colors and ranges of iterations". When you select this option, a new window appears on the screen. It begins by looking like the following:

Enter Upper Limit Number and Use Arrows to Set Colors:
Start Iters   End Iters   Color #1   Color #2
       0

You are now ready to select colors for the group beginning with zero iterations. You first type in the number of iterations that is to be the end of this group. When you hit the Enter key, two colors will appear, one under Color #1 and the other under Color #2. (If the value that you inserted under End Iters is greater than the maximum number of iterations that you specified earlier, the program will automatically replace it with the maximum number of iterations.) The up and down arrows will now change the first color, cycling through the 16 shades that make up the EGA selection of colors. When you have found the one that you want for this group, hit the Enter key. What you have selected is the color that you want for all even numbered values of iterations within the designated group. You can now use the up and down arrow keys to select the color that you want for the odd numbered values of iterations within the group. If you want to preserve the maximum amount of detail in the display, choose a different color for this; if not, you may make it the same as the first color and the same color will apply to all iteration values within the group. After you hit the Enter key again, if your value for the end iterations was equal to the maximum number of iterations, the window will terminate. Otherwise, the last value for the end number of iterations will be placed in the next row for starting number of iterations and your cursor will be placed for you to insert the next value for the end number of iterations. You can then select colors as you did before. You can continue this process until you reach the maximum number of iterations or until you have inserted twelve groups of colors. If you reach the twelfth group without specifying the maximum number of iterations, the end value of iterations is automatically changed for you to the maximum number of iterations. Also, if you ever specify an ending value of iterations that is less than the starting value, the program automatically replaces it with the starting value plus one.

The two color schemes described above give us a whole lot of information about the points which blow up, but tell us very little about those that don't. Therefore, another color technique is also provided. It assigns black to all points that blow up, and assigns points that don't blow up to one of the available colors, depending upon the magnitude of the value of the iterated equation after the maximum number of iterations occurs. This option is chosen by selecting, "Cycle colors for closed solution values". You will now see a display like the following:

Select palette number with up and
down arrows. Select color with
left and right arrows:

Background	0
Palette # 1	1
Palette # 2	2
Palette # 3	3
Palette # 4	4
Palette # 5	5
Palette # 6	20
Palette # 7	7

Each of the numbers on the right is surrounded by a block of color. Using the arrows, you can select a background and seven foreground colors from the 64 EGA palette colors. When you have properly selected your colors, hit Enter to terminate the color selection process.

Once you have finished selecting the color option, the program begins to generate the selected curve. The program automatically enters the proper parameters in the iterated equation to generate the curve you selected and also selects the proper limits of x and y for the selected curve.

To give you some idea of what can be done with the traditional Mandelbrot set, Plate 5 is a Mandelbrot set using the first color option and choosing colors as shown in Table 4-1.

Lower Bound	Upper Bound	Color #1	Color #2
0	20	1	1
20	30	14	9
30	35	4	4
35	50	12	12
50	100	14	14
100	512	0	0

Table 4-1. Colors for Mandelbrot Set using First Color Option

Julia and Dragon Curves

We've now discussed what happens when you select the Mandelbrot set or the Mandelbrot-like set for dragons. Now suppose that, instead, you selected the Julia set or the Dragon curve. For the Julia set, you must have on your disk the "mandel00.pcx" file containing information on the original Mandelbrot set. If you do, when you select the Julia set, this Mandelbrot set will be displayed together with a cursor arrow that you can move with the arrow keys to select the point where you want the fixed parameter for a Julia set. Remember that the cusps of the curve produce the most interesting Julia sets. As you move the cursor with the arrow keys, the real (P) and imaginary (Q) values of the Julia set constant appear at the bottom of the display. Once you have properly positioned the cursor, hit the Enter key. The program will then ask for the number of iterations as it did for the Mandelbrot set. When this has been entered, a new window will appear which will allow you to select the color options as for the Mandelbrot set. After you set the color options, the program will begin to generate the Julia set. The dragon curve is specified in just the same way, except that the initial file that must be present on your disk is called *drgset00.pcx*. Plate 6 is a typical Julia set having the constant real value of P =

0.383725 and the imaginary value of Q = 0.147851 and the colors given in Table 4-2, using the third color option. Plate 7 is a typical dragon, having the constant real value of P = 1.646009 and the imaginary value of Q = 0.967049 and the colors shown in Table 4-3, using the third color option.

Palette	Color
Background	0
Palette # 1	57
Palette # 2	58
Palette # 3	59
Palette # 4	60
Palette # 5	61
Palette # 6	62
Palette # 7	63

Table 4-2. Colors for Julia Set with Third Color Option

Palette	Color
Background	0
Palette # 1	1
Palette # 2	52
Palette # 3	62
Palette # 4	38
Palette # 5	44
Palette # 6	20
Palette # 7	7

Table 4-3. Colors for Dragon Curve Set with Third Color Option

Creating Your Own Curves

We now come to the last option for generating a curve, which you choose by selecting, "Select Parameters for curve". When you do this, you will see the following display:

Curve for x = (a+ib)*z*z + (c+id)*z + (e+if)

Select three lines with up and down arrows.
On each line enter two values separated by comma
a, ib:
c, id:
e, if:
start x, start y:

This option gives you total flexibility over the system parameters. The program is set up so that the line in which you don't enter parameters selects the variables that are varied and therefore are the screen coordinates for your display. You can also enter a number less than -10000 for each of the parameters on a line and have them become the negative of the variable parameter values. Thus, by leaving out the bottom line, you will have a Julia-type set, whereas leaving out one of the other lines will give you a Mandelbrot-like set. As a test case, we generated a curve having the following entries:

a, ib: 0.5, 0.5
c, id: 0.8, 0.6
start x, start y: 0, 0;

After these numbers have been entered, the display will request, "Enter name of file to save display". You then type in the desired file name. The program will then give you an opportunity to select the number of iterations and the color options in the same way as for the curves described above. The curve resulting from the set of parameters listed above is not very exciting, but you can no doubt select parameters which give some new and interesting displays.

Expanding an Existing Set

Returning to the first menu display, the second option is, "Expand a Section of an Existing Set". If you have already completed a set and stored it on disk, you may select this option and then type in the proper file name when requested. If you chose a suitable file, the program will display it on the screen, together with a cursor in the form of an upper left hand corner for a rectangle. You may move this cursor in large increments (ten pixels) with the arrow keys or in single pixel increments with the SHIFT arrow keys. As you begin to move the cursor, the minimum x and maximum y values will appear at the bottom of the screen. (The screen coordinates for the PC are designated so that the top left hand corner of the screen is (0,0). The column coordinate increases toward the right and the row coordinate increases downward. However, to be more conventional, we have defined the coordinates so (0,0) is at the bottom left and x increases toward the right and y increases upward.) When you get the top corner where you want it, hit Enter and a cursor in the form of a lower right corner will appear. This cursor is limited so that it must always be in a position so that it, together with the previous cursor, delineate the bounds of a rectangle which will be the boundary of the new display. As you begin to move this cursor with the arrow keys, the maximum value for x and the minimum value for y will appear at the bottom of the screen. When you have designated the rectangle that you want for the bounds of the display that is to be created, hitting the Enter key will record the bounds selected. When you expand a curve, the same number of iterations and color options that were selected for the original display are preserved for the expanded display.

Some of the most interesting displays are produced by expanding on the original sets. As an example of the hidden characteristics that you can uncover, take a look at the picture shown in Plate 8. This is an expansion of the Mandelbrot set having the following parameters: $XMax$ = -1.252442, $XMin$ = -1.258917, $YMax$ = 0.385815, $YMin$ = 0.374419, and $max\_iterations$ = 512. Suddenly we see a replica of the original Mandelbrot set.

Completing an Unfinished Display

One of the problems with creating fractal displays is that many such displays take a long time to generate. At some point in this process you may absolutely have to terminate the process to use your computer for some other job. If you have been running this program, you can terminate it at any time by striking a key. The program will then complete the column that it is working on, save the partially generated display, and return to DOS. When you want to complete this unfinished display, you can select the third beginning option, "Complete an Unfinished Set". This will only work if you actually have an unfinished display file stored on your disk. When you select this option, you will be requested to, "Enter name of file to complete: ". At this point you had better have the name of an incomplete file to type in; otherwise the program will display an error message and return you to DOS. If you do type in the name of a legitimate file, the program will display the partially completed picture and obtain all of the parameters needed to complete the picture from the disk file. The program will begin drawing the picture at the byte boundary nearest the end of the display. This may result in a little overlap (but no more that seven columns in the worst case). You can then allow the program to complete the drawing, or let it work for a while and then save another partially completed picture.

Quitting

The last of the initial options is pretty obvious. When you select "Quit", the program terminates and returns you to DOS. In fact, this is the only way to leave this program without resetting the computer or prematurely terminating a display generation process, since when the program finishes creating a display it goes through the following procedure. First it waits for any keystroke. When a keystroke is received, the screen is returned to text mode and the time that was required to generate the display together with the output file name is displayed. Then the program awaits another keystroke. When it is received, the program returns to the opening menu, ready to create another display. It is at this point that you must select "Quit" if you want to terminate the program.

How the Program Works

Figure 4-3 is a listing of the fractal generating program. The whole program consists of one gigantic *while* loop, which continues as long as the parameter *key* is not equal to 6. On each pass through the loop, the user has an opportunity to set parameters and generate a set display on the screen. Finally, on the pass in which *key* is equal to 6 because the option "Quit" was selected, the loop terminates the program and returns to DOS.

Returning to the very beginning of the program, you will note some define statements. These are a convenience for help in understanding the operation of the program. A little later you will see a *switch* statement which selects things to be done on the basis of the option chosen from the menu. If these *switch* cases were simply labeled by number, you would have to go back and check the *menu* function each time to see what was going on. By using define statements to assign to each number a word which indicates the meaning of the option, we make it possible to understand what each case is doing without having to continuously refer back and forth. Next, the functions and variables used in the program are defined. We then start the main program, which first sets *key* to zero and then begins the *while* loop that we referred to earlier. At the beginning of the program, all of the equation parameters and starting values are initialized to 10001. Next the *menu* function is called. This function will be described in detail later. Right now, we'll just say that it allows you to select one of the six program options and then returns the value of the selected option in the variable *key*.

```
/*

    mandel = ADVANCED PROGRAM TO MAP THE
    MANDELBROT SET
    By Roger T. Stevens 08/26/90

*/

#include <process.h>
#include <ctype.h>
#include <time.h>
#include "ftools.h"

#define NEWSET    0
#define EXPAND    1
#define COMPLETE  2
#define QUIT      3
#define MANDELBROT 0
#define JULIA     1
#define DRGSET    2
#define DRAGON    3
#define SETPARAMS 4
```

```
int menu (int types);
int set_colors(void);
void move_cursor(int type,int color,int min_col, int min_row);
int restore_parameters(char file_name[]);
void get_iterations();
void get_starters(void);
void set_parameters(void);
void setMode(int mode);
void set_julia_colors(void);

double XMax, XMin, YMax, YMin, TXMax, TXMin, TYMax, TYMin, Pval, Qval,
        a, b, c, d, e, f;
int colors[15][3], max_iterations, color_option, CURSOR_X, CURSOR_Y;
unsigned char PALETTE[16]={0,1,2,3,4,5,20,7,56,57,58,59,60,61,62,63};
const int maxcol = 640;
const int maxrow = 350;
const int max_colors = 16;
unsigned plotting_type,key,set_type;
int max_size = 4,length;
int LINEWIDTH=1, OPERATOR=0x00;
int color, m, row, col,error,response,repeat=0x30,start_col=0,old_color=0;
unsigned long int PATTERN=0xFFFFFFFF;
double A[640], B[350], C[640], D[350], E[640], F[350], x_starter[640],
    y_starter[350], threshold;
clock_t start, end;
FILE *f1;
char file_name[13];
double deltaX, deltaY,start_x,start_y;

main()
{
    double X, Y, Xsquare, Ysquare,old_x,old_y,y;
    int i,j;
    float elapsed_time;

    key = 0;
    while (key != 3)
    {
        file_name[0] = NULL;
        a = 10001;
```

77

```
b = 10001;
c = 10001;
d = 10001;
e = 10001;
f = 10001;
start_x = 10001;
start_y = 10001;
key = menu(0);
switch(key)
{
    case QUIT:
        setMode(3);
        exit(0);
    case COMPLETE:
        gotoxy(12,13);
        cprintf("Enter name of file to complete:  ");
        cscanf("%s",file_name);
        if ((strchr(file_name,'.'))==NULL)
            strcat(file_name,".PCX");
        error = restore_screen(file_name);
        if (error == 0)
            exit(0);
        start_col = error;
        error = restore_parameters(file_name);
        if (error == 0)
        {
            printf("Error = %d while getting"
                " parameters\n",error);
            exit(0);
        }
        remove(file_name);
        set_parameters();
        break;
    case EXPAND:
        gotoxy(12,13);
        cprintf("Enter name of file to expand: ");
        cscanf("%s",file_name);
        if ((strchr(file_name,'.'))==NULL)
            strcat(file_name,".PCX");
        error = restore_screen(file_name);
```

```
            if (error == 0)
                 exit(0);
            f1 = fopen(file_name,"rb");
            error = restore_parameters(file_name);
            if (error == 0)
                 exit(0);
            getch();
            move_cursor(0,15,0,0);
            move_cursor(1,15,CURSOR_X,CURSOR_Y);
            start_col = 0;
            XMax = TXMax;
            XMin = TXMin;
            YMax = TYMax;
            YMin = TYMin;
            setMode(3);
            get_iterations();
            color_option = menu(1);
            if (color_option == 0)
                 set_colors();
            if (color_option == 2)
                 set_julia_colors();
            set_parameters();
            setMode(16);
            cls(7);
            break;
     case NEWSET:
            set_type = menu(2);
            switch(set_type)
            {
                 case JULIA:
                        error = restore_screen("mandel00.pcx");
                        if (error != 0)
                        {
                              strcpy(file_name,"julia000.pcx");
                              move_cursor(2,15,0,0);
                              XMax = 1.6;
                              XMin = -1.6;
                              YMax = 1.2;
                              YMin = -1.2;
                              a = 1;
```

```
                b = 0;
                c = 0;
                d = 0;
                e = Pval;
                f = Qval;
                set_parameters();
                setMode(3);
                get_iterations();
                color_option = menu(1);
                if (color_option == 0)
                        set_colors();
                if (color_option == 2)
                        set_julia_colors();
                setMode(16);
                for (i=0; i<16; i++)
                        setEGApalette(i,PALETTE[i]);
                cls(7);
                break;
        }
        printf("\nRequired Mandelbrot Set"
                " 'mandel00.pcx' doesn't exist.");
        printf("\nGenerating this Mandelbrot Set");
        delay(5000);
case MANDELBROT:
        strcpy(file_name,"mandel00.pcx");
        XMax = 1.2;
        XMin = -2.0;
        YMax = 1.2;
        YMin = -1.2;
        a = 1;
        b = 0;
        c = 0;
        d = 0;
        get_starters();
        set_parameters();
        get_iterations();
        color_option = menu(1);
        if (color_option == 0)
                set_colors();
        if (color_option == 2)
```

```
            set_julia_colors();
        setMode(16);
        for (i=0; i<16; i++)
            setEGApalette(i,PALETTE[i]);
        cls(7);
        break;
case DRAGON:
        error = restore_screen("drgset00.pcx");
        if (error != 0)
        {
            strcpy(file_name,"dragon00.pcx");
            move_cursor(2,15,0,0);
            XMax = 1.6;
            XMin = -0.6;
            YMax = 1.0;
            YMin = -1.0;
            a = -Pval;
            b = -Qval;
            c = Pval;
            d = Qval;
            e = 0;
            f = 0;
            set_parameters();
            setMode(3);
            get_iterations();
            color_option = menu(1);
            if (color_option == 0)
                    set_colors();
            if (color_option == 2)
                    set_julia_colors();
            setMode(16);
            for (i=0; i<16; i++)
                    setEGApalette(i,PALETTE[i]);
            cls(7);
            break;
        }
        printf("\nRequired Set for Dragons"
            " 'drgset00.pcx' doesn't exist.");
        printf("\nGenerating this Set");
        delay(5000);
```

```
case DRGSET:
    strcpy(file_name,"drgset00.pcx");
    XMax = 4.2;
    XMin = -2.2;
    YMax = 1.5;
    YMin = -1.5;
    get_starters();
    a = -10001;
    b = -10001;
    e = 0;
    f = 0;
    set_parameters();
    get_iterations();
    color_option = menu(1);
    if (color_option == 0)
        set_colors();
    if (color_option == 2)
        set_julia_colors();
    setMode(16);
    for (i=0; i<16; i++)
        setEGApalette(i,PALETTE[i]);
    printf("Color option is: %d",color_option);
    getch();
    cls(7);
    break;
case SETPARAMS:
    gotoxy(12,14);
    cprintf("Enter name of file to save"
        " display: ");
    cscanf("%s",file_name);
    XMax = 3.2;
    XMin = -2.2;
    YMax = 1.5;
    YMin = -1.5;
    set_parameters();
    get_iterations();
    color_option = menu(1);
    if (color_option == 0)
        set_colors();
    if (color_option == 2)
```

```
                    set_julia_colors();
                setMode(16);
                for (i=0; i<16; i++)
                    setEGApalette(i,PALETTE[i]);
                cls(7);
                break;
        }
}
start = clock();
threshold = ((deltaX < deltaY ? deltaX : deltaY) / 2.0);
for (col=start_col; col<maxcol; col++)
{
    if (kbhit() != 0)
    {
        end = clock();
        save_screen(0,0,col,349,file_name);
        printf("\nElapsed time was %f seconds\n",
            (end - start)/CLK_TCK);
        printf("File name is: %s\n",file_name);
        setMode(3);
        getch();
        exit(0);
    }
    for (row=0; row<maxrow; row++)
    {
        X = x_starter[col];
        Y = y_starter[row];
        Xsquare = Ysquare = 0.0;
        color = 0;
        old_x = 0;
        old_y = 0;
        while ((color<max_iterations) && ((Xsquare +
            Ysquare) < 4.0))
        {
            Xsquare = X*X;
            Ysquare = Y*Y;
            y = 2*A[col]*X*Y + B[row]*Xsquare -
                B[row]*Ysquare + C[col]*Y + D[row]*X + F[row];
            X = A[col]*Xsquare - A[col]*Ysquare
                -2*B[row]*X*Y + C[col]*X - D[row]*Y + E[col];
```

```
                    Y = y;
                    if (old_color == max_iterations)
                    {
                        if ((color & 15) == 0)
                        {
                            old_x = X;
                            old_y = Y;
                        }
                        else
                            if ((fabs(old_x - X) + fabs(old_y - Y)) <
                                    threshold)
                                color = max_iterations-1;
                    }
                    color++;
                }
                switch(color_option)
                {
                    case 0:
                        i=0;
                        while (color > colors[i][0])
                            i++;
                        if ((color % 2) == 0)
                            plot(col,row,colors[i][2]);
                        else
                            plot(col,row,colors[i][1]);
                        break;
                   case 1:
                        plot(col,row,color%16);
                        break;
                   case 2:
                        if (color < max_iterations)
                            plot(col,row,0);
                        else
                        plot(col,row,((int)((Xsquare + Ysquare) *
                            6.0) % 6) + 1);
                }
                old_color = color;
            }
        }
        save_screen(0,0,639,349,file_name);
```

```
                end = clock();
                getch();
                setMode(3);
                printf("\nElapsed time was %f seconds\n",(end - start)/CLK_TCK);
                printf("File name is: %s\n",file_name);
                getch();
        }
}


/*
```

┌───┐
│   │
│   menu() = Permits the user to select from various options   │
│   │
└───┘

```
*/

int menu (int types)
{
        char TextData[7][48] = {"Generate a New Set",
                "Expand a Section of an Existing Set",
                "Complete an Unfinished Set",
                "Quit"};
        char TextData2[3][55] = {"Select colors and ranges of"
                " iterations",
                "Cycle through colors as iterations or values change",
                "Cycle colors for closed solution values"};

        char TextData3[5][55] = {"Mandelbrot Set","Julia Set",
                "Mandelbrot-like Set for Dragons","Dragon Curve",
                "Select parameters for curve"};
        char TextData4[7][48] = {"a, ib: ",
                "c, id: ",
                "e, if: ",
                "start x, start y: "};
        int flag=0;
        char ch1;
        int i,k=0, k2=0;
        int location[4] = {11,11,11,22};

        window(1,1,80,25);
        textbackground(0);
```

```
clrscr();
switch(types)
{
    case 0:
        window(10,6,59,13);
        m = 3;
        break;
    case 1:
        window(10,6,64,12);
        m = 2;
        break;
    case 2:
        window(10,6,59,14);
        m = 4;
}
textbackground(1);
clrscr();
gotoxy(3,2);
textcolor(10);
cprintf("Make your choice with the up and down arrows:");
do
{
    for (i=0; i<=m; i++)
    {
        if (i==k)
        {
            textcolor(1);
            textbackground(15);
        }
        else
        {
            textcolor(15);
            textbackground(1);
        }
        gotoxy(3,i+4);
        switch(types)
        {
            case 0:
                cprintf("%s",TextData[i]);
                break;
```

```
                    case 1:
                        cprintf("%s",TextData2[i]);
                        break;
                    case 2:
                        cprintf("%s",TextData3[i]);
                }
        }
        ch1 = getch();
        if (ch1 == 0x00)
        {
            ch1 = getch();
            switch(ch1)
            {
                case 'P':
                    ++k;
                    k = k % (m+1);
                    break;
                case 'H':
                    -k;
                    if (k<0)
                        k = m;
            }
        }
}
while (ch1 != 0x0D);
if (k > 3)
{
    window(1,1,80,25);
    textbackground(0);
    clrscr();
    window(10,6,61,14);
    m = 3;
    textbackground(1);
    clrscr();
    gotoxy(3,2);
    textcolor(11);
    cprintf("Curve for z = (a+ib)*z*z + (c+id)*z + (e+if)");
    textcolor(10);
    gotoxy(3,3);
    cprintf("Select three lines with up and down arrows.");
```

```
gotoxy(3,4);
cprintf("On each line enter two values separated by"
    " comma");
for(;;)
{
    if ((flag == 14) || (flag == 13) || (flag == 11) ||
        (flag == 7))
        break;
    for (i=0; i<=m; i++)
    {
        if (i==k2)
        {
            textcolor(1);
            textbackground(15);
        }
        else
        {
            textcolor(15);
            textbackground(1);
        }
        gotoxy(3,i+5);
        cprintf("%s",TextData4[i]);
    }
    gotoxy(location[k2],k2+5);
    ch1 = getch();
    if (ch1 == 0x00)
    {
        ch1 = getch();
        switch(ch1)
        {
            case 'P':
                ++k2;
                k2 = k2 % (m+1);
                break;
            case 'H':
                -k2;
                if (k2<0)
                    k2 = m;
        }
    }
```

```
        else
        if ((isdigit(ch1)) || (ch1 == '-') || (ch1 == '.'))
        {
            cprintf("%c",ch1);
            ungetch(ch1);
            switch(k2)
            {
                case 0:
                    cscanf("%f,%f",&a,&b);
                    flag |= 1;
                    break;
                case 1:
                    cscanf("%f,%f",&c,&d);
                    flag |= 2;
                    break;
                case 2:
                    cscanf("%f,%f",&e,&f);
                    flag |= 4;
                    break;
                case 3:
                    cscanf("%f,%f",&start_x,&start_y);
                    flag |= 8;
                    break;
            }
        }
    }
    window(1,1,80,25);
    return(k);
}


set_colors() = Sets limits and Colors for fractal generation


int set_colors(void)
{
    int color_set[2] = {1,1};
    int i, j, k;
    char ch1;;
```

```
textbackground(4);
clrscr();k = 0;
window(10,4,70,22);
textbackground(0);
clrscr();
gotoxy(3,1);
cprintf("Enter Upper Limit Number and Use Arrows to"
    " Set Colors:");
textcolor(14);
gotoxy(3,3);
cprintf("Start Iters  End Iters  Color #1  Color #2");
i = 0;
colors[0][0] = 0;
colors[1][0] = 0;
while (colors[i][0] < max_iterations)
{
    i++;
    textcolor(15);
    gotoxy(6,i+5);
    cprintf("%d",colors[i-1][0]);
    gotoxy(20,i+5);
    cscanf("%d",&colors[i][0]);
    if (colors[i][0] <= colors[i-1][0])
    {
        colors[i][0] = colors[i-1][0] + 1;
        gotoxy(20,i+5);
        cprintf("%d",colors[i][0]);
    }
    if ((i == 13) || (colors[i][0] > max_iterations))
    {
        colors[i][0] = max_iterations;
        gotoxy(20,i+5);
        cprintf("%d",colors[i][0]);
    }
    gotoxy(30,i+5);
    textcolor(color_set[0]);
    cprintf("\xDB\xDB\xDB\xDB\xDB\xDB");
    gotoxy(40,i+5);
    textcolor(color_set[1]);
    cprintf("\xDB\xDB\xDB\xDB\xDB\xDB");
```

```
getch();
for (k=0; k<2; k++)
{
    gotoxy(36+10*k, i+5);
    do
    {
        ch1 = getch();
        if (ch1 == 0x00)
        {
            ch1 = getch();
            switch(ch1)
            {
                case 'P':
                    ++color_set[k];
                    color_set[k] = color_set[k] % 16;
                    break;
                case 'H':
                    -color_set[k];
                    if (color_set[k] < 0)
                        color_set[k] = 15;
            }
        }
        gotoxy(30+10*k,i+5);
        textcolor(color_set[k]);
        cprintf("\xDB\xDB\xDB\xDB\xDB\xDB");
    }
    while (ch1 != 0x0D);
}
colors[i][1] = color_set[0];
colors[i][2] = color_set[1];
}
window(1,1,80,25);
clrscr();
textcolor(15);
return(i);
}
```

```
get_iterations() = Read in maximum number of iterations
```

```c
*/

void get_iterations()
{
    textbackground(0);
    clrscr();
    window(15,8,66,11);
    textbackground(4);
    clrscr();
    gotoxy(3,2);
    textcolor(15);
    cprintf("Enter number of iterations desired (16-512): ");
    cscanf("%d",&max_iterations);
    if (max_iterations < 16)
        max_iterations = 16;
    if (max_iterations > 512)
        max_iterations = 512;
    getch();
}

/*
```

```
get_starters() = Read in starting values for x and y
```

```c
*/

void (get_starters(void)
{
    textbackground(0);
    clrscr();
    window(20,9,66,15);
    textbackground(3);
    clrscr();
    gotoxy(3,2);
    textcolor(0);
    gotoxy(8,3);
```

```
        cprintf("Normal is 0 for Mandlebrot: ");
        gotoxy(8,4);
        cprintf("Normal is 0.5 for Dragon: ");
        gotoxy(3,2);
        cprintf("Enter starting value of x: ");
        cscanf("%lf",&start_x);
        gotoxy(3,5);
        cprintf("Enter starting value of y (normal is 0): ");
        cscanf("%lf",&start_y);
        getch();
        window(1,1,80,25);
        textbackground(0);
        textcolor(15);
}


/*

    ┌──────────────────────────────────────────────────────────────┐
    │  set_parameters() = Sets the equation parameters               │
    └──────────────────────────────────────────────────────────────┘

*/

void set_parameters(void)
{
        int i;

        deltaX = (XMax - XMin)/(maxcol);
        deltaY = (YMax - YMin)/(maxrow);
        for (i=0; i<maxcol; i++)
        {
            if (a > 10000)
                A[i] = XMin + i * deltaX;
            else
            {
                if (a < -10000)
                    A[i] = -XMin - i * deltaX;
                else
                    A[i] = a;
            }
            if (c > 10000)
                C[i] = XMin + i * deltaX;
```

```
            else
            {
                if (c < -10000)
                    C[i] = -XMin - i * deltaX;
                else
                    C[i] = c;
            }
            if (e > 10000)
                E[i] = XMin + i * deltaX;
            else
            {
                if (e < -10000)
                    E[i] = -XMin - i * deltaX;
                else
                    E[i] = e;
            }
            if (start_x > 10000)
                x_starter[i] = XMin + i * deltaX;
            else
            {
                if (start_x < -10000)
                    x_starter[i] = -XMin - i * deltaX;
                else
                    x_starter[i] = start_x;
            }
        }
        for (i=0; i<maxrow; i++)
        {
            if (b > 10000)
                B[i] = YMax - i * deltaY;
            else
            {
                if (b < -10000)
                    B[i] = -YMax + i * deltaY;
                else
                    B[i] = b;
            }
            if (d > 10000)
                D[i] = YMax - i * deltaY;
            else
```

```
        {
            if (d < -10000)
                D[i] = -YMax + i * deltaY;
            else
                D[i] = d;
        }
        if (f > 10000)
            F[i] = YMax - i * deltaY;
        else
        {
            if (f < -10000)
                F[i] = -YMax + i * deltaY;
            else
                F[i] = f;
        }
        if (start_y > 10000)
            y_starter[i] = YMax - i * deltaY;
        else
        {
            if (start_y < -10000)
                y_starter[i] = -YMax + i * deltaY;
            else
                y_starter[i] = start_y;
        }
    }
}

/*
```

```
┌─────────────────────────────────────────────────────────┐
│ ┌───────────────────────────────────────────────────── │
│ │ set_julia_colors() = Sets the colors for a Julia set   │
│ └───────────────────────────────────────────────────── │
└─────────────────────────────────────────────────────────┘
```

```
*/

void set_julia_colors(void)
{
    int color_set[2] = {1,1},palette=0;
    int i, j, k;
    char ch1=0;
```

```
textbackground(4);
clrscr();
k = 0;
window(20,4,60,16);
textbackground(0);
clrscr();
for (i=0; i<16; i++)
    setEGApalette(i,PALETTE[i]);
gotoxy(3,1);
textbackground(0);
textcolor(15);
cprintf("Select palette number with up and\n");
gotoxy(3,2);
cprintf("down arrows. Select color with\n");
gotoxy(3,3);
cprintf("left and right arrows:");

while (ch1 != 0x0D)
{
    textbackground(0);
    gotoxy(3,5);
    cprintf("Background:    %2d",PALETTE[0]);
    for (i=1; i<8; i++)
    {
        gotoxy(3,5+i);
        textbackground(0);
        cprintf("Palette # %d  ",i);
        textbackground(i);
        cprintf("  %2d  ",PALETTE[i]);
    }
    gotoxy(18,k+5);
    ch1 = getch();
    if (ch1 == 0x00)
    {
        ch1 = getch();
        switch(ch1)
        {
            case 'M':
                ++palette;
                if (palette == 64)
```

```
                          palette = 0;
                      break;
                  case 'K':
                      - -palette;
                      if (palette == -1)
                              palette = 63;
                      break;
                  case 'P':
                      ++k;
                      if (k == 8)
                          k = 0;
                      palette = PALETTE[k];
                      break;
                  case 'H':
                      - -k;
                      if (k == -1)
                          k = 7;
                      palette = PALETTE[k];
              }
          }
          setEGApalette(k,palette);
      }
  }
```

Figure 4-3. Listing of Advanced Set Generation Program

Next, we enter a *switch* statement which performs functions appropriate to the menu option that was selected. The first option to be processed is *Quit*. When this option is selected, all that the program does is reset the display screen to the text mode and then exit to DOS.

The next option is *Complete*. This option permits the completion of a partially generated display file. It begins by moving to a blank position on the menu display and displaying, "Enter name of file to complete". It then reads in a character string to the *file_name* variable. It next checks whether the string contains a period. If so, it assumes that a complete file name was entered. If there is no period, the program assumes that the extender to the file name was not entered, so it appends the standard extender for a display file, namely .PCX to the file name. It then calls the *restore_screen* function to read the display file to the screen. If reading of this file was not successful, the function returns a zero, which results in the program terminating and returning to DOS. If the file was read successfully, the number that is returned is that of the column at which the display generation was originally terminated. The program sets up *start_col* to be this number. This is where the program will begin the generation of column data, so that the part of the display that was already generated does not have to be repeated. Next, the program calls the function *restore_parameters*. This function will also be described in detail later. What it does is read the various parameters that are needed for establishing the iterated equation, colors, etc., from the end of the display file. If the operation is not successful, the program displays an error message and returns to DOS. Otherwise, the program removes the partially completed file from the disk. (At the completion of display generation, the display will be saved to a disk file having the same name as the partially completed file that we have just erased.) The program then calls the function *set_parameters*, which will be described below. This uses the parameter information that was recovered from the partially complete file to set up all the necessary parameters. This marks the end of the part of the program done in response to the particular menu command. The program then jumps to the actual curve computation, which is described below.

Next we come to the portion of the *switch* statement that is performed when the option is selected to expand an existing function. This begins by moving to an empty part of the menu window and asking for the name of the file containing the display that is to be expanded. The program then reads in a character string to the *file_name* variable. It next checks whether the string contains a period. If so, it assumes that a complete file name was entered. If there is no period, the program assumes that the extender to the file name was not entered, so it appends the standard extender for a display file, namely .PCX to the file name. It then calls the *restore_screen* function to read the display file to the screen. If reading of this file was not successful, the function returns a zero, which results in the program terminating and returning to DOS. If the file was read successfully, it calls the function *restore_parameters*, which reads the various parameters that are needed for establishing the iterated equation, colors, etc., from the end of the display file. Note that these will be the same for the expanded display as they were for the original display that was generated. If the operation is not successful, the program displays an error message and returns to DOS. If successful, the program calls the *move_cursor* function which was described in Chapter 3. This function allows the user to move an upper left hand corner cursor around the screen with the arrow keys, displaying the corresponding x and y values at the bottom of the screen. When the cursor is properly positioned, the Enter key is hit, whereupon the function terminates, leaving the cursor and the coordinate values on the screen. Next, the *move_cursor* function is called again, with a different type specified. For this type, a lower right hand corner is displayed. The coordinate values for the corner previously specified are passed to the function to limit it so that it can never be moved above or to the left of the previously specified corner position. When the arrow keys have been used to select the desired location for the bottom right hand corner, the function terminates. The starting column is then set to zero and the maximum and minimum values for the coordinates of the display are set up. The display mode is then reset to text and the function *get_iterations* is called. This function allows the user to decide how many iterations of the fractal equation are desired (within the limits of 16 to 512). Once the iterations have been selected, the function *set_parameters* is called to set up the equation parameters. The display is then reset to the graphics mode, and the screen cleared to a light gray background, which completes the necessary operations during this *switch* statement.

If the option selected was to generate a new set, the *menu* function is called again (using a different type number) to permit the user to select the type of set that he wants to generate. The necessary actions for each desired selection are performed within a *switch* statement. If the option selected is to create a Julia set, the program calls the function *restore_screen*, which attempts to read and display the file *mandel00.pcx*. If the file is found successfully, a set of statements are conditionally performed. They begin by storing the proper file name for a Julia set. Then the *move_cursor* function is called. The type used is such that the cursor displayed is an arrow. The arrow is moved with the arrow keys until the desired point on the Mandelbrot set at which a Julia set to be generated is found. Hitting the Enter key then terminates the function. The program then calls the menu function to permit the user to select the desired color option. If the first color option was selected, the program calls the function *set_colors*, which permits the user to select the colors for that option. If the second color option was selected, no further action is necessary. If the third color option was selected, the function *set_julia_colors* is called to permit selecting the colors for that option. The *set_mode* function is then called to place the display in the high resolution EGA graphics mode. The *setEGApalette* function is then called 16 times to set the 16 EGA palette registers to the 16 desired colors, which have been stored in the PALETTE array. The screen is then cleared to light gray, which completes the preliminary actions for this type of new set. If it was impossible to read the *mandel00.pcx* file, the program displays a warning message, waits five seconds, and then proceeds to prepare for generating the initial Mandelbrot set.

If the user chose to generate a Mandelbrot set, the *file_name* variable is properly initialized so that the Mandelbrot set display that is ultimately generated will be stored in a correctly named file. The program then sets up the proper coefficients for the Mandelbrot set and the proper bounds for the first running of the Mandelbrot set. The function *get_starters* is then called to permit the user to enter the desired starting values of x and y for each set of iterations. (Normally these values are both zero for the Mandelbrot set.) The *set_parameters* function is then called to prepare the parameters for running the program. The *get_iterations* function is then called. This gives the user the opportunity to enter the desired maximum number of iterations for the iterated equation. The program then proceeds with selecting the color option, setting the graphics mode, setting the palette registers, and clearing the screen to light gray as was done for the Julia set.

If the user elected to generate a dragon curve, everything proceeds almost the same as for the Julia set. The only differences are that the initial file that is displayed to provide a map for selecting a dragon is called *drgset00.pcx* and that the bounds and equation parameters are set up differently to be appropriate for generating a dragon curve. In the same way as for the Julia set, if the required file cannot be read in, the program displays a warning message and then proceeds to generate this initial map display.

If the user elected to generate the Mandelbrot-like equivalent of the dragon, the program proceeds in the same manner as for the Mandelbrot set, except that the name of the file where the display is to be stored is different and the bounds and equation parameters are set appropriately for the dragon equivalent curve.

Finally, if the user chose to set his own equation parameters, before leaving the *menu* function, the user is given the opportunity to set up the equation parameters, including the values for *start_x* and *start_y*. The program then gives him an opportunity to select a name for the file in which the display is to be stored. The program then sets up an appropriate set of bounds for the display and proceeds for number of iterations, color options, etc. as for each of the selections previously described.

The program next sets the clock starting time and then computes the value of the threshold which is used in terminating iterations. This threshold is half the value of *deltaX* or *deltaY*, whichever is smaller. The program then begins a *for* loop which is iterated once for each column of the display. At the beginning of each iteration, the program checks to see if a key has been pressed. If so, the partially completed display is saved to a disk file and the program then terminates, displaying the elapsed time and name of the output file. If no key was pressed, the program continues.

Next comes the inner *for* loop which is iterated once for every row of the display. Within this loop, the parameters x and y are set to the starting values. The square parameters, the old values, and the color are all initialized to zero. Next a *while* loop is iterated until the sum of the squares of the x and y parameters exceeds a value of 4. (It can be shown mathematically that if this occurs, the iterated equation will eventually go to infinity.) We next compute the new values of the parameters.

Most of the computation time for these sets is spent in iterating those values for which the equation does not ever go to infinity, so the *while* loop tends to go through the maximum number of iterations. To reduce this large number of computations, one must know something about the behavior of the equation in such cases. If you modify the program to print out the equation values after each iteration, you will find that usually when the equation does not go to infinity, it either settles down to some permanent value or else cycles back and forth between several different values. Each time that the previous running of the while loop results in a case where the equation doesn't blow up, the maximum number of iterations is stored in *old_color*. On the next running of the *while* loop, on every sixteenth iteration, we store the values of x and y in *old_x* and *old_y*. For the other fifteen iterations, we compare the stored values with the values on the current iteration and if the differences are within the threshold, we set the number of iterations to maximum and terminate the loop. We ought to get a match if the values have settled down or if they are recycling within sixteen iterations. Thus, for example, if our maximum number of iterations is 512, we may be able to ascertain that the equation is not going to go to infinity within 16 or at most 32 iterations instead of having to run through all 512. This results in a substantial speed up of the program.

Once the program leaves the *while* loop, it selects a color to be plotted, based upon the color option selected. For the first color option, the program enters a while loop which cycles through the iteration values in the *colors* array. These values mark the lower bound of each color range. The loop stops when the number of iterations is going to exceed the next bound, and selects the correspondingly specified color from the array (depending upon whether the number of iterations is odd or even) for display. The appropriate color is plotted to the screen at the row and column currently being processed. If the second color option is selected, the color is taken to be the number of iterations modulo 16. For the third color option, all cases where the equation goes to infinity are colored with the background color, while the other cases are plotted in a color that is based on the magnitude of the equation value when it settles down.

Ultimately, all three loops complete their iterations and the display is complete. The function *save_screen* is then called to save the display in the form of a .PCX disk file. The program then waits for a key stroke. When this occurs, the screen is returned to the text mode, and the time and output file name displayed. The program then waits for another key stroke. When this occurs, the program returns to the original menu to allow for generating another display. If you wish to terminate at this point, you select the *Quit* option.

The menu Function

The *menu* function presents the display and provides for the user interactions to select several of the different options that are offered by the program. At the very beginning, this function creates a full screen window, sets the background color to black, and then clears the screen. The function begins by creating a full-sized screen window and then clearing the screen to a black background. Next, a switch statement occurs which creates a window of the proper size and then sets the parameter *m* to one less than the number of options that will be allowed for that particular menu. The background color is then set to blue (1) and the window is cleared to that background color. The text color is set to light cyan (10) and the legend, "Make your choice with the up and down arrows:" is displayed at the top of the window. The function then begins a *do-while* loop. This loop begins with a *for* loop. At the beginning of this function are four sets of character strings, containing the menu selections for each of four different menu types. The *for* loop prints out the proper set of character strings, all in intense white on a blue background, except for the first string, which is reversed to be blue on a white background. Next, the function gets a character from the keyboard. If a special key was selected (one having a first character of 00, then the second character from this key is read). Another *switch* statement is entered which increments or decrements k. This is the selection indicator and also the designator for the reverse colored line. It is incremented if a down arrow (the second character is P) was typed and decremented if an up arrow (the second character is H was typed. Modulo arithmetic is used to assure that the reverse colored line rolls over to the top when a down arrow is typed for a last line location or rolls over to the bottom when an up arrow is typed for a top line location. Since after each character selection the entire *do-while* loop is reiterated, the menu is rewritten, but with the reverse colored line moved in accordance with the arrow selection. (Note that no other character than the up and down arrows and the Enter key has any effect on this loop.) The loop terminates when the Enter key is typed. As long as k is no greater than 3 (which must be the case for the first two menu types) the function now ends by going back to a full-sized screen window and then returning k to indicate which option was selected. If k is greater than 3 (for menu type 2) the function sets up a full-sized window, clears the screen to black, and then opens a new window, sets the background to blue and clears the window to that background color. It then prints three lines of headings for the parameter selection display and then enters an infinite *for* loop. The function breaks from this loop when one of four values of flag is encountered. These values are those which occur when three of the four parameter lines have had data entered into them. Next another *for* loop is entered, which prints out the remainder of the display data, with the first line in reverse color. The inputs from the keyboard are then checked, permitting selecting a desired line with the up and down arrows. If an arrow key is not selected, then the user should be entering numerical data on one of the lines. The function checks whether the character is a number, a minus sign, or decimal point, which are the permissible first characters of a data input. If the key input is anything else, it is disregarded and the infinite loop continues. If the character indicates the beginning of numerical data, the character is echoed to the screen and then put back into the keyboard buffer. Then two floating point numbers, separated by a comma, are read and put into the proper parameters by the correct case of a *switch* statement for the data line being entered.

The set_colors function

This function is used to enter the appropriate color information when the first color option has been selected. The function begins by setting the background color to dark red (4) and clearing the screen to that color. The function then opens a window and fills it with the black background color. Next, the heading "Enter Upper Limit Number and Use Arrows to Set Colors", is displayed at the top of the window in bright white, and after skipping a line, the column headings are displayed in yellow:

Start Iters End Iters Color #1 Color #2

Next the function initializes the first two members of the *colors* array to zero as well as the index parameter i. The *colors* array consists of three arrays. The first set, *colors[nn][1]*, contains upper limits of the number of iterations. The second set, *colors[nn][2]*, contains the palette number of the color that is to be used for all odd numbers of iterations beginning just after the previous member of the first set and ending with the number of iterations specified in the current member of the first set. The third set, *colors[nn][0]*, contains the palette number of the color that is to be used for all even numbers of iterations beginning just after the previous member of the first set and ending with the number of iterations specified in the current member of the first set. The function next enters a *while* loop to fill this array. The first member of the first set is already initialized to zero. The loop first checks whether the current value of the first array is less than the maximum number of iterations. If it is not, the loop terminates. Otherwise the index is incremented. The text color is set to bright white (15). The loop then displays the previous member of the first array under "Start

Iters" and then moves the cursor under "End Iters". The function then reads an integer from the keyboard and places it in the current member of the first color array. The function checks whether the number that was entered is less than or equal to the number in the previous member of the array. If it is, this number is changed in the array and on the display to one more that the value of the previous member. Next, the function then checks whether this is the fourteenth member of the color array (the last one permitted) or whether a number has been entered that is greater than the maximum number of iterations. In either case, it is time to provide an orderly finish of the data by setting the current member of the first color array to the maximum number of iterations. The function then changes the text color to blue and prints blocks of blue under "Color #1" and "Color #2". A *for* loop is then begun which iterates once for each color block. It begins by properly positioning the cursor next to the selected color block. A *do-while* loop then reiterates until the Enter key is pressed. Within this loop, only the up and down arrow keys are recognized. The up arrow causes the number of the current member of the color array (second array on the first pass through the for loop and third array on the second pass through the *for* loop) to be decremented while the down arrow causes it to be incremented. Also, when the number goes below zero it is reset to 15 and when it goes above 15 it is reset to zero. After each key entry, the text color is set to the number that went into the current member of the color array and the block of color is redisplayed in the corresponding color. When the first color block has been set to the desired color and the Enter key pressed, a second pass through the for loop is used to set the desired color for the second block. (The first block is the color for odd numbers of iterations and the second block the color for even numbers of iterations.) After both color blocks have been set, the original *while* loop iterates again to generate the next line of color data. Finally, as mentioned above, this loop terminates when the number of iterations in the first array becomes equal to the maximum number of color iterations. A full screen-sized window is then generated and the screen cleared to black. The text color is reset to white and the function returns the number of color selections made.

The get_iterations Function

This function permits the user to specify the maximum number of iterations for the iterated equation. It begins by clearing the screen to black (0). It then creates a window for the display and clears the window to red (4). Next, the legend, "Enter number of iterations desired (16-512):" is displayed. The function then reads in an integer from the keyboard to the variable *max_iterations*. If this value is less than 16, it is reset to 16; if it is greater than 512, it is reset to 512. The function then waits for another keystroke, and when it occurs, returns to the calling program.

The get_starters Function

This function permits the user to specify the starting values of x and y for the iterated equation. The function begins by clearing the screen to black and then creating a window for the display. The window is cleared to a background of cyan (3). The cursor in position, the text color set to black (0), and the function displays:

Enter starting value of x:

Normal is 0 for Mandelbrot:

Normal is 0.5 for Dragon:

The function then reads the floating point number for *start_x* from the keyboard input. Next, the function displays:

Enter starting value of y (normal is 0):

The function then reads the floating point number for *start_y* from the keyboard input. The function then waits for another character input from the keyboard and then sets up a full-sized screen window and fills it with a black background. It then sets the text color to bright white and then returns to the calling program.

The set_parameters Function

This function is used to generate the values for the iterated equation parameters, after the generic parameter values have been entered from the keyboard or read from the disk file. The equation basically takes the form:

$$z_n = (A + iB)z_{n-1}^2 + (C + id)z_{n-1} + D + iF \qquad \text{(Equation 4-14)}$$

106

There are also the starting values of x and y to be considered. All of the values except one pair are held constant for a particular display. That pair varies over the range required to fill the display. The way that this is accomplished is to have an array of all possible column values for each real parameter and an array of all possible row values for the imaginary parameters. If the parameter was originally assigned a normal coefficient, the entire array for that parameter is filled with the coefficient value. If the coefficient was assigned a value of greater than 10,000 (which would not normally be in the range that would be considered), values are computed for each row and column of the display and put in their appropriate places in the array(s). If the coefficient is assigned a value less than -10,000, the same computation takes place, but the negative of the computed value is assigned to each array member. This is all done with a series of *if* and *else* statements. Running this function takes only a small amount of time and the memory storage requirements are not excessive. The beauty of this approach is that a single equation can be iterated for all possible cases with the minimum of repetitive computations.

The set_julia_colors Function

This function sets up eight of the EGA palette colors for generating a Julia type set. The function begins by clearing the screen to a red background (4) and then opening an appropriate window, setting the background color to black (0) and clearing the window background to this color. The function then sets the EGA palette to the standard sixteen colors. It then sets the background to black and the text color to bright white. The legend, "Select palette number with up and down arrows. Select color with left and right arrows:", is then displayed. The function then enters a *while* loop which is reiterated until the Enter key is pressed. The display then continues with two columns, one showing the palette numbers from 0 to 7 and the other showing a block for each corresponding palette color, with the number of the color (from 0 to 63) within the block. These are created by setting the text background to the appropriate palette number and then printing out some spaces and the color number with a white foreground and the designated color as the background, within a *for* loop. Next, the function positions the cursor at the selected color row (the first one upon initial entry) and reads a character from the keyboard. Other than the Enter key, only the arrow keys are recognized. (These are special keys that output two characters, the first being 00 and the next a recognized ASCII code.) Now a *switch* statement is used to decide what to do for a particular arrow key. If the up or down arrow key is pressed, the parameter k, which designates the index for the palette register being selected, is decremented or incremented. If it exceeds the limits of 0 to 7, it is reset. In addition, the parameter *palette*, which is the index for the selected color, is set to the current color for this palette register. If the left or right arrows are pressed, the *palette* parameter is decremented or incremented, within the limits of 0 to 63. The *switch* statement is then complete and the selected color is sent to the selected palette register. The loop continues until all color selections have been completed and the Enter key pressed. You will note that in selecting colors for the Julia set, only eight of the sixteen palette registers may be changed in color. You'll also note that although we have 64 color choices for the Julia set colors, in setting colors for the Mandelbrot set our program only permitted selecting the 16 standard colors. These were my own choices. You may want to modify one or both of the color selecting functions to provide greater (or less) variety, as you might desire. Furthermore, if you are going to convert to VGA or extended VGA modes, you may want to make some choices which involve selecting 256 colors from 256K shades.

CHAPTER 5

The Core Program

We look at a lot of interesting sets in the following chapters that produce fractal patterns, never seen before in any publication. After looking at the simple equations that were iterated to produce Mandelbrot and Julia sets and dragon curves, you may think that almost any polynomial could be iterated to produce an interesting fractal display. This is not true. There are many polynomials that don't have any convergence zones, or produce uninteresting displays. However, we'll find a lot of interesting polynomials and establish criteria for detecting them. When we generate the displays, not only are all of the options in the advanced program of the previous chapter inappropriate, but they might make it difficult to generate new sets. On the other hand, there are some parts of the program, involving inserting and storing parameters, that will be the same for a lot of different functions. Therefore, instead of writing a separate program for each fractal and having a lot of repetition, we develop a core program which will be the same for every fractal in the following chapters. The actual portion of the program that scans through the display and performs the iterations of mathematical functions will be called *fractal*. It is this function only, which will be different for each fractal we investigate. The core program, listed in Figure 5-1, is a bare bones program that includes only the essentials common to all of the fractal programs that we create in the following chapters. What we will be changing for each new fractal is the function *fractal*. It is in the listing as a simple program for the Mandelbrot set. You can try this out while you are debugging the *core* program. Once it is working, you can substitute any of the corresponding functions listed in the following chapters for this function or any of your own that you may want to generate.

```
/*
```

```
core = Generic Program to be used for generating various fractals

By Roger T. Stevens 9-3-90
```

```
*/
```

```c
#include <stdio.h>
#include <dos.h>
#include <complex.h>
#include <conio.h>
#include <math.h>
#include <stdlib.h>
#include "ftools.h"

void fractal(void);

#define Min(x,y) ((x)<(y) ? (x) : (y))
#define Max(x,y) ((x)>(y) ? (x) : (y))

double XMax, XMin, YMax, YMin, Pval, Qval, a, b, c, d, e, f, g, h,
      TXMax, TXMin, TYMax, TYMin, start_x, start_y;
int colors[15][3], max_iterations, color_option, CURSOR_X, CURSOR_Y;
unsigned char PALETTE[16]={0,1,2,3,4,5,20,7,56,57,58,59,60,61,62,63};

char *ptr;
const int maxcol = 639;
const int maxrow = 349;
double max_size = 1000.0;
int index,old_index;
double x,y,p,q,old_x,old_y;
double deltaP, deltaQ,threshold;
int i,j, row, col;
char filename1[13],filename[13];

main()
{
    max_iterations = 64;
    setMode(3);
```

```
window(1,1,80,25);
textbackground(0);
clrscr();
textbackground(1);
window(9,9,62,19);
clrscr();
gotoxy(3,2);
textcolor(15);
printf("Enter parameters for display:\n");
gotoxy(8,3);
printf("X Max: ");
cscanf("%lf",&XMax);
gotoxy(8,4);
printf("X Min: ");
cscanf("%lf",&XMin);
gotoxy(8,5);
printf("Y Max: ");
cscanf("%lf",&YMax);
gotoxy(8,6);
printf("Y Min: ");
cscanf("%lf",&YMin);
gotoxy(8,7);
printf("P: ");
cscanf("%lf",&Pval);
gotoxy(8,8);
printf("Q: ");
cscanf("%lf",&Qval);
gotoxy(3,9);
printf("\nEnter name of file for output data: ");
cscanf("%s",filename1);
ptr = strchr(filename1, '.');
if (ptr == NULL)
{
    strncpy(filename,filename1,6);
    strcat(filename,"00.pcx");
}
else
    strcpy(filename,filename1);
setMode(16);
cls(7);
```

```
        fractal();
        save_screen(0,0,maxcol,maxrow,filename);
        getch();
        getch();
        move_cursor(2,15,0,0);
        setMode(3);
}


/*
```

┌───┐
│ ┌───┐ │
│ │ fractal() = Function to Generate a Mandelbrot Set   │ │
│ └───┘ │
└───┘

```
*/

void fractal(void)
{
    complex c,z;
    int color;

    deltaP = (XMax - XMin)/640;
    deltaQ = (YMax - YMin)/350;
    for (col=0; col<640; col++)
    {
            if (kbhit() != 0)
            {
                save_screen(0,0,col,maxrow,filename);
                exit(0);
            }
        for (row=0; row<350; row++)
        {
            c = complex(XMin + col * deltaP,YMax - row * deltaQ);
            z = (0,0);
            color = 0;
            while ((color < max_iterations) && (norm(z) < max_size))
            {
                z = z*z + c;
                color++;
            }
            if (color >= max_iterations)
```

```
                color = 0;
            else
                color = color%15 + 1;
            plot (col,row,color);
        }
    }
}
```

Figure 5-1. Core Program Listing

Description of the Core Program

The core program begins by creating a full-sized window and clearing the screen to black (0). The program then creates a suitably sized window to obtain input parameters. It sets the text background to blue (1) and clears the window to this color. The program then displays the heading, "Enter parameters for display:", in bright white and displays "X Max: ", on the next line. The program then waits for a floating point number representing the maximum value for the *x* boundary of the display to be input from the keyboard. When you enter this parameter and type the *Enter* key, the value is placed in the parameter *XMax*. The program then moves down a line, displays, "X Min: ", the minimum *x* boundary parameter, and repeats the process to read in this parameter. The process is then repeated for *YMax*, *YMin*, *Pval*, and *Qval*. Note that the boundary values are required for all types of sets that are to be generated, but the *Pval* and *Qval* values are used only when you are generating a Julia-like set. The *core* program provides the opportunity to make these inputs so that it can handle all cases. However, your specialized *fractal* function will not use any entries of these two last values if you are creating Mandelbrot-like sets. Next, in a similar way, the user is given an opportunity to enter the maximum number of iterations of the iterated equation desired, and the name of the file in which the completed picture is to be stored. Observe that the program is set up to handle two different cases of file name input. It searches the string input for a period (the character that separates the main file name from the extension in DOS), and if the period is found, the program assumes that the user entered the entire file name, including the extension, exactly as desired. If the period is not found, the program assumes that the user inserted a file name without an extension. In this case, the program truncates the entered file name to six characters, if necessary, and then

113

appends the numbers 00, followed by .PCX. This is the generally accepted extension for ZSoft files for saving graphics screens, and is the format used by our function for saving the screen display (as described in Chapter 3).

The program next sets the system to the high resolution EGA graphics mode (mode 16 = 640 x 350 pixels by 16 colors). It then clears the screen to light gray and then calls the function *fractal* to actually generate the fractal curve. (Light gray is used instead of black, since Mandelbrot-like sets usually have large black areas, so that if a different starting background is used, the generation of each black pixel on the screen can be observed and the user knows about where the program is, instead of looking at nothingness and wondering what is going on.)

After the *fractal* function is finished, the program saves the completed display to the disk. It then waits for two keyboard entries. (Sometimes after the screen is saved, the program seems to behave peculiarly and skip one keyboard entry call, so this assures that you will not lose the display before you want to.) Next the *move_cursor* function (which was described in Chapter 3) is called to display an arrow cursor on the screen and give the user the opportunity to move it around. As the cursor moves, the *x* and *y* coordinates are shown at the bottom of the screen. This permits using the cursor to determine what boundaries might be interesting for the next running of the program. The user can record these and enter them at the appropriate time on the next run.

The Sample *fractal* Function

The sample *fractal* function generates the ordinary Mandelbrot set. It begins by computing *deltaP* and *deltaQ*, the *x* and *y* increments for a movement of one pixel on the display. The function then begins a *for* loop that iterates once for each column in the display. The function then checks for a keyboard entry; if one has occurred, it saves the incomplete display to disk and then exits from the program back to DOS. Note that although we have saved the incomplete file, this program does not have any provision for completing this saved display as presently written. If you need to do this, you will have to modify the program accordingly.

The function next enters an inner *for* loop, which is iterated once for each row of the display. This loop begins by computing the value of *c* for this particular column and row combination, then sets the initial value of *z* and the value of *color* to zero. Then a *while* loop is entered which iterates until either color (which is incremented on each pass) reaches the maximum number of iterations specified or until the square of the magnitude of *z* (*norm(z)*) is greater than the maximum size specified. During each iteration of the loop, the Mandelbrot equation is recalculated, using complex numbers directly. On each iteration, *color* is incremented. Upon exiting the *while* loop, if the maximum number of iterations occurred, the color is set to black (0). Otherwise, the color cycles through the remaining fifteen EGA colors, depending upon the number of iterations that occurred. When all loops are complete, the function returns to the main program.

Note that complex numbers are used throughout this function, which at present requires that you have Turbo C++ or Zortech C++ version 2.12. Hopefully you will soon be able to get a Microsoft version of C++ that also has this capability. If you don't have the complex number capability, you can use the functions described in Chapter 2 to get your program running as effectively, although in a less elegant manner.

CHAPTER 6

Using the Distance Method with the Mandelbrot Set

In this chapter, we take a look at a different way to generate the Mandelbrot set. The technique is called the distance estimation technique. It depends upon the fact that it is possible to make an estimate of the distance from any given point to the nearest point on the Mandelbrot set, and that this estimate:

1. Is always an underestimate, so that there is no possibility of coming up with an estimate that is inside the Mandelbrot set, and

2. Gets better as the distance from the point to the Mandelbrot set decreases.

Apart from any other considerations, plotting the Mandelbrot set with the colors representing the distance from any point outside the set to the edge of the set makes an interesting display. However, it turns out that we can increase the speed with which the display is generated by computing only certain distances and getting intermediate results by interpolation. The distance estimation technique can be conveniently extended to obtain the normal to the set at each significant point, which has important implications for three dimensional modeling. We'll just consider two dimensions here, but later we'll expand the technique to three dimensions.

Mathematics of the Distance Estimation Method

We will start as usual with the equation for the Mandelbrot set:

$$z_n = z_{n-1}{}^2 + c \qquad \text{(Equation 6-1)}$$

The potential of the Mandelbrot set, G(c), is given by:

$G(c) = \ln|z_n(c)| / 2^n$ $\qquad\qquad$ (Equation 6-2)

Then, at any point c, the distance, D, to the Mandelbrot set can be estimated by:

$D = G(c) / 2|G'(c)| = (|z| \ln|z|) / (2|z'|$ $\qquad\qquad$ (Equation 6-3)

This is the distance estimate which has the two characteristics described above. To compute the desired derivative, we note that:

$z'_1 = 1$ $\qquad\qquad$ (Equation 6-4)

and

$z'_n = 2z_{n-1} z'_{n-1} + 1$ $\qquad\qquad$ (Equation 6-5)

We could compute each step of the derivative along with the corresponding step of the original iterated equation. However that would mean that we would have to compute the derivative for points inside the Mandelbrot set, where we don't need it. Most of the time spent computing the Mandelbrot set is used in processing the points that are within the boundaries of the set. Each one of these requires a maximum number of iterations. If we use a separate loop to iterate the derivative equation, and only enter it when a point is not within the Mandelbrot set, we save a lot of computation time.

Function to Implement Distance Algorithm

Figure 6-1 is a listing of the functions to be inserted into the core program that implement the distance method of generating the Mandelbrot set. The function begins by evaluating *deltaP* and *deltaQ* which are respectively the changes in *x* and *y* for a change of one pixel on the display. Next *delta* is evaluated. It is one-half of *deltaQ*. The function begins the outer *for* loop, which iterates once for each column of the display. The loop begins each iteration by computing the value of the real part of the constant term. Next, it checks for a keystroke. If one has occurred, it saves the unfinished display to a disk file and then exits back to DOS. The function then enters the inner *for* loop, which is ordinarily iterated for every row of the display. The function determines the imaginary value of the constant term at the pixel being evaluated. It then uses the function *mdist* to obtain an estimate of the distance from the beginning of the column to the Mandelbrot set. If this distance is less than *delta* (that is smaller than one half a pixel width), then the color is set to zero (black), and the point plotted to the screen. For larger distances, the function computes end, which is a number of pixels based upon the distance, but confined within the bounds of 1 to 20. The function then adds this to the current row number, determines the value of the constant term at this new point, and uses *mdist* to find the distance to the Mandelbrot set boundary from this new point. The function then determines the distance increment between the distance of the beginning point and that of the end point for each pixel. A *for* loop is then entered which iterates *end* times. For each iteration, *row* is incremented, the function interpolates between the two distances to estimate the distance at each pixel, and the color for each distance is obtained and the pixel plotted to the screen in the proper color.

If the maximum row is reached before this loop is complete, the loop is terminated. When this loop is completed, the function returns to the *for* loop that is counting rows with the *row* parameter increased by some number that depends upon the distances and represents those pixels that were written by distance interpolation rather than completely iterating the iterated equations. Thus the row *for* loop skips those rows and proceeds from its new setting.

```
/*
```

fractal() = Computes the Mandelbrot Set using the distance estimation method.

By Roger T. Stevens 10-16-90

```
*/
```

```
float delta;
```

```c
void fractal(void)
{
    double distance, distance2, deltaD, temp;
    int k,end,color;

    deltaP = (XMax - XMin)/640;
    deltaQ = (YMax - YMin)/350;
    delta = deltaQ / 2;
    for (col=0; col<640; col++)
    {
        p = XMin + col * deltaP;
        if (kbhit() != 0)
        {
            save_screen(0,0,col,maxrow,filename);
            exit(0);
        }
        for (row=0; row<350; row++)
        {
            q = YMax - row * deltaQ;
            if ((distance = mdist()) < delta)
            {
                color = 0;
                plot(col,row,color);
            }
            else
            {
                end = Max(1,Min(20, (int)(distance/(2*deltaQ))));
                q = YMax - (row + end) * deltaQ;
                distance2 = mdist();
                deltaD = (distance - distance2) / end;
                for (k=0; k<=end; k++)
                {
                    row++;
                    temp = 1 + ((distance + distance) / delta);
                    color = (int)(temp / sqrt(temp)) % 15 + 1;
                    plot(col,row,color);
                    if (row>=350)
                        break;
                    distance -= deltaD;
                }
```

```
                        row-;
                }
            }
        }
}

/*
```

┌──┐
│ ┌──┐ │
│ │   mdist() = Function to compute distance to edge of Mandelbrot Set │ │
│ └──┘ │
└──┘

```
*/
double mdist()
{
    int i,flag,row_dist;
    static int old_index;
    double dist=0, temp, xsq, ysq, xprime, yprime, orbit_x[512],
    orbit_y[512], denom, old_x, old_y;

    i = 0;
    flag = 0;
    xsq = 0;;
    ysq = 0;
    x = 0;
    y = 0;
    xprime = 0;
    yprime = 0;
    index = 0;
    orbit_x[0] = 0;
    orbit_y[0] = 0;
    old_x = 0;
    old_y = 0;
    while ((index < max_iterations) && (xsq + ysq < max_size))
    {
        index++;
        y = 2*x*y + q;
        orbit_y[index] = y;
        x = xsq -ysq + p;
        orbit_x[index] = x;
        xsq = x*x;
        ysq = y*y;
```

```
            if (old_index == max_iterations)
            {
                if ((index & 15) == 0)
                {
                    old_x = x;
                    old_y = y;
                }
                else
                    if ((fabs(old_x - x) + fabs(old_y - x)) < delta)
                        index = max_iterations-1;
            }
        }
        if (xsq + ysq > max_size)
        {
            while ((i<index) && (!flag))
            {
                temp = 2 * (orbit_x[i] * xprime - orbit_y[i] * yprime) + 1;
                yprime = 2 * (orbit_y[i] * xprime + orbit_x[i] * yprime);
                xprime = temp;
                if (Max(fabs(xprime),fabs(yprime)) > 1e14)
                    flag = 1;
                i++;
            }
            if (!flag)
            {
                dist = log(xsq + ysq) * sqrt((xsq + ysq) / (xprime * xprime + yprime *
yprime));
            }
        }
        return dist;
    }
```

Figure 6-1. Functions to Be Added to Core Program to Generate the Mandelbrot Set with the Distance Estimation Technique

Now let's look at the *mdist* function. Both this function and the *fractal* function must be added to the *core* program to use the distance estimation method. The prototype for the *fractal* function is already included at the beginning of the *core* program, but you will have to add a prototype for the *mdist* function if you want everything to behave properly . The function initializes a bunch of parameters to zero. It then enters the *while* loop to compute the iterated equation. This loop is repeated until the square of the result of the equation exceeds the maximum size or until the maximum number of iterations occurs. Within the loop, the new values of x and y are calculated in the same way as for other Mandelbrot sets, and each set of values is also stored in an array. In addition, we use the technique of periodically comparing sets of values, when we think we may be within the Mandelbrot set, so that if cycling or repetition of values occurs, we may know that the iterated equation will never blow up and can consequently set the index to the maximum number of iterations and quit the loop without further ado. (Note that the procedure we described above for estimating points with the distance estimation method substantially reduces the amount of time required to process pixels outside the Mandelbrot set, but is of no help within the Mandelbrot set.) The above technique substantially reduces the time to process points within the Mandelbrot set, so that the combination of the two makes a very fast running program, indeed. Once we leave this *while* loop, if the termination was caused by the iterated expression exceeding the maximum size, we enter another *while* loop which computes the derivative. This loop only has to repeat for the same number of iterations performed by the original loop before it terminated. If either the real or imaginary part of the derivative gets too large, we terminate the loop and the function returns a distance of zero; otherwise, once the loop has completed, we calculate the distance and return it.

The display of the Mandelbrot set with colors indicating distance from the boundary, as generated by the program described above, is illustrated in Plate 9.

CHAPTER 7

Transcendental Functions

If you have exhausted the possibilities of Mandelbrot/Julia sets and dragon curves and are looking for new mathematical expressions for creating fractal displays, where is a good place to turn? Look at Taylor's theorem. It says that any function which is continuous and has derivatives may be expanded into a *Taylor's series*:

$$f(x) = f(a) + f'(a)(x - a) / 1! + f''(a)(x - a)^2 / 2! +$$
$$f'''(a)(x - a)^3 / 3! + ... + f^{(n-1)}(a)(x - a)^{n-1} / (n - 1)!$$

(Equation 7-1)

where a can be any quantity as long as its derivatives are finite. However, if you are going to use the series to approximate a function for some value of x you need to select an a that is close in value to x if you wish to minimize the number of terms needed for the series to give a reasonable approximation. A particular case of the Taylor's series is called the *Maclaurin's series*, where a is taken to be zero . Now let's look at the series obtained for some of the transcendental functions with which we are familiar:

$$e^x = 1 + x + x^2/2! + x^3/3! + x^4/4! + ...$$

(Equation 7-2)

$$\sin x = x - x^3/3! + x^5/5! - x^7/7! + ...$$

(Equation 7-3)

$$\cos x = 1 - x^2/2! + x^4/4! - x^6/6! + ...$$

(Equation 7-4)

$$\sinh x = x + x^3/3! + x^5/5! + x^7/7! + ...$$

(Equation 7-5)

$$\cosh x = 1 + x^2/2! + x^4/4! + x^6/6! + ...$$

(Equation 7-6)

Now particularly observe what happens when we truncate the series of Equation 7-6 at two terms. It begins to look like the equation for the Mandelbrot set, with a little scaling and displacement. This suggests that the transcendental functions might be a fertile field for the generation of fractals. This turns out to be true. Many beautiful fractal displays can be generated by iterating transcendental functions.

The *cos* Set

The cosine fractals are generated by the iterated equation:

$$z_n = \cos(z_{n-1}) + c \qquad \text{(Equation 7-7)}$$

where both z and c are complex numbers. Figure 7-1 lists a fractal function for use with the core program to generate the cosine fractals. This function generates a Mandelbrot-type curve but you can easily alter it to produce Julia-type curves instead. Note that the function is designed with a compiler that supports the complex number type. What do you do if your compiler doesn't supply such support? We've already given some functions to support mathematical operations on complex numbers in Chapter 2. The critical thing for this function is the trigonometric identity:

$$\cos(x + iy) = \cos x \cosh y - i \sin x \sinh y \qquad \text{(Equation 7-8)}$$

With this you can define the real and imaginary parts of the cosine using the trig and hyperbolic functions that are a part of your C library. Another possibility is to use the Taylor series given in equation 7-4 to approximate the cosine.

```
/*
```

```
fractal() = Computes and displays the cosine fractal
```

```
*/

void fractal(void)
{
    complex c,z,zsq;
```

```
        int color;

        deltaP = (XMax - XMin)/640;
        deltaQ = (YMax - YMin)/350;
        for (col=0; col<640; col++)
        {
            if (kbhit() != 0)
            {
                save_screen(0,0,col,maxrow,filename);
                exit(0);
            }
            for (row=0; row<350; row++)
            {
                c = complex(XMin + col * deltaP,YMax - row *deltaQ);
                z = (0,0);
                color = 0;
                while ((color < max_iterations) && (norm(z) < max_size))
                {
                    z = cos(z) + c;
                    color++;
                }
                if (color >= max_iterations)
                    color = 0;
                else
                    color = color%15 + 1;
                plot (col,row,color);
            }
        }
    }
```

Figure 7-1 Listing of Function to Generate Cosine Fractals

You need enough terms to do a fairly precise approximation, however. Remember that we were pointing out that the first two terms of the series for the hyperbolic cosine looked a lot like the Mandelbrot equation. Not too surprisingly, if you approximate the hyperbolic cosine by just these two terms, you get a Mandelbrot set, rather than the new set that you were looking for. This is a good example of how truncating the Taylor series too soon can give you some other fractal than the one you were expecting.

Another important thing to note is that the cosine fractal is periodic. Plate 11, which is the overall view of the cosine fractal, shows the periodicity. Plate 12 is an expansion of the cosine fractal. Table 7-1 shows the parameters that were used to generate three fractal pictures, including the two color plates.

The *sine* Set

The sine fractals are generated by the iterated equation:

$$z_n = \sin(z_{n-1}) + c \qquad \text{(Equation 7-9)}$$

where both z and c are complex numbers. Figure 7-2 lists a fractal function with the core program that generates the sine fractals. This function generates a Mandelbrot-type curve but you can easily alter it to produce Julia-type curves instead.

	Plate 11	Plate 12	Not shown
X Maximum	5.0000	1.150235	-4.182951
X Minimum	-7.0000	0.924883	-4.207904
Y Maximum	8.0000	1.994261	1.329093
Y Minimum	-8.0000	1.627507	1.1289681
Maximum iterations	64	64	64

Table 7-1. Parameters for Cosine Fractals

As with the program for generating cosine fractals, there is a mathematical identity that makes it possible to handle the sine of a complex number. It is:

$$\sin(x + iy) = \sin x \cosh y + i \cos x \sinh y \qquad \text{(Equation 7-10)}$$

Using this identity you can obtain the real and imaginary parts of the sine using the trig and hyperbolic functions that are a part of your C library. As with the cosine set, you can also use the Taylor series given in equation 7-3 to approximate the sine.

However, as with the cosine, if you don't use enough terms of the Taylor series to give a precise approximation, you will get a set that may be quite different from what you expected.

As with the cosine, the sine fractal is periodic. Plate 13, which is the overall view of the sine fractal, shows the periodicity. Plate 14 is an expansion of the sine fractal, and plate 15 is another expansion. Table 7-2 shows the parameters used to generate these color plates.

The *exp* Set

The exp fractals are generated by the iterated equation:

$$z_n = c(exp)z_{n-1} \qquad \text{(Equation 7-11)}$$

where both z and c are complex numbers.

```
/*

┌─────────────────────────────────────────────────────────┐
│  fractal() = Computes and displays the sine fractal       │
└─────────────────────────────────────────────────────────┘

*/

void fractal(void)
{
    complex c,z,zsq;
    int color;

    deltaP = (XMax - XMin)/640;
    deltaQ = (YMax - YMin)/350;
    for (col=0; col<640; col++)
    {
        if (kbhit() != 0)
        {
            save_screen(0,0,col,maxrow,filename);
            exit(0);
        }
        for (row=0; row<350; row++)
        {
```

```
c = complex(XMin + col * deltaP,YMax - row *deltaQ);
z = (0,0);
color = 0;
while ((color < max_iterations) && (norm(z) < max_size))
{
    z = sin(z) + c;
    color++;
}
if (color >= max_iterations)
    color = 0;
else
    color = color%15 + 1;
plot (col,row,color);
    }
  }
}
```

Figure 7-2 Listing of Function to Generate Sine Fractals

	Plate 13	Plate 14	Plate 15
X Maximum	5.0000	-4.031643	-4.182951
X Minimum	-7.0000	-4.370892	-4.207904
Y Maximum	8.0000	1.444176	1.329093
Y Minimum	-8.0000	0.893989	1.289681
Maximum iterations	64	64	64

Table 7-2. Parameters for Sine Fractals

In this case, the constant term is a multiplier rather than being summed in, as with the dragon curves. This was done because summing the constant term yields very uninteresting fractals. Figure 7-3 lists a fractal function for use with the core program to generate the exponential fractals. This function generates a Mandelbrot-type curve but you can easily alter it to produce Julia-type curves instead. This function is also designed for use with a compiler that supports the complex number type. Using the previously described mathematical functions for complex numbers and the identity you can obtain the real and imaginary parts of the equation with the trig and hyperbolic functions that are a part of your C library.

$$e^{(x+iy)} = \cosh x \cosh y + \sinh x \cosh y$$
$$+ i(\cosh x \cosh y + \sinh x \sin y)$$

(Equation 7-12)

Again it is possible, if you want to try it, to use the Taylor series given in equation 7-2 to approximate the exponential function. The same warning applies, that if you use too few terms of the series, you will get a fractal image that might be quite unlike the one for the exponential function.

Plate 16 is the overall view of the exponential fractal. The parameters used for generating this display were: $XMax = 2.0000$, $XMin = 0.50000$, $YMax = 1.0000$, and $YMin = 1.0000$. The maximum number of iterations was 64.

The *cosh* Set

The hyperbolic cosine fractals are generated by the iterated equation:

$$z_n = \cosh(z_{n-1}) + c$$

(Equation 7-13)

where both z and c are complex numbers. Figure 7-4 lists a fractal function for use with the core program to generate the sine fractals. This function generates a Mandelbrot-type curve but you can easily alter it to produce Julia-type curves instead. This function, like those above, is designed for use with a compiler that supports the complex number type.

```
/*

    fractal() = Computes and displays the exp fractal

*/

void fractal(void)
{
    complex c,z,zsq;
    int color;
```

```
deltaP = (XMax - XMin)/640;
deltaQ = (YMax - YMin)/350;
for (col=0; col<640; col++)
{
    if (kbhit() != 0)
    {
        save_screen(0,0,col,maxrow,filename);
        exit(0);
    }
    for (row=0; row<350; row++)
    {
        c = complex(XMin + col * deltaP,YMax - row * deltaQ);
        z = (0,0);
        color = 0;
        while ((color < max_iterations) && (norm(z) < max_size))
        {
            z = c* exp(z);
            color++;
        }
        if (color >= max_iterations)
            color = 0;
        else
            color = color%15 + 1;
        plot (col,row,color);
    }
}
}
```

Figure 7-3 Listing of Function to Generate Exponential Fractals

Using the identity given below, you can rewrite the function in terms of standard C library functions and operators:

$$\cosh(x + iy) = \cosh x \cos y + i \sinh x \sin y \qquad \text{(Equation 7-14)}$$

If you want to approximate this function, do so with the Taylor series given in equation 7-6, but use enough terms to produce a fractal picture that really looks like the exponential set, rather than something different.

Another important thing to note is that the hyperbolic cosine fractal is periodic in the imaginary direction. This is different from the sine and cosine fractals, which are periodic in the real direction. Plate 17, which is the overall view of the hyperbolic cosine fractal, shows the periodicity. Plate 18 is an expansion of the hyperbolic cosine fractal. Table 8-3 shows the parameters that were used to generate three fractal displays, including the two color plates.

The *sinh* Set

The hyperbolic sine fractals are generated by the iterated equation:

$$z_n = \sinh(z_{n-1}) + c \qquad\qquad \text{(Equation 7-15)}$$

where both z and c are complex numbers.

```
/*

    fractal() = Computes and displays the hyperbolic cosine fractal

*/
void fractal(void)
{
    complex c,z,zsq;
    int color;

    deltaP = (XMax - XMin)/640;
    deltaQ = (YMax - YMin)/350;
    for (col=0; col<640; col++)
    {
        if (kbhit() != 0)
        {
            save_screen(0,0,col,maxrow,filename);
            exit(0);
        }
        for (row=0; row<350; row++)
        {
```

```
            c = complex(XMin + col * deltaP,YMax - row *deltaQ);
            z = (0,0);
            color = 0;
            while ((color < max_iterations) && (norm(z) < max_size))
            {
                z = cosh(z) + c;
                color++;
            }
            if (color >= max_iterations)
                color = 0;
            else
                color = color%15 + 1;
            plot (col,row,color);
        }
    }
}
```

Figure 7-4 Listing of Function to Generate Hyperbolic Cosine Fractals

	Plate 17	Not shown	Plate 18
X Maximum	5.0000	0.455399	2.760563
X Minimum	-7.0000	-0.014085	1.884194
Y Maximum	8.0000	1.123209	-1.272206
Y Minimum	-8.0000	0.481375	-2.189172
Maximum iterations	64	64	64

Table 7-3. Parameters for Hyperbolic Cosine Fractals

Figure 7-5 lists a fractal function for use with the core program to generate the sine fractals. This function generates a Mandelbrot-type curve but you can easily alter it to produce Julia-type curves instead. This function, like those above, is designed for use with a compiler that supports the complex number type. Using the identity given below, you can rewrite the function in terms of standard C library functions and operators:

$$\sinh(x + iy) = \sinh x \cos y + i \cosh x \sin y \qquad \text{(Equation 7-16)}$$

If you want to approximate this function, do so with the Taylor series given in Equation 8-5, but use enough terms to produce a fractal picture that looks like the exponential set, rather than something different.

Another important thing to note is that the hyperbolic sine fractal, like the hyperbolic cosine fractal, is periodic in the imaginary direction. This is different from the sine and cosine fractals, which are periodic in the real direction. Plate 19, which is the overall view of the hyperbolic cosine fractal, shows the periodicity. Plate 20 is an expansion of the hyperbolic sine fractal. Table 7-4 shows the parameters that were used to generate three hyperbolic sine fractals, including the two color plates.

	Plate 19	Plate 20	Not shown
X Maximum	6.0000	-0.859155	-1.470674
X Minimum	-6.0000	-2.136150	-1.570595
Y Maximum	8.0000	-0.217765	-0.564560
Y Minimum	-8.0000	-0.951289	-0.633919
Maximum iterations	64	64	64

Table 7-4. Parameters for Hyperbolic Sine Fractals

```
/*

    fractal() = Computes and displays the hyperbolic sine fractal

*/

void fractal(void)
{
    complex c,z,zsq;
    int color;

    deltaP = (XMax - XMin)/640;
    deltaQ = (YMax - YMin)/350;
    for (col=0; col<640; col++)
    {
        if (kbhit() != 0)
```

```
            {
                  save_screen(0,0,col,maxrow,filename);
                  exit(0);
            }
            for (row=0; row<350; row++)
            {
                  c = complex(XMin + col * deltaP,YMax - row *deltaQ);
                  z = (0,0);
                  color = 0;
                  while ((color < max_iterations) && (norm(z) < max_size))
                  {
                        z = sinh(z) + c;
                        color++;
                  }
                  if (color >= max_iterations)
                        color = 0;
                  else
                        color = color%15 + 1;
                  plot (col,row,color);
            }
      }
}
```

Figure 7-5. Listing of Function to Generate Hyperbolic Sine Fractals

CHAPTER 8

Orthogonal Polynomials

Not every polynomial results in a beautiful fractal picture when iterated. In fact most polynomials that you select by chance result in uninteresting displays, many of them with a blank screen. I have not seen any advanced mathematics that sets up criteria for polynomial suitability for fractal generation. However, I have discovered a number of interesting fractals that can be generated from what are known as orthogonal polynomials. Most orthogonal polynomials have arisen from the study of the solutions of differential equations. A system of polynomials is considered to be orthogonal with respect to a weight function $w(x)$, if over the interval $a<x<b$ the following relationship holds:

$$\int_a^b w(x)f_2(x)f_m(x)\,dx=0 \qquad \text{(Equation 8-1)}$$

This definition can result in a lot of different polynomials, depending upon what weight function is selected. We can standardize orthogonal polynomials using the following definitions:

$$\int_a^b w(x)\,f_n^2(x)\,dx=h_n \qquad \text{(Equation 8-2)}$$

$$f_n(x)=k_nx^n+k_n'x^n+\cdots \qquad \text{(Equation 8-3)}$$

There are several interesting relationships which are fulfilled by orthogonal polynomial systems. The first is the differential equation:

$$g_2(x)f_n'' + g_1(x)f_n' + a_nf_n = 0$$

(Equation 8-4)

where $g_2(x)$ and $g_1(x)$ are independent of n and a_n is a constant depending solely on n. Orthogonal polynomials also obey the recurrence relationship:

$$f_{n+1} = (a_n + xb_n)f_n - c_{n-1}$$

(Equation 8-5)

where

$$b_n = k_{n+1}/k_n$$

(Equation 8-6)

$$a_n = b_n(k'_{n+1}/k_{n+1} - k'_n/k_n)$$

(Equation 8-7)

$$c_n = (k_{n+1}k_{n-1}h_n) / (k_n^2 h_{n-1})$$

(Equation 8-8)

Creating Fractals with Orthogonal Polynomials

Fractals are created with orthogonal polynomials in the usual manner, namely at each point over a selected area of the complex plane an iterated equation is evaluated. For Mandelbrot-like sets, the iterated equation sets a new value of z equal to the orthogonal polynomial of the old z either with a constant, which is determined by the position on the complex plane, added to the polynomial (for Mandelbrot/Julia-like sets) or multiplied by the polynomial (for dragon-like sets). Usually, either adding the constant or multiplying by it will yield an interesting looking set, but not both. You have to try both ways and see which sets you like best. For example, the T Tchebychev fifth order polynomial, T_5, is:

$$T_5 = 16z^5 - 20z^3 + 5z$$

(Equation 8-9)

The iterated equation for creating fractals using the Tchebychev T polynomial is:

$$z_n = c(16z_{n-1}^5 - 20z_{n-1}^3 + 5z_{n-1})$$

(Equation 8-10)

In modifying the *fractal* function to use with the *core* program, you will probably want to create one or more temporary variables to store powers of z. You select those for a particular polynomial so as to reduce the number of multiplications as much as possible in order to speed up operation. Figure 8-1 is a listing of the *fractal* function for the Tchebychev T_5 polynomial; it is typical. All you need to do is select the polynomial that you want to work with and insert the proper equation into the *fractal* function.

The T Tchebychev Polynomials

There are four different kinds of Tchebychev polynomials, T_n, U_n, C_n, and S_n. We shall list the coefficients for all types, but will only give examples of displays generated by T_5 and C_6, leaving it to you to investigate what the other two types look like. Tchebychev polynomials are well known in electrical engineering because they describe the locations of poles and zeroes for creating frequency filters, but as far as we know, nobody has ever generated a Tchebychev fractal before, or even attempted to connect the fractal diagram to filter response characteristics. Table 8-1 lists the coefficients for the Tchebychev T polynomial. Table 8-2 lists the coefficients of the Tchebychev U polynomial. Table 8-3 lists the coefficients for the Tchebychev C polynomial. Table 8-4 lists the coefficients for the Tchebychev S polynomial. Table 8-5 lists the parameters used to generate the Tchebychev fractal displays that are shown in the color plates. Plate 21 is the overall view of the Tchebychev T fractal. Plate 22 is the overall view of the Tchebychev C fractal. Both of these fractals were generated using the constant c as a multiplier rather than as a term added to the polynomial. Figure 8-2 lists the function to generate the Tchebychev C_6 polynomial.

```
/*

    fractal() = Computes and displays the Tchebychev T5 fractal

*/

void fractal(void)
{
        complex c,z,zcube;
```

```
        int color;

        deltaP = (XMax - XMin)/640;
        deltaQ = (YMax - YMin)/350;
        for (col=0; col<640; col++)
        {
            if (kbhit() != 0)
            {
                save_screen(0,0,col,maxrow,filename);
                exit(0);
            }
            for (row=0; row<350; row++)
            {
                c = complex(XMin + col * deltaP,YMax - row *deltaQ);
                z = (0,0);
                color = 0;
                while ((color < max_iterations) && (norm(z) < max_size))
                {
                    zcube = z*z*z;
                    z = c*(16*z*z*zcube - 20*zcube + 5*z);
                    color++;
                }
                if (color >= max_iterations)
                    color = 0;
                else
                    color = color%15 + 1;
                plot (col,row,color);
            }
        }
    }
```

Figure 8-1 Listing of Function to Generate the Tchebychev T_5 Fractals

	z^0	z^1	z^2	z^3	z^4	z^5	z^6	z^7
T_0	1							
T_1		1						
T_2	-1		2					
T_3		-3		4				
T_4	1		-8		8			
T^5		5		-20		16		
T_6	-1		18		-48		32	
T_7		-7		56		-112		64

Table 8-1. Coefficients of the Tchebychev T Polynomial

	z^0	z^1	z^2	z^3	z^4	z^5	z^6	z^7
C_0	2							
C_1		1						
C_2	-2		1					
C_3		-3		1				
C_4	2		-4		1			
C^5		5		-5		1		
C_6	-2		9		-6		1	
C_7		-7		14		-7		1

Table 8-2. Coefficients of the Tchebychev C Polynomial

	z^0	z^1	z^2	z^3	z^4	z^5	z^6	z^7
U_0	1							
U_1		2						
U_2	-1		4					
U_3		-4		8				
U_4	1		-12		16			
U^5		6		-32		32		
U_6	-1		24		-80		64	
U_7		-8		80		-192		128

Table 8-3. Coefficients of the Tchebychev U Polynomial

	z^0	z^1	z^2	z^3	z^4	z^5	z^6	z^7
S_0	1							
S_1		1						
S_2	-1		1					
S_3		-2		1				
S_4	1		-3		1			
S^5		3		-4		1		
S_6	-1		6		-5		1	
S_7		-4		10		-6		1

Table 8-4. Coefficients of the Tchebychev S Polynomial

	Plate 21 Tchebychev T_5	Plate 22 Tchebychev C_6
X Maximum	1.60000	1.00000
X Minimum	-1.60000	-1.00000
Y Maximum	0.75000	0.32000
Y Minimum	-0.75000	-0.32000
Maximum Iterations	64	64

Table 8-5. Parameters for Tchebychev Fractals

```
/*

    fractal() = Computes and displays the Tchebychev C₆ fractal

*/

void fractal(void)
{
    complex c,z,zsq;
    int color;

    deltaP = (XMax - XMin)/640;
    deltaQ = (YMax - YMin)/350;
    for (col=0; col<640; col++)
```

```
deltaQ = (YMax - YMin)/350;
for (col=0; col<640; col++)
{
    if (kbhit() != 0)
    {
        save_screen(0,0,col,maxrow,filename);
        exit(0);
    }
    for (row=0; row<350; row++)
    {
        c = complex(XMin + col * deltaP,YMax - row *deltaQ);
        z = (0,0);
        color = 0;
        while ((color < max_iterations) && (norm(z) < max_size))

        {
            zsq = z*z;
            z = c*(zsq*zsq*zsq - 6*zsq*zsq + 9*zsq - 2);
            color++;
        }
        if (color >= max_iterations)
            color = 0;
        else
            color = color%15 + 1;
        plot (col,row,color);
    }
}
}
```

Figure 8-2 Listing of Function to Generate the Tchebychev C_6 Fractals

Legendre Polynomials

The Legendre polynomial P_6 generates a rather interesting fractal which is reminiscent in shape of the Mandelbrot set except that instead of having a body and one "head", it has five successively smaller circles. This fractal was generated by adding the constant c to the polynomial at each iteration. The fractal is shown in Plate 23. Table 8-6 gives the coefficients for the Legendre polynomials. Note that the table lists a denominator for each polynomial. The entire polynomial is divided by this

143

denominator. Table 8-7 gives the parameters that were used to generate the color plates of the Legendre, Laguerre, and Hermite polynomials. Figure 8-3 lists the function used with the core program to generate the Legendre P_6 polynomial.

Laguerre Polynomials

The Laguerre polynomial L_4 generates the fractal picture shown in Plate 24. The constant c is added to the polynomial at each iteration. Table 8-8 gives the coefficients for the Laguerre polynomials. Like the Legendre polynomial, each Laguerre polynomial has a denominator listed. The entire polynomial must be divided by this denominator. The function to create the Laguerre fractal is listed in Figure 8-4.

	denom	z^0	z^1	z^2	z^3	z^4	z^5	z^6	z^7
P_0	1	1							
P_1	1		1						
P_2	2	-1		3					
P_3	2		-3		5				
P_4	8	3		-30		35			
P_5	8		15		-70		63		
P_6	16	-5		105		-315		231	
P_7	16		-35		315		-693		429

Table 8-6. Coefficients of the Legendre Polynomial

	Plate 23 Legendre	Plate 24 Laguerre	Plate 25 Hermite
X maximum	0.60000	4.00000	0.10000
X minimum	-0.60000	0.25000	-0.10000
Y maximum	0.40000	1.40000	0.06000
Y minimum	-0.40000	-1.40000	-0.60000
Max iter	64	64	64

Table 8-7. Parameters for Legendre, Laguerre, and Hermite Polynomial Fractals

```
/*
```

┌───┐
│ legend = Fractal function to generate Legendre Fractal   │
└───┘

```
*/

void fractal(void)
{
    complex c,z,zsq;
    int color;

    deltaP = (XMax - XMin)/640;
    deltaQ = (YMax - YMin)/350;
    for (col=0; col<640; col++)
    {
            if (kbhit() != 0)
            {
                save_screen(0,0,col,maxrow,filename);
                exit(0);
            }
        for (row=0; row<350; row++)
        {
            c = complex(XMin + col * deltaP,YMax - row * deltaQ);
            c = complex(XMin + col * deltaP,YMax - row * deltaQ);
            z = (0,0);
            color = 0;
            while ((color < max_iterations) && (norm(z) < max_size))
            {
                zsq = z*z;
                z = .125*(35*zsq*zsq -30*zsq + 3) + c;
                color++;
            }
            if (color >= max_iterations)
                color = 0;
            else
                color = color%15 + 1;
            plot (col,row,color);
        }
    }
```

```
        }
```
Figure 8-3. Listing of Function to Generate Legendre Fractal

Hermite Polynomials

The Hermite polynomial H_4 generates the fractal picture shown in Plate 25. The constant c is added to the polynomial at each iteration. Table 8-8 gives the coefficients for the Laguerre polynomials. Like the Legendre polynomial, each Laguerre polynomial has a denominator listed. The entire polynomial must be divided by this denominator.

```
/*

    ┌─────────────────────────────────────────────────────────────┐
    │  laguer = Fractal function to generate Laguerre Fractal       │
    └─────────────────────────────────────────────────────────────┘

*/

void fractal(void)
{
    complex c,z,zsq;
    int color;

    deltaP = (XMax - XMin)/640;
    deltaQ = (YMax - YMin)/350;
    for (col=0; col<640; col++)
    {
            if (kbhit() != 0)
            {
                save_screen(0,0,col,maxrow,filename);
                exit(0);
            }
        for (row=0; row<350; row++)
        {
            c = complex(XMin + col * deltaP,YMax - row * deltaQ);
            c = complex(XMin + col * deltaP,YMax - row * deltaQ);
            z = (0,0);
            color = 0;
            while ((color < max_iterations) && (norm(z) <
```

```
max_size))
        {
            zsq = z*z;
            z = (zsq*zsq -16*zsq*z + 72*zsq - 96*z + 24.0) /
        24.0 + c;
            color++;
        }
        if (color >= max_iterations)
            color = 0;
        else
            color = color%15 + 1;
        plot (col,row,color);
    }
  }
}
```

Figure 8-4. Listing of Function to Generate Laguerre Fractal

	denom	z^0	z^1	z^2	z^3	z^4	z^5	z^6
L_0	1	1						
L_1	1	1	-1					
L_2	2	2	-4	1				
L_3	6	6	-18	9	-1			
L_4	24	24	-96	72	-16	1		
L^5	120	120	-600	600	-200	25	-1	
L_6	720	720	-4320	5400	-2400	450	-36	1

Table 8-8. Coefficients of the Laguerre Polynomial

```
/*
```

```
    hermite = Fractal function to generate Hermite Fractal
```

```
*/

void fractal(void)
{
```

```
        complex c,z,zsq;
        int color;

        deltaP = (XMax - XMin)/640;
        deltaQ = (YMax - YMin)/350;
        for (col=0; col<640; col++)
        {
                if (kbhit() != 0)
                {
                    save_screen(0,0,col,maxrow,filename);
                    exit(0);
                }
            for (row=0; row<350; row++)
            {
                c = complex(XMin + col * deltaP,YMax - row * deltaQ);
                c = complex(XMin + col * deltaP,YMax - row * deltaQ);
                z = (0,0);
                color = 0;
                while ((color < max_iterations) && (norm(z) < max_size))
                {
                    zsq = z*z;
                    z = 16*zsq*zsq -48*zsq + 12) + c;
                    color++;
                }
                if (color >= max_iterations)
                    color = 0;
                else
                    color = color%15 + 1;
                plot (col,row,color);
            }
        }
    }
```

Figure 8-5. Listing of Function to Generate Hermite Fractal

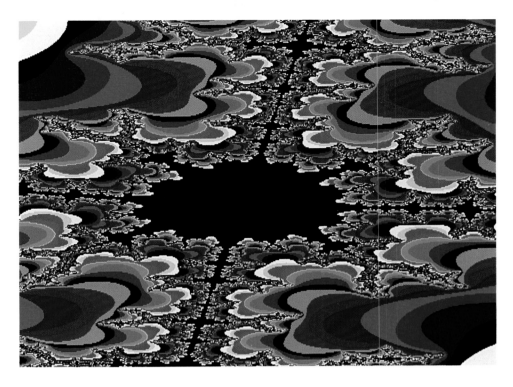

Plate 1   Expansion of the Mandelbrot Set

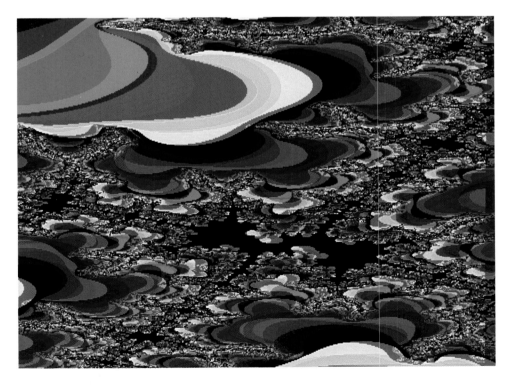

Plate 2   Expansion of the Julia Set

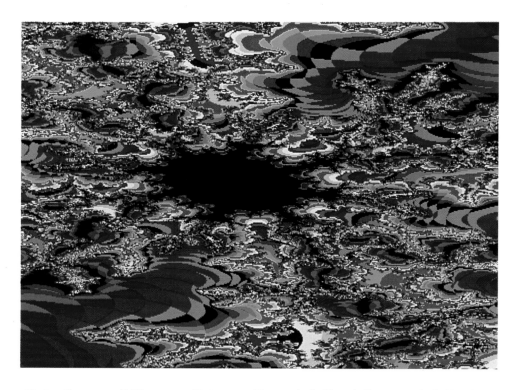

Plate 3   **Difference Between Expanded Mandelbrot and Julia Sets**

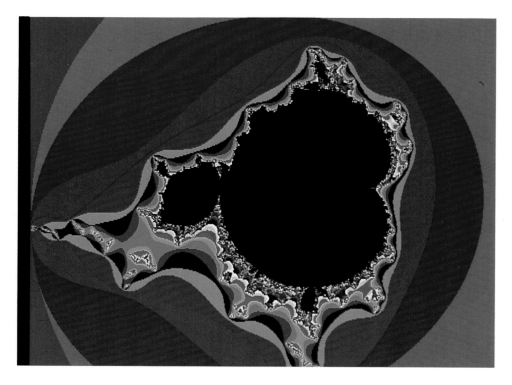

Plate 4   **Distorted Mandelbrot Set Starting with X and Y of 0.3**

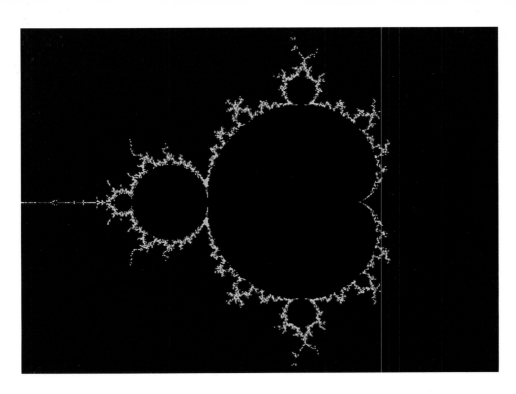

Plate 5   The Mandelbrot Set Using Color Assignment

Plate 6   Julia Set Using Julia Set Color Assignment

Plate 7   Dragon Curve

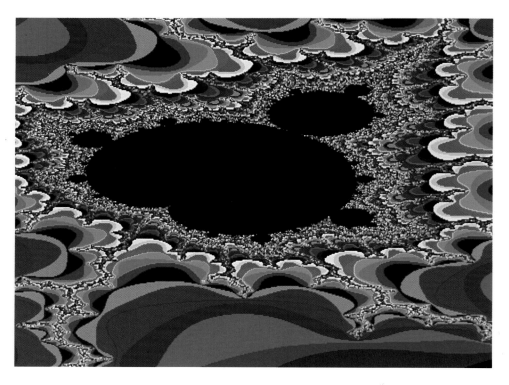

Plate 8   Major Expansion of the Mandelbrot Set

Plate 9   Mandelbrot Set Using the Distance Estimating Method

Plate 10   Three Dimensional Mandelbrot Set Using the Distance
                  Estimating Method

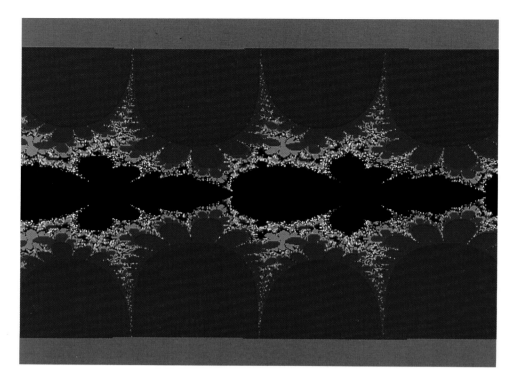

Plate 11   **The Cosine Set**

Plate 12   **Expansion of the Cosine Set**

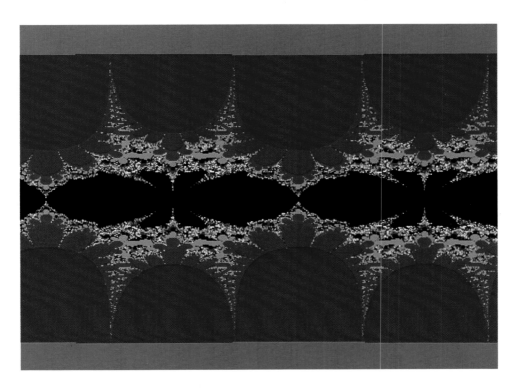

Plate 13   The Sine Set

Plate 14   Expansion of the Sine Set

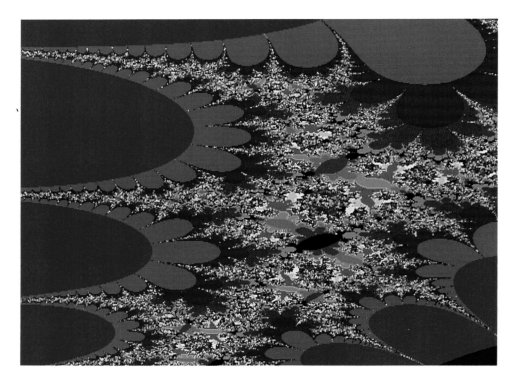

Plate 15   **Another Expansion of the Sine Set**

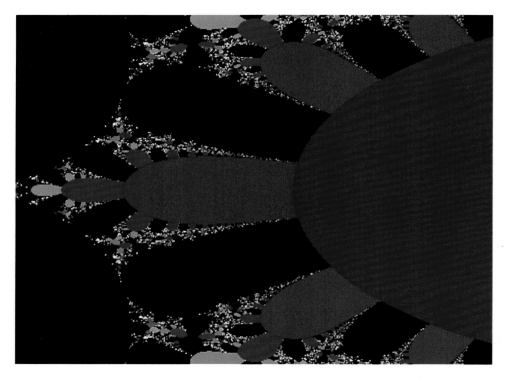

Plate 16   **The Exponential Set**

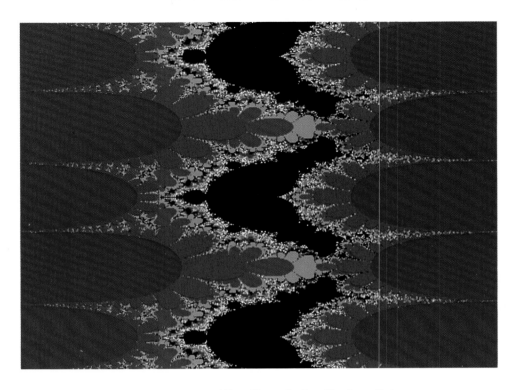

Plate 17   The Hyperbolic Cosine Set

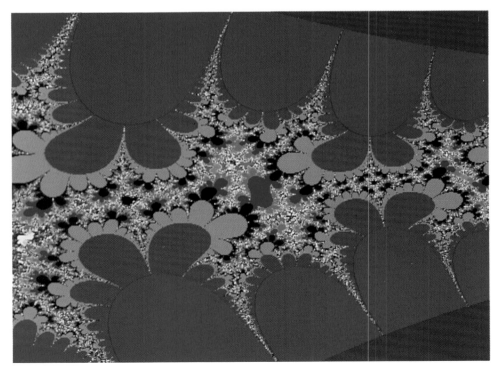

Plate 18   Expansion of the Hyperbolic Cosine Set

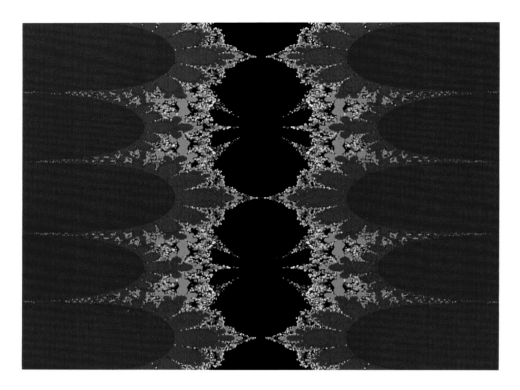

Plate 19   The Hyperbolic Sine Set

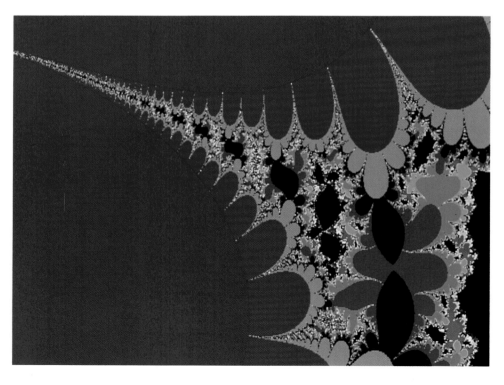

Plate 20   Expansion of the Hyperbolic Sine Set

Plate 21   The Tchebychev T Polynomial Set

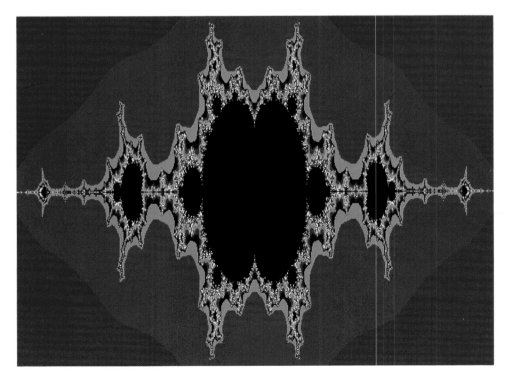

Plate 22   The Tchebychev C Polynomial Set

Plate 23   The Legendre Polynomial Set

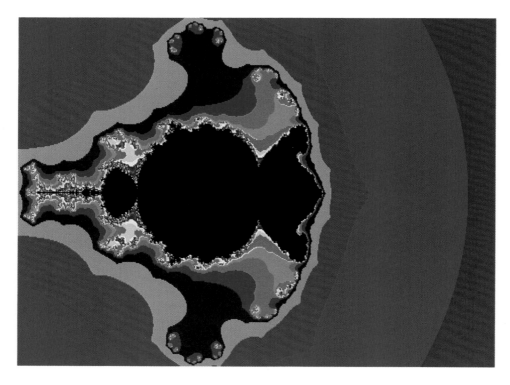

Plate 24   The Laguerre Polynomial Set

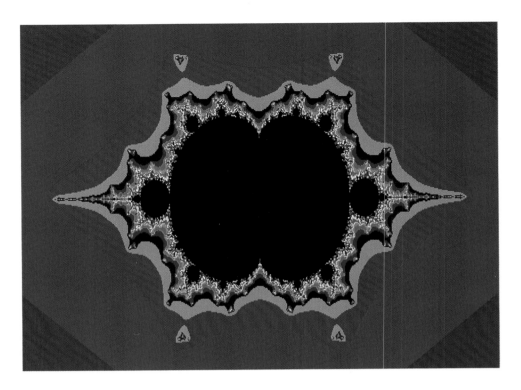

Plate 25 **The Hermite Polynomial Set**

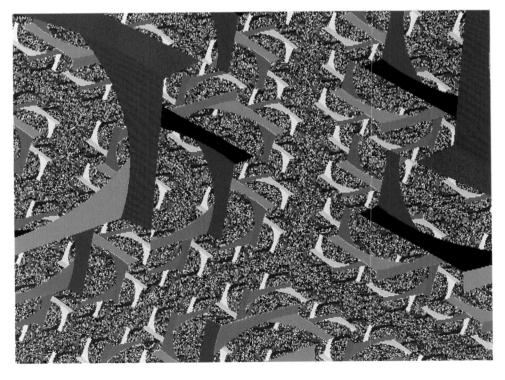

Plate 26 **First Barnsley Fractal**

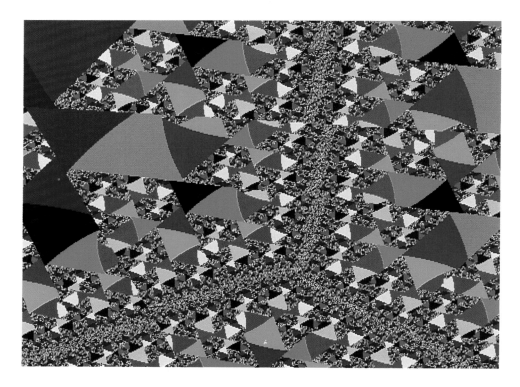

Plate 27   Second Barnsley Fractal

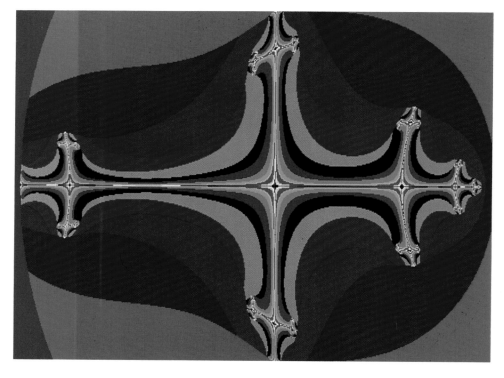

Plate 28   Third Barnsley Fractal

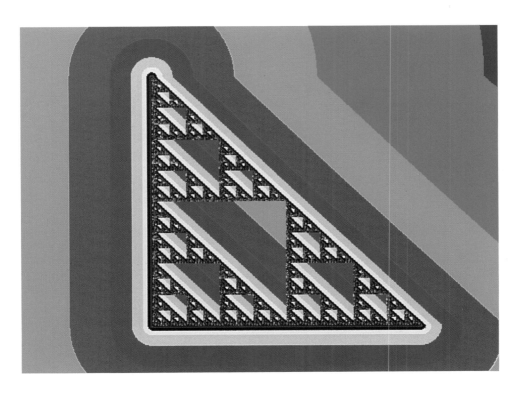

Plate 29   Sierpinski Triangle

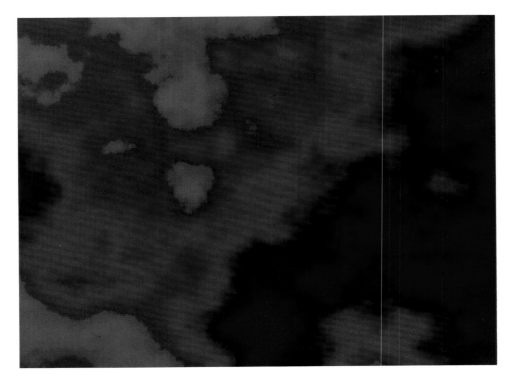

Plate 30   A Typical Plasma Display

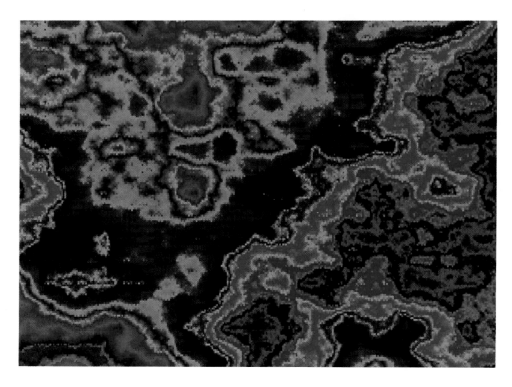

Plate 31   Plasma Display After Color Cycling

Plate 32   Three Dimensional Representation of a Plasma Display

	z^0	z^1	z^2	z^3	z^4	z^5	z^6	z^7
H_0	1							
H_1		2						
H_2	-2		4					
H_3		-12		8				
H_4	12		-48		16			
H^5		120		-160		32		
H_6	-120		720		-480		64	
H_7		-1680		3360		-1344		128

Table 8-9. Coefficients of the Hermite Polynomial

CHAPTER 9

Some Barnsley Fractals

Michael Barnsley, at Georgia Institute of Technology, is the discoverer of iterated function systems (a technique for generating fractals of which more will be said in Chapter 13). He has written a book called *Fractals Everywhere*, which provides a wealth of information on many different fractals. One type of fractal in the book, is that in which at each iteration of an equation, there are two courses of action possible. One course is selected at each iteration, depending upon the value of the equation after the preceding iteration. The result is a fractal that looks much different from any we have seen thus far. We are going to look at three of these fractals, plus a representation of the well-known Sierpinski triangle.

The First Barnsley Fractal

The first Barnsley fractal is defined in the following manner:

$$z_n = cz_{n-1} - c \qquad \text{when the real part of} \qquad z_{n-1} >= 0$$

and

$$z_n = cz_{n-1} + c \qquad \text{otherwise}$$

(Equation 9-1)

The *fractal* function to insert into the *core* program to generate this fractal is listed in Figure 10-1. This is a Julia-type fractal, so that the starting value of z is varied over the complex plane, while the value of c is kept constant. The parameters that were used to generate this picture were: *XMax = 1.0000, XMin = 0.0000, YMax = 1.0000, YMin = 0.0000, P = 0.60000,* and *Q = 1.10000.* The maximum number of iterations was 64. The resulting fractal is shown in Plate 26.

```
/*

    ┌─────────────────────────────────────────────────────────┐
    │ fractal() = Computes the first Barnsley fractal          │
    └─────────────────────────────────────────────────────────┘
*/

void fractal(void)
{
    int color;
    double px, py, qx, qy;

    max_size = 4;
    p = Pval;
 q = Qval;
    deltaP = (XMax - XMin)/640;
    deltaQ = (YMax - YMin)/350;
    for (col=0; col<640; col++)
    {
        if (kbhit() != 0)
            {
                save_screen(0,0,col,maxrow,filename);
                exit(0);
            }
        for (row=0; row<350; row++)
        {
            x = XMin + col * deltaP;
            y = YMax - row * deltaQ;
            color = 0;
            while ((color < max_iterations) && (x*x + y*y <
                max_size))
            {
                px = p*x;
                qx = q*x;
                py = p*y;
                qy = q*y;
                if (x >= 0)
                {
                    x = px - p - qy;
                    y = py - q + qx;
                }
```

```
                else
                {
                    x = px + p - qy;
                    y = py + q + qx;
                }
                color++;
            }
            if (color >= max_iterations)
                color = 0;
            else
                color = color%15 + 1;
            plot (col,row,color);
        }
    }
}
```

Figure 9-1. Listing of fractal Function for the First Barnsley Fractal

The Second Barnsley Fractal

The second Barnsley fractal is defined in the following manner:

$$z_n = cz_{n-1} - c \qquad \text{when imaginary part of} \qquad cz_{n-1} >= 0$$

and

$$z_n = cz_{n-1} + c \qquad \text{otherwise}$$

(Equation 9-2)

The fractal function for the *core* program to generate this fractal is listed in Figure 9-2. You will note that the two alternate iteration equations are exactly the same as for the first Barnsley fractal, but the condition for choosing between them is different. The result is an entirely different fractal picture. This fractal is also of the Julia-type requiring P and Q input parameters. The parameters that were used to generate this picture were: *XMax = 1.0000, XMin = 0.0000, YMax = 1.0000, YMin = 0.0000, P = 0.60000,* and *Q = 1.10000.* The maximum number of iterations was 64. The resulting fractal is shown in Plate 27.

```
/*

┌─────────────────────────────────────────────────────────┐
│  ┌──────────────────────────────────────────────────┐   │
│  │  fractal() = Computes the second Barnsley fractal  │   │
│  └──────────────────────────────────────────────────┘   │
└─────────────────────────────────────────────────────────┘

*/

void fractal(void)
{
    int color;
    double px, py, qx, qy;
    max_size = 4;
    p = Pval;
 q = Qval;
    deltaP = (XMax - XMin)/640;
    deltaQ = (YMax - YMin)/350;
    for (col=0; col<640; col++)
    {
        if (kbhit() != 0)
            {
                save_screen(0,0,col,maxrow,filename);
                exit(0);
            }
        for (row=0; row<350; row++)
        {
            x = XMin + col * deltaP;
            y = YMax - row * deltaQ;
            color = 0;
            while ((color < max_iterations) && (x*x + y*y <
        max_size))
            {
                px = p*x;
                qx = q*x;
                py = p*y;
                qy = q*y;
                if (qx + py >= 0)
                {
                    x = px - p - qy;
                    y = py - q + qx;
                }
                else
```

```
            {
                x = px + p - qy;
                y = py + q + qx;
            }
            color++;
        }
        if (color >= max_iterations)
            color = 0;
        else
            color = color%15 + 1;
        plot (col,row,color);
    }
  }
}
```

Figure 9-2. Listing of the fractal Function for the Second Barnsley Fractal

The Third Barnsley Fractal

The third Barnsley fractal is defined in the following manner:

$$z_n = z_{n-12} - 1.0 \qquad\qquad \text{when real part of} \qquad z_{n-1} \geq 0$$

and

$$z_n = z_{n-12} - 1.0 + px \qquad\qquad \text{otherwise}$$

(Equation 9-3)

where px is the real part of c multiplied by the real part of z_{n-1}. The *fractal* function to insert into the core program to generate this fractal is listed in Figure 9-3. This is very similar to the equation for the Julia set except that the constant term can take on either of the two alternatives. As a matter of fact, if the P(the real part of c is set equal to zero, the equation becomes that of a Julia set (similar to what Mandelbrot calls the San Marcos dragon). This fractal, since it is of the Julia type requires a constant parameter to be entered, but only P (the real part); the imaginary part, Q, is not used. The parameters that were used to generate this picture were: *XMax = 1.7000, XMin = -2.1000, YMax = 1.0300, YMin = -1.0300*, and *P = 1.00000*. The maximum number of iterations was 64. The resulting fractal is shown in Plate 28.

155

```c
/*

┌────────────────────────────────────────────────────────────┐
│  fractal() = Function to generate Barnsley's third fractal   │
└────────────────────────────────────────────────────────────┘

*/

void fractal(void)
{
    int color;
    double xsq, ysq, xy;

    max_size = 4;
    p = Pval;
    q = Qval;
    deltaP = (XMax - XMin)/640;
    deltaQ = (YMax - YMin)/350;
    for (col=0; col<640; col++)
    {
        if (kbhit() != 0)
            {
                    save_screen(0,0,col,maxrow,filename);
                    exit(0);
            }
        for (row=0; row<350; row++)
        {
            x = XMin + col * deltaP;
            y = YMax - row * deltaQ;
            xsq = 0;
            ysq = 0;
            color = 0;
            while ((color < max_iterations) && (xsq + ysq < max_size))
            {
                xsq = x*x;
                ysq = y*y;
                xy = x*y;
                if (x >= 0)
                {
                    x = xsq - ysq - 1.0;
                    y = 2 * xy;
```

```
            }
            else
            {
                x = xsq - ysq - 1.0 + p*x;
                y = 2 * xy;
            }
            color++;
        }
        if (color >= max_iterations)
            color = 0;
        else
            color = color%15 + 1;
        plot (col,row,color);
        }
    }
}
```

Figure 9-3. Listing of the fractal Function for the Third Barnsley Fractal

The Ubiquitous Sierpinski Triangle

No matter what technique you use for creating fractals, there always seems to be a variation of it that produces a Sierpinski triangle. In Chapter 13, we shall be looking at a way to generate a Sierpinski triangle with the L-systems technique. There are also ways to create it with iterated function systems, and by taking a solid triangle and cutting smaller triangles out of it. The method used here is a modification of one developed by Barnsley. It is based upon a very simple iterated function:

$z_n = 2z_{n-1} - i$ when imaginary part of $z_{n-1} < 0.5$

or, otherwise

$z_n = 2z_{n-1} - 1$ when real part of $z_{n-1} < 0.5$

or otherwise

$z_n = 2z_{n-1}$ (Equation 9-4)

The *fractal* function to insert into the *core* program to generate this fractal is listed in Figure 9-4. This fractal is of the Julia-type but the constant is zero so that it doesn't have to be entered. The parameters that were used to generate this picture were: *XMax = 1.3000*, *XMin = -0.5000*, *YMax = 1.2200*, and *YMin = -0.2200*. The maximum number of iterations was 64. The resulting fractal is shown in Plate 29.

```
/*

    sierp = Fractal function to generate Sierpinski Triangle

*/

void fractal(void)
{
    double x,y;
    int color;

    deltaP = (XMax - XMin)/640;
    deltaQ = (YMax - YMin)/350;
    for (col=0; col<640; col++)
    {
        if (kbhit() != 0)
        {
            save_screen(0,0,col,maxrow,filename);
            exit(0);
        }
        p = XMin + col * deltaP;
        for (row=0; row<350; row++)
        {
            q = YMax - row * deltaQ;
            x = p;
            y = q;
            color = 0;
            while ((color < max_iterations) && (x*x + y*y < max_size))
            {
                x = 2 * x;
                y = 2 * y;
                if (y > 1.0)
```

```
                y- -;
            else
            {
                if (x > 1.0)
                    x- -;
            }
            color++;
        }
        if (color >= max_iterations)
            color = 0;
        else
            color = color%15 + 1;
        plot (col,row,color);
        }
    }
}
```

Figure 9-4. Listing of the Fractal Function for the Sierpinski Triangle

CHAPTER 10

Plasmas

If you have a VGA display, you can generate a very interesting kind of fractal called a plasma. To really be effective, this fractal requires a 256 color display mode, so I don't recommend that you try doing anything similar on an EGA display, since there aren't enough colors to make the display effective. The plasma cloud technique was first written by Bret Mulvey in Pascal. The program included in this book is written in C. It does not require any assembly language routines.

The Plasma Program

Figure 10-1 lists the plasma program. The plasma program produces a varicolored cloud-like display. It is achieved by first establishing a color for each of the four corners of the screen, and then recursively finding new points midway between these original ones and selecting a proper color for them. The first thing that the program does is to set the graphics mode using the *setMode* function. This function makes use of the ROM BIOS video services to set the graphics mode of the display to 320 by 200 pixels by 256 colors. Next, the program sets up the initial colors for the 256 color registers of the VGA. (Be aware that the default VGA colors are superfluous. They begin with the same 64 colors that are available for the EGA. The next 64 colors are shades of gray for a gray scale depiction. After that, the reasons for color selection are even more obscure.) We are going to split the palette into black plus three groups of 85 colors each. The first color in each group will be one of the three primary display colors, *blue, green,* and *red* respectively.

```
/*

    plasma = Creates a plasma display on a VGA

*/
```

```c
#include <dos.h>
#include <stdio.h>
#include <stdlib.h>
#include <time.h>
#include <conio.h>

void plot(int x, int y, int color);
void setMode(int mode);
void setVGApalette(unsigned char *buffer);
void set_color(int xa, int ya, int x, int y, int xb, int yb);
void initPalette(void);
void subdivide(int x1, int y1, int x2, int y2);
void rotate_colors(void);
void setVGAreg(int reg_no, int red, int green, int blue);
void screen_save(void);

union REGS reg;
struct SREGS inreg;

int Xres=319, Yres=199, scale_factor=1;
int interval=24, index=25;
unsigned char Pal_Array[256][3];
char ch, file_name[13];

void main()
{
    printf("\nEnter file name: ");
    scanf("%s",&file_name);
    setMode(0x13);
    initPalette();
    randomize();
    plot(0,0,random(255) + 1);
    plot(Xres,0,random(255) + 1);
    plot(Xres,Yres,random(255) + 1);
    plot(0,Yres,random(255) + 1);
    subdivide(0,0,Xres,Yres);
    ch = getch();
    if ((ch == 'S') || (ch == 's'))
        screen_save();
    rotate_colors();
```

```
        getch();
        setMode(0x03);
}



/*

    ┌─────────────────────────────────────────────────┐
    │   setMode() Sets Video Mode                       │
    └─────────────────────────────────────────────────┘
*/

void setMode(int mode)
{
        reg.h.ah = 0;
        reg.h.al = mode;
        int86 (0x10,&reg,&reg);
}

/*

    ┌─────────────────────────────────────────────────┐
    │   plot() = Function to plot point to VGA 256 Color Screen │
    └─────────────────────────────────────────────────┘
*/

void plot(int x, int y, int color)
{
        unsigned int offset;
        char far *address;
        offset = 320 * y + x;
        address = (char far *)(0xA0000000L + offset);
        *address = color;
}



/*

    ┌─────────────────────────────────────────────────┐
    │   setVGAreg() = Function to set individual VGA color register │
    └─────────────────────────────────────────────────┘
*/
```

```c
void setVGAreg(int reg_no, int red, int green, int blue)
{
    reg.x.ax = 0x1010;
    reg.x.bx = reg_no;
    reg.h.ch = red;
    reg.h.cl = green;
    reg.h.dh = blue;
    int86(0x10,&reg,&reg);
}


/*
```

```
    setVGApalette() = Function to set all 256 color registers
```

```c
*/
void setVGApalette(unsigned char *buffer)
{
    reg.x.ax = 0x1012;
    segread(&inreg);
    inreg.es = inreg.ds;
    reg.x.bx = 0;
    reg.x.cx = 256;
    reg.x.dx = (int)&buffer[0];
    int86x(0x10,&reg,&reg,&inreg);
}


/*
```

```
    subdivide() = Divides up a display section and fills with color.
```

```c
*/

void subdivide(int x1, int y1, int x2, int y2)
{
    int index;
    int x, y, color;

    if ((x2-x1<2) && (y2-y1<2))
        return;
    x = (x1 + x2) >> 1;
```

```
        y = (y1 + y2) >> 1;
        set_color(x1,y1,x,y1,x2,y1);
        set_color(x2,y1,x2,y,x2,y2);
        set_color(x1,y2,x,y2,x2,y2);
        set_color(x1,y1,x1,y,x1,y2);
        color = (readPixel(x1,y1) + readPixel(x2,y1) +
            readPixel(x2,y2) + readPixel(x1,y2) + 2) >> 2;
        plot(x,y,color);
        subdivide(x1,y1,x,y);
        subdivide(x,y1,x2,y);
        subdivide(x,y,x2,y2);
        subdivide(x1,y,x,y2);
}
```

```
/*
```
┌───┐
│ set_color() = Picks the new color for the pixel   │
└───┘
```
*/
```

```
void set_color(int xa, int ya, int x, int y, int xb, int yb)
{
        long color;

        color = abs(xa - xb) + abs(ya - yb);
        color = random(color<<1) - color;
        color += (readPixel(xa,ya) + readPixel(xb,yb) + 1) >> 1;
        if (color < 1)
            color = 1;
        if (color > 255)
            color = 255;
        if (readPixel(x,y) == 0)
        plot(x,y,color);
}
```

```
/*
```
┌───┐
│ initPalette() = Sets the colors of the VGA plaette   │
└───┘
```
*/
```

```
void initPalette(void)
{

    int max_color = 63;
    int index;

    Pal_Array[0][0] = 0;
    Pal_Array[0][1] = 0;
    Pal_Array[0][2] = 0;

    for (index=1; index<86; index++)
    {
        Pal_Array[index][0] = 0;
        Pal_Array[index][1] = (index*max_color) / 85;
        Pal_Array[index][2] = ((86 - index)*max_color) / 85;
        Pal_Array[index+85][0] = (index*max_color) / 85;
        Pal_Array[index+85][1] = ((86 - index)*max_color) / 85;
        Pal_Array[index+85][2] = 0;
        Pal_Array[index+170][0] = ((86 - index)*max_color) / 85;
        Pal_Array[index+170][1] = 0;
        Pal_Array[index+170][2] = (index*max_color) / 85;
    }
    setVGApalette(Pal_Array[0]);
}

/*
```

```
    readPixel()= Reads a pixel from the Screen
```

```
*/

int readPixel(int x, int y)
{
    #include <dos.h>

    union REGS reg;

    reg.h.ah = 0x0D;
    reg.x.cx = x;
    reg.x.dx = y;
```

```
  int86 (0x10,&reg,&reg);
      return (reg.h.al);
}


/*
```

┌──┐
│ ┌──┐ │
│ │   rotateColors() = Rotates the VGA colors   │ │
│ └──┘ │
└──┘

```
*/

void rotate_colors(void)
{
      int i, j, k, old_red, old_green, old_blue, new_red, new_green, new_blue,
          last_step=32;
      char ch;

      for(;;)
      {
          if (kbhit() != 0)
          {
              ch = getch();
              if ((ch == 'S') || (ch == 's'))
              {
                  screen_save();
                  ch = getch();
              }
              if (ch == 0x0D)
                  break;
              else
              {
                  if ((ch - '0' <= 9) && (ch - '0' > 0))
                      last_step = 4* (int)(ch - '0');
                  getch();
              }
          }
          old_red = Pal_Array[255][0];
          old_green = Pal_Array[255][1];
          old_blue = Pal_Array[255][2];
          new_red = rand() % 63;
          new_green = rand() % 63;
```

```c
            new_blue = rand() % 63;
            for (j=1; j<last_step; j++)
            {
                outportb(0x3C8,0);
                for (i=1; i<255; i++)
                {
                    Pal_Array[i][0] = Pal_Array[i+1][0];
                    Pal_Array[i][1] = Pal_Array[i+1][1];
                    Pal_Array[i][2] = Pal_Array[i+1][2];
                }
                Pal_Array[255][0] = old_red +
                    ((new_red-old_red)*j)/last_step;
                Pal_Array[255][1] = old_green +
                    ((new_green-old_green)*j)/last_step;
                Pal_Array[255][2] = old_blue +
                    ((new_blue-old_blue)*j)/last_step;
                outportb(0x3C8,0);
                for (i=0; i<256; i++)
                {
                    if (i%63 == 0)
                    {
                        while ((inportb(0x3DA) & 0x08) != 0);
                        while ((inportb(0x3DA) & 0x08) == 0);
                    }
                    outportb(0x3C9,Pal_Array[i][0]);
                    outportb(0x3C9,Pal_Array[i][1]);
                    outportb(0x3C9,Pal_Array[i][2]);
                }
            }
        }
    }
}

/*

    screen_save() = Save screen to disk file

*/

void screen_save(void)
{
```

```
    int row, col, color;
    FILE *fsave;

    sound (256);
    while (file_name[6] < 0x3A)
    {
        if ((fsave = fopen (file_name,"rb")) != NULL)
        {
            file_name[7]++;
            if (file_name[7] >= 0x3A)
            {
                file_name[7] = 0x30;
                file_name[6]++;
            }
            fclose(fsave);
        }
        else
        {
            fclose(fsave);
            fsave = fopen(file_name,"wb");
            fwrite(&Xres,1,2,fsave);
            fwrite(&Yres,1,2,fsave);
            for (col=0; col<=Xres; col++)
            {
                for (row=0; row<=Yres; row++)
                {
                    color = readPixel(col,row);
                    fwrite(&color,1,2,fsave);
                }
            }
            fclose(fsave);
            break;
        }
    }
    nosound();
}
```

Figure 11-1. Listing of the plasma Program

As the register number increases, in the first group, the blue component decreases from maximum blue to zero and the green component increases from zero to maximum green. The next group begins with maximum green and as the register number increases, the green component decreases from maximum to zero while the red component increases from zero to maximum red. Finally, in the third group, as the register number increases the red component decreases from maximum to zero and the blue component increases from zero to maximum blue. If you will look at the listing for the function *initPalette*, you'll see that *Pal_Array* is an array of 256 sets (one for each color register) of three values (one for each primary color). The first register is initialized to all zeroes for black. You can see how the *for* loop then sets the values of the array for the colors described above. After all the register values have been set, the function *setVGApalette* is called. This function makes use of the ROM BIOS video services of DOS to set the 256 color register values from an array (in this case *Pal_Array*) whose address is given in register *d*.

Next, the program calls *randomize* to choose a seed for the random number that gives a different display for each running of the program. The program then plots a randomly colored point at each corner of the display. (In Chapter 3, we described how a point is plotted in a particular color to the EGA/VGA in the 16 color mode, using a single memory address, but four actual memory planes for color storage that are controlled by the internal registers of the EGA or VGA card. In the 256 color mode plotting a point is much simpler. Each pixel of the display is assigned one byte of memory; plotting is accomplished simply by sending the color, from 0 to 256, to that memory address. Inside the VGA card, funny things happen. Each set of four adjacent pixel addresses are distributed one each to the four memory planes, so that each memory plane is only one-fourth full. This doesn't concern us in plotting, however, so our plotting routine is very simple as can be seen from the listing.)

Subdividing the Display

Next, the *subdivide* function is called to recursively fill in the rest of the points on the display. The function is called with the coordinates of two points specified. The function takes these to be the upper left and lower right corners of a box of four points, one at each corner. If the difference between the *x* coordinate is less than two and the difference between the *y* coordinates is less than two, then the display has been filled, and the function terminates. (On the first pass through the function, the

170

coordinates represent the corners of the full display screen.) Otherwise, the function next determines the coordinates of the point at the center of the box. It then calls the function *set_color* four times to select the color and plot each of the points midway between two corners of the box. This function begins by setting color to the absolute value of the difference in the *x* coordinates of the two points plus the absolute value of the difference in the *y* coordinates of the two points. The function then chooses a random variable between 0 and twice the value of *color* and subtracts color from it to yield a random variable between *-color* and *+color*. Note that the limits of this variable are smaller and smaller as the two coordinates get closer together. As this function repeats recursively, large color changes are permitted between widely spaced points, but the amount of permissible maximum color change gets smaller and smaller as the points approach each other. This results in maximum color changes over the entire screen, but very smooth changes as we move in any direction.

The next thing that occurs is that the function reads the colors of the two pixels from the screen and then takes their average. It then sets the value of *color* to this average plus the random value obtained previously. The midpoint is then plotted to the screen in this resulting color if this midpoint has not been colored already. (Note that this check is necessary, since the midpoint of the side of a square is likely to be the midpoint of the side of the adjacent square also. If we were to just color over it, there would be a discontinuity between the shading on one side of the line and the other. By only plotting when the point has not been written to, we make sure that a selected color is not changed.) This ends the *set_color* function. As noted above, it is called four times to paint the pixels at the midpoint of each of the four sides of the box. The *subdivide* function then colors the pixel in the center of the box to the average of the colors of the four midpoints just painted on the display. It then calls *subdivide* recursively four times to operate upon each of the smaller boxes defined by the four original box corners, the four midpoints, and the center of the original box. The recursion continues for smaller and smaller boxes until every pixel on the screen is colored in.

Dynamically Changing the Color Registers

At this point, the program pauses until you strike a key. This permits you to view the plasma cloud that has just been generated. Once a key has been struck, the program calls *rotate_colors* which dynamically changes the color registers. Earlier in the chapter, we described a function which changed the colors of all of the VGA registers to the contents of an array. We would like to use this technique repeatedly to modify the display and produce a continuously shifting color display. All of this color changing takes place in an infinite *for* loop. We only get out of this loop when the *Enter* key is struck. Alternately, if a key between 1 and 9 is struck, the program changes the value of *last_step*. We will discuss the effect of this later.

Next, the function saves the contents of *Pal_Array* for last color register. A random number between 0 and 63 is obtained for each color component. The function then begins a pair of *for* loops. The first is iterated *last_step* times; the inner loop iterates for every color register except the first and last. (The first register defines the color black. This is left untouched.) For each of these registers, the array that defines the color of the next higher register is transferred down one. We now have rotated all of the register definitions by one. Now, for each color component of the array position defining the last color register, the function substitutes the sum of the color component that was there previously plus the new color component that was found randomly divided by *last_step*. You can see that the value of *last_step* is going to make a big difference in the coloring of the display. When it is small, the color of in the last color register changes to the two randomly selected value in just a few iterations, making for dramatic color changes adjacent to each other. When the value is large, the increments of color change per iteration are very small, so that adjacent shades change very slowly. As mentioned above, this value is controlled by a keyboard entry, being four times the number entered on the keyboard.

If we changed our color array and dumped the contents out to control the VGA color registers, we would have very objectionable blinking and blanking as the display colors changed. To avoid this, we want the display screen blanked during the vertical retrace as the color register changes . Unfortunately, the ROM BIOS video service which dumps the contents of an array into all the color registers in one pass is too slow for a single vertical retrace. If we tried to use it, we would at least be synched to the display, but unfortunately the color changing would overlap the beginning of the display resulting in some snow and blanking of the top of the display. Ideally, we should use assembly language; hopefully it would be fast to complete the color transfer during the vertical retrace. However, we are going to use C language functions instead. You will see that before entering the loop, we send data to an output port that sets up the VGA to accept color register change data. Inside the loop, the first thing we do for the zero register and every 64 registers from there on, is read a register which contains a bit indicating whether the vertical retrace is occurring. This is done with a *while* loop which continues to repeat until the condition is met. Since the statement ends with a semicolon, nothing else occurs within the loop. The first loop is set up so that it continues as long as the vertical retrace is taking place. The second *while* loop then iterates until the vertical retrace begins again. This assures that when we leave the pair of loops, we are exactly at the beginning of the vertical retrace, giving us maximum time. If we just made use of the second loop, we would proceed on as soon as we saw that the vertical retrace was occurring, but because of the varied timing with which we might enter the loop, we wouldn't know whether we were at the beginning of the vertical retrace or somewhere near its end. Once we get the indication of the beginning of the vertical retrace, we send data to the color registers for 64 registers. The inner workings of the VGA card are set up so that sending successive bytes to the one data register causes it to send first red, then green, and then blue bytes to the associated sections of the color register and then increment a counter so that the next three bytes are sent to the next color register. Note that we are using four vertical retraces to send all of the color data to the 256 registers. This is enough time so we don't see any ill effects on the display with the 386 computer I am using. If you find that your computer requires more time, you can change the if statement at the beginning of the loop uses a smaller modulus than 64.

Saving the Screen

In the next chapter, we use a technique for creating a three dimensional fractal. As has been mentioned, the three-dimensional representation of a plasma makes a remarkably life-like mountain. Since we are more interested in the three-dimensional aspects, we aren't going to save the plasma fractals as ordinary .PCX files, but rather as .ZBF files, where the suffix means a special data file arranged for ray tracing using the z-buffering technique. The file is simple; it is also large, since we make no effort to compress it. It consists of two words at the beginning for x and y resolution, followed by a word representing the height at every pixel on the screen. The height is simply the plasma color value, from 0 to 255. We'll use this file as data for rendering a three-dimensional display, after which, hopefully, we'll save the final display in .PCX form. The function simply reads each pixel from the screen and saves it as an integer to the disk file. The order of reading is important because of the way that the z-buffering function works; we need to read all the way down successive columns, rather than reading across rows as is done with the .PCX file. The screen saving function is activated at any time that a plasma has been created, or at any point while colors are being cycled, by typing an *S* or an *s* on the keyboard. (It doesn't really matter when you activate the function, the same information will be stored anyway.)

What Else to Do

You'll find that this program gives an interesting, hypnotic, infinitely varying, color display. However, we have just touched the surface of what you can do with the color registers. We have been straightforward in how we cycle colors; you can think of other interesting ways to do it. You can also have a similar routine that rotates through the color registers in the opposite direction. Then one key could control the direction of color cycling and permit you to reverse it whenever you wish. You can also add this color cycling to the Mandelbrot set or one of the other set-generating programs, provided that you have set that program to be in the 256 color mode.

CHAPTER 11

Three Dimensional Techniques

In Chapter 10, a function called *screen_save* was described as part of the plasma program. This function created a file containing one integer representing height for each pixel of the plasma display and it was suggested that plasmas make good mountains when represented three-dimensionally. In this chapter, we'll look at the techniques for creating such a three dimensional display using two separate programs.

The first, *rend.cpp*, will render the plasma file, using a simple ray-tracing technique that depends upon the z-buffering technique. The result will be a raw data file that contains three bytes for each pixel; red green, and blue. The number of different color shades described in this way can be very large. The VGA can display a maximum of 256K colors; We need a program to assign the proper colors to the VGA so a realistic picture can be drawn. This program is called *process.cpp*. It takes the raw data file and turns it into an actual VGA display on the screen.

The rend.cpp Program

Figure 11-1 is a listing of the *rend.cpp* program. This is designed to be a stand-alone program, so that some of the functions duplicate those described for the *ftools.cpp* package. The program begins by setting the display to text mode, defining a full-screen window, and clearing the screen. A menu window is then set up and cleared to a blue background. The program then displays, "Enter parameters for display", and starts with the first parameter, *LightPhi*. The program then reads a floating-point number for this parameter from the keyboard and stores it in the proper location. This process is repeated for *LightTheta* and *ViewPhi*. The program then performs a similar process to read the red, green, and blue components of ambient, diffuse, specular, background, and *alt_background.*

```
/*
```

```
    rend = Rendering program for 3D plasmas, etc.

    By Roger T. Stevens        10-29-90
```

```
*/
```

```
#include <dos.h>
#include <iostream.h>
#include <stdio.h>
#include <math.h>
#include <string.h>
#include <conio.h>
#include <stdlib.h>
#include <ctype.h>

#define MIN(x,y) ((x)<(y) ? (x) : (y))
#define MAX(x,y) ((x)>(y) ? (x) : (y))
#define Max(x,y,z) (x>y && x>z ? x : (y>z ? y : z))
#define Min(x,y,z) (x<y && x<z ? x : (y<z ? y : z))

void cls(int color);
void plot(int x, int y, int color);
void setMode(int mode);
void Intensity(int i, int j);

char ObjectFile[32];
char file_in[32] = {"mandis01"};
int Xres, Yres;
int Height[2][800];
int max_color=63,max_iterations,flag;
int Scaling;
struct Vector
{
    float x,
```

```
          y,
          z;
}    view,
     light,
     color_vec,
     Pix,
     newPix,
     oldPix,
     ambient,
     diffuse,
     specular,
     background,
     alt_background;
float ViewPhi=65, SinViewPhi, CosViewPhi, LightPhi=75, LightTheta=-35, Xmax=1.2,
     Xmin=-2.0, Ymax=1.2, Ymin=-1.2,   Zmax=1.0, Zmin=0;
FILE *fget, *fsave;
int m,i, j, k, p, p0, p1, horizon;
float h,temp;
char FileNameOut[32];
int Tilt,Flip;
int b = 2;
int Type, type, integer;
char red[800],green[800], blue[800];

/*
```

┌───┐
│ Main Program   │
└───┘

```
*/

main(void)
{
     setMode(3);
     window(1,1,80,25);
     textbackground(0);
     clrscr();
     textbackground(1);
     window(9,9,68,22);
     clrscr();
     gotoxy(3,2);
```

```
textcolor(15);
cprintf("Enter parameters for display:\n");
gotoxy(8,3);
cprintf("Light Phi: ");
cscanf("%f",&LightPhi);
gotoxy(8,4);
cprintf("Light Theta: ");
cscanf("%f",&LightTheta);
gotoxy(8,5);
cprintf("View Phi: ");
cscanf("%f",&ViewPhi);
gotoxy(8,6);
cprintf("Ambient Light Color (r,g,b): ");
cscanf("%f,%f,%f",&ambient.x, &ambient.y, &ambient.z);
gotoxy(8,7);
cprintf("Diffuse Light Color (r,g,b): ");
cscanf("%f,%f,%f",&diffuse.x, &diffuse.y, &diffuse.z);
gotoxy(8,8);
cprintf("Specular Light Color (r,g,b): ");
cscanf("%f,%f,%f",&specular.x, &specular.y, &specular.z);
gotoxy(8,9);
cprintf("Background Light Color (r,g,b): ");
cscanf("%f,%f,%f",&background.x, &background.y, &background.z);
gotoxy(8,10);
cprintf("Alternate Background Light Color (r,g,b): ");
cscanf("%f,%f,%f",&alt_background.x, &alt_background.y, &alt_background.z);
gotoxy(3,11);
cprintf("Enter name of file for output data: ");
cscanf("%s",file_in);
printf("Z-Buffer Rendering Program\n\n");
ViewPhi *= 0.0174533;
LightPhi *= 0.0174533;
LightTheta *= 0.174533;
strcpy(ObjectFile, file_in);
strcpy(FileNameOut,ObjectFile);
strcat(ObjectFile, ".zbf");
strcat(FileNameOut, ".raw");
printf("\nSaving %s \n",FileNameOut);
fsave = fopen(FileNameOut,"wb");
printf("\nLoading %s\n",ObjectFile);
```

```
fget = fopen(ObjectFile,"rb");
SinViewPhi = sin(ViewPhi);
CosViewPhi = cos(ViewPhi);
view.x = 0;
view.y = -CosViewPhi;
view.z = SinViewPhi;
light.x = sin(LightTheta) * cos(LightPhi);
light.y = sin(LightTheta) * sin(LightPhi);
light.z = cos(LightTheta);
fread(&Xres,2,1,fget);
fread(&Yres,2,1,fget);
printf("Resolution is %d pixels by %d rows.\n",Xres, Yres);
printf("Hit any key to continue...\n");
getch();
setMode(0x13);
fread(&Scaling,2,1,fget);
fwrite(&Xres,2,1,fsave);
fwrite(&Yres,2,1,fsave);
fread(&Height[0][0],2,Yres+1,fget);
for (i=0; i<Xres; i++)
{
    fread(&Height[(i+1)%2][0],2,Yres+1,fget);
    horizon = (float)(Height[i % 2][0]) * CosViewPhi;
    for (j=0; j<Yres; j++)
    {
        if (j < 160)
        {
            red[j] = background.x*max_color;
            green[j] = background.y*max_color;
            blue[j] = background.z*max_color;
        }
        else
        {
            red[j] = alt_background.x*max_color;
            green[j] = alt_background.y*max_color;
            blue[j] = alt_background.z*max_color;
        }
    }
    for (j=1; j<Yres; j++)
    {
```

```c
p1 = (float)(j) * SinViewPhi +
    (float)(Height[i % 2][j]) * CosViewPhi;
if (p1 > horizon)
{
    Intensity(i, j);
    oldPix.x = color_vec.x;
    oldPix.y = color_vec.y;
    oldPix.z = color_vec.z;
    if ((p1 <= Yres) && (p1 >= 0))
    {
        plot(i, p1, Height[i%2][j]);
        red[p1] = oldPix.x;
        green[p1] = oldPix.y;
        blue[p1] = oldPix.z;
        p = p1 - 1;
        Intensity(i, j-1);
        newPix.x = color_vec.x;
        newPix.y = color_vec.y;
        newPix.z = color_vec.z;
        while (p >= horizon)
        {
            h = (float)(p - horizon) / (float)(p1 -
horizon);
            Pix.x = ((oldPix.x * h) + (newPix.x * (1 - h)));
            Pix.y = ((oldPix.y * h) + (newPix.y * (1 - h)));
            Pix.z = ((oldPix.z * h) + (newPix.z * (1 - h)));
            plot(i, p, Height[i%2][j]);
            red[p] = Pix.x;
            green[p] = Pix.y;
            blue[p] = Pix.z;
            p—;
        }
    }
    horizon = p1;
}
p0 = p1;
}
```

```
            fwrite(&i,2,1,fsave);
            fwrite(&red[0],1,Yres+1,fsave);
            fwrite(&green[0],1,Yres+1,fsave);
            fwrite(&blue[0],1,Yres+1,fsave);
        }
        fclose(fget);
        fclose(fsave);
        getch();
        setMode(3);
    printf("\n  ┌──────────────────────────────┐ \n")
    ;
    printf(   "||                                  || \n");
    printf(   "||            Processing Complete.  || \n");
    printf(   "||      Data in File: %12s          ||\n",
        FileNameOut);
    printf(   "||                                  || \n");
    printf(   "└──────────────────────────────┘ \n");
        getch();
    }
```

```
/*
```

┌──┐
│ cls() = Clears the Screen   │
└──┘

```
*/
```

```
void cls(int color)
{
    union REGS reg;
    reg.x.ax = 0x0600;
    reg.x.cx = 0;
    reg.x.dx = 0x184F;
    reg.h.bh = color;
    int86(0x10,&reg,&reg);
}
```

```
/*
```

┌──┐
│ setMode() = Sets video mode   │
└──┘

```
*/
```

```c
union REGS reg;

void setMode(int mode)
{
    reg.h.ah = 0;
    reg.h.al = mode;
    int86 (0x10,&reg,&reg);
}

/*
```

```
┌─────────────────────────────────────────────────────────────┐
│   ┌─────────────────────────────────────────────────────────┐ │
│   │  Intensity() = Finds light intensity at a point          │ │
│   └─────────────────────────────────────────────────────────┘ │
└─────────────────────────────────────────────────────────────┘
```

```c
*/

void Intensity(int i, int j)
{
    Vector n1, n2, difference, normal, reflected;
    float CosTheta, CosAlpha, temp, maximum;

    n1.x = (Xmax-Xmin)/(Xres+1);
    n1.y = 0;
    n1.z = (float)( Height[(i+1)%2][j] - Height[i%2][j]) / 256.0;
    n2.x = 0;
    n2.y = (Ymax-Ymin)/(Yres+1);
    n2.z = (float)(Height[i%2][j+1] - Height[i%2][j]) / 256.0;
    normal.x = - n1.z * n2.y;
    normal.y = - n1.x * n2.z;
    normal.z = n1.x * n2.y;
    temp = sqrt(normal.x * normal.x + normal.y * normal.y + normal.z * normal.z);
    if (temp != 0)
    {
        normal.x /= temp;
        normal.y /= temp;
        normal.z /= temp;
    }
    CosTheta = normal.x * light.x + normal.y * light.y + normal.z * light.z;
    if (CosTheta < 0)
    {
        color_vec.x = ambient.x * max_color;
        color_vec.y = ambient.y * max_color;
```

```
        color_vec.z = ambient.z * max_color;
    }
    else
    {
        reflected.x = (normal.x - light.x) * (2.0*CosTheta);
        reflected.y = (normal.y - light.y) * (2.0*CosTheta);
        reflected.z = (normal.z - light.z) * (2.0*CosTheta);
        CosAlpha = view.x * reflected.x + view.y * reflected.y +
            view.z * reflected.z;
        color_vec.x = ((specular.x * pow(CosAlpha, b) + ambient.x
            * diffuse.x + (diffuse.x * CosTheta)) * max_color);
        color_vec.y = (specular.y * pow(CosAlpha, b) + ambient.y
            * diffuse.y + (diffuse.y * CosTheta)) * max_color;
        color_vec.z = (specular.z * pow(CosAlpha, b) + ambient.z
            * diffuse.z + (diffuse.z * CosTheta)) * max_color;
    }
    maximum = Max(color_vec.x, color_vec.y, color_vec.z);
    if (maximum > max_color)
    {
        color_vec.x *= (max_color / maximum);
        color_vec.y *= (max_color / maximum);
        color_vec.z *= (max_color / maximum);
    }
}


/*
    ┌─────────────────────────────────────────────────────────────┐
    │ plot() = Function to plot point to VGA 256 color screen       │
    └─────────────────────────────────────────────────────────────┘
*/

void plot(int x, int y, int color)
{
    unsigned int offset;
    char far *address;
    offset = 320 * y + x;
    address = (char far *)(0xA0000000L + offset);
    *address = color;
}
```

Figure 11-1. Listing of the rend.cpp Program

Each light vector is read in a format that demands three-floating point keyboard inputs, separated by commas. Each component is stored in the proper location. Next, the program asks for the name of the disk file to be operated upon. It reads a string from the keyboard and places it in *file_in*. It then displays, "Z-buffer Rendering Program". Next, *ViewPhi*, *LightPhi* and *LightTheta* are all converted to radians so that they will work properly with the sine and cosine functions. The program then copies the file name that was input to *ObjectFile* and *FileNameOut*. The extension *.zbf* is added to *ObjectFile* and the extension *.raw* is added to *FileNameOut*. The two new file names are displayed and the files opened. Next, the sine and cosine of the viewing angle phi are obtained and stored in appropriately named variables. The components of the viewing and light vectors are then computed. Next the x and y resolutions are read from the *.zbf* input file and displayed. The user is given an opportunity to abort if necessary, through a computer reset. If he wishes to continue, he hits any key and the program proceeds. The screen mode is set to graphics mode 13H (320 pixels by 200 rows by 256 colors). *Scaling* is then read. This is an obsolete variable that was part of the input file, but is no longer used. The resolution values are then written to the output file. Next, the first column of height data is read, and the program is ready to begin data processing.

Three-Dimensional Geometry

Figure 11-2 shows the geometry for projecting a three-dimensional representation upon a two-dimensional screen. The distance d is that from the observer to the screen and y is the distance from the observer to the projection of the observed point on the y axis. The coordinates v_y and v_x (not shown) are the coordinates of the point on the screen. The triangle formed by the observer, the observed point, and the projection on the y axis is similar to the one formed by the observer, the projection of the observed point on the screen, and the z coordinate of that projected point, so that the ratio of the two sides is the same for each triangle. Thus:

$$z/y = v_y/d \qquad \text{(Equation 11-1)}$$

The projection of z on the screen (resulting from the correction for y) is therefore:

$$v_y = dz/y \hspace{4cm} \text{(Equation 11-2)}$$

Exactly the same geometry applies to scaling x, giving

$$v_x = dx/y(\hspace{4cm} \text{Equation 11-3}$$

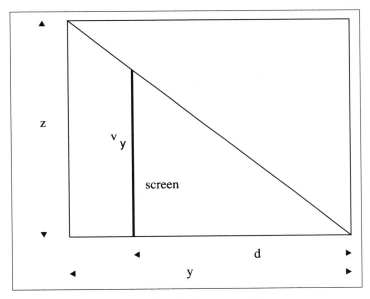

Figure 11-2. Geometry for Projecting *y* on a Screen

Looking at a three-dimensional figure with this orientation is not very interesting, so we normally will want to rotate the three-dimensional display into an orientation that shows more interesting detail. We can rotate around any of the three axes of the coordinate system, but we aren't going to be this general. Instead, we will only allow rotation around the x axis, by the angle view phi. If we call the original coordinate (x_0, y_0, z_0) and the final coordinate (x, y, z), then the rotation is expressed by:

$$\begin{bmatrix} x \\ y \\ z \end{bmatrix} = \begin{bmatrix} 1 & 0 & 0 \\ 0 & \cos \text{ViewPhi} & \sin \text{ViewPhi} \\ 0 & -\sin \text{ViewPhi} & \cos \text{ViewPhi} \end{bmatrix} \begin{bmatrix} x_0 \\ y_0 \\ z_0 \end{bmatrix}$$ (Equation 11-4)

Applying this transformation, we have:

$v_y = d(-y_0 \sin \text{ViewPhi} + z_0 \cos \text{ViewPhi}) / (y_0 \cos \text{ViewPhi} + z_0 \sin \text{ViewPhi})$

(Equation 11-5)

and

$v_x = dx / (y0 \cos \text{ViewPhi} + z_0 \sin \text{ViewPhi})$ (Equation 11-6)

We have a certain amount of flexibility in how we define *d* so to simplify things, we will define *d* as:

$d = y0 \cos \text{ViewPhi} + z_0 \sin \text{ViewPhi}$ (Equation 11-7)

As a result, we have:

$v_x = x$ (Equation 11-8)

and

$v_y = -y_0 \sin \text{ViewPhi} + z_0 \cos \text{ViewPhi}$ (Equation 11-9)

You will see these transformations applied later in the program.

Processing the Display Data

The program next begins a *for* loop which is iterated once for each column of the display. Each iteration begins by reading the next column of height data. The *Height* array is arranged so that two columns of data are preserved at any given time, with the latest column of data alternating between two buffers. A value for the horizon is computed which is the transformed data for the (0,0) point in the input data file. The program next enters a *for* loop which sets the background color for the entire row. For most mountain scenes, this background will be a sky color. Some mountains, however, will have a few holes near the bottom of the display. These don't look realistic if colored to match the sky, so an alternate (mountain-colored) background is used after we pass row 160 (which is near the bottom of the screen). After this *for* loop is completed, another *for* loop is entered to process the scene data. First, the projected value onto the screen of the input data for the particular column and row being examined is computed. If this is greater than the horizon, the *Intensity* function is called to find the proper color for this point. These color values are stored in *old_pix*. Then, if the row is within display bounds, the point is plotted to the screen, using a color equivalent to the height value, and the color information is transferred to a color array containing all the color information for the current column. We then set *p* to be one column less than the point just plotted on the screen. Next, *Intensity* is called to find the colors for the point on the input matrix one row below the point which was previously examined. These are stored in *new_pixel*. If the two adjacent points of the input matrix do not represent adjacent rows on the screen, we have to fill in between the two specified rows somehow. This is done by interpolating between the colors in *old_pixel* and *new_pixel* and coloring the intervening pixels accordingly. This data is stored in the color data array and a representation plotted to the screen. The *horizon* variable is then set to the value of *p1* and the process continues. After the loops have completed, there is a display on the screen that shows the shape of the ultimate display, but does not have the proper colors. It gives you some idea, however, of whether you have zeroed in on the proper angle to see what you wanted to. After each column of color data has been accumulated, it is written to a raw data output file. When all data has been processed, the input and output files are closed, and the program awaits an input from the keyboard. After you are through viewing the screen, a keyboard input will cause the program to return to the text mode and display a box which indicates that processing is complete and gives the name of the file where the output data has been stored.

The *Intensity* Function

The *Intensity* function determines what the color components are for the particular pixel being processed. This function begins by finding a vector normal to the surface at the point that is being examined. It does this by creating two vectors along the surface, one between two adjacent rows of the surface and one between two columns. These two vectors are orthogonal. The function then takes the cross product of these two vectors and normalizes it to produce a unit vector that is normal to the surface. (This is not necessarily the ideal way to find a normal, but it will serve for most purposes.) We next find the cosine of an angle *theta* which is the angle between the light source vector and the normal vector. This is found by taking the dot product of the two vectors. If this angle is less than zero, we return the ambient light value. (This is the light from a surface when it is not directly illuminated by the light source.) If the angle is greater than zero, the color of the pixel is made up of the sum of three components. The first is the ambient color. The second is the diffuse color (the natural color of the object) multiplied by the cosine of *theta*. The third is the reflected light using the Phong shading model. This is obtained by taking the cosine of the angle between the reflected light vector and the viewing vector and raising it to some selected power (2.0 in this case). The result is then multiplied by the specified reflected color. The resulting colors are then checked to see if the sum exceeded the maximum color value (63) in any case. If so, we scale down all of the colors by dividing by the ratio of the maximum to 63. By applying this to all colors, the general hue does not change.

Processing Color Data

We now have a color data file, but it is much more color information than we can use with a VGA display. To produce our actual rendered display, we make use of the program *process.cpp* This program is listed in Figure 11-2 and is also a stand-alone program. Some functions are duplicated from elsewhere in the book.

The file generated by the ray tracer is set up to provide three bytes of data for each pixel of the color display. Each byte contains a number from 0 to 63, representing a shade of color. One byte gives the shade of red, another the shade of green, and the third the shade of blue. Together, each set of bytes can represent 262,144 different shades of color. This is adequate to represent the coloring of any scene with more precision than our human eye can distinguish. However, our VGA display card can, at the most, display only 256 different colors at any one time. This severely limits our ability to create a realistic scene from our original data file. However, it is not as bad as it seems. For one thing, most scenes do not require anywhere near the full range of colors. The program to be described above tallies the number of shades of color used in a scene. For the two sample pictures in the color plate section, only a few hundred colors were needed. Although this exceeds the 256 that can be handled by the VGA, many of these colors are used in shading a surface and are thus very close to each other, so that the number of colors can be reduced to 256 without major degradation of the picture. Of course, we could have a prettier and more realistic picture if we had more colors to work with, but by using a few tricks we can make the VGA displays look pretty good.

The program operates by first halving the number of shades of each primary color from 0 to 63 to 0 to 31. Since we are only going to be able to display 256 out of a possible 262,144 colors anyway, it doesn't matter very much if we cut the number of possible values of each color in half. Fortunately, this results in a total maximum number of color shades of 32,768. This is a size that we can contain within an array in a C program. Next, we will look at every set of three bytes that represent a color in the file and increment the member of the array representing this color so that when we are finished the array contains the number of occurrences of each of the 32,768 shades of color. The program sorts these according to the number of occurrences and assigns the 256 VGA colors to the 256 shades that occur most often. For colors not included in the first 256, the program compares each of these colors with the 256 selected for display and assigns the color to whichever of the 256 is **the** closest least squares fit to the actual color.

```
/*

    process = Program to process raw VGA color data

*/
#include <dos.h>
```

```c
#include <stdio.h>
#include <alloc.h>
#include <stdlib.h>
#include <conio.h>

void gotoxy(int x, int y);
void plot(int x, int y, int color);
void setMode(int mode);
void setVGApalette(unsigned char *buffer);
void sort(unsigned int start, unsigned int end);

typedef struct
{
    char Red;
    char Green;
    char Blue;
}
RGB;

enum { red=0,grn=1,blu=2 };

union REGS reg;
struct SREGS inreg;

#define  MAXXRES          320

unsigned int Col_Array[256][2];
unsigned char Pal_Array[256][3];
RGB Color,Color2;

int i,k,xres, yres, last_color,scanline,r1,r2,g1,g2,b1,b2;
unsigned char r[MAXXRES], g[MAXXRES], b[MAXXRES];
FILE *file_1;
unsigned char far *color_hist;
long int color_no;
unsigned int j;
unsigned char frequency[8192];
unsigned int hues[8192];

void main(argc,argv)
```

```
int argc;
char *argv[];

{
    int index;
    int rgbindex;
    int x1;
    unsigned int d1, temp_d;
    unsigned char d2;

    setMode(3);
    if (argc != 2)
    {
        printf("VGA Color Processor by Roger Stevens\n");
        printf("Usage: %s filename.RAW\n",argv[0]);
        exit(1);
    }
    if ((file_1 = fopen(argv[1],"rb"))==NULL)
    {
        printf("Couldn't open file %s\n",argv[1]);
        exit(1);
    }

    color_hist = farmalloc(32768);
    for (i=0;i<256;i++)
    {
        Pal_Array[i][red] = 0;
        Pal_Array[i][grn] = 0;
        Pal_Array[i][blu] = 0;
    }
    for (j=0; j<32768; j++)
        color_hist[j] = 0;
    xres = yres = 0;
    fread(&xres,sizeof(int),1,file_1);
    fread(&yres,sizeof(int),1,file_1);
    printf("VGA 256 Color Processor by Roger Stevens\n");
    printf("Image file resolution is: %d by %d\n",xres,yres);
    for (i=0;i<256;i++)
    {
        Pal_Array[i][red] = 0;
```

```
        Pal_Array[i][grn] = 0;
        Pal_Array[i][blu] = 0;
    }
x1 = 0;
printf("Collecting color data [  ]");
while (!feof(file_1))
{
    fread(&scanline,sizeof(int),1,file_1);
        if (scanline >= xres)
        {
            printf("\nFaulty data file.\n");
            exit(1);
        }
    gotoxy(24,3);
    printf("%d",scanline);
    fread(&r[0],sizeof(char),yres+1,file_1);
    fread(&g[0],sizeof(char),yres+1,file_1);
    fread(&b[0],sizeof(char),yres+1,file_1);
    for (index=0;index<=yres;index++)
    {
        Color.Red  = (r[index] & 0x3e);
        Color.Green = (g[index] & 0x3e);
        Color.Blue = (b[index] & 0x3e);
        color_no = (Color.Red >> 1) | (Color.Green << 4) |
            (Color.Blue << 9);
        if (color_hist[color_no] < 255)
            color_hist[color_no]++;
    }
    x1 += 1;
}
last_color = -1;
for (j=0; j<32768; j++)
{
    if (color_hist[j] > 0)
    {
        last_color++;
        hues[last_color] = j;
        frequency[last_color] = color_hist[j];
    }
}
```

192

```
printf("\nThere are %d colors.",last_color);
printf("\nStarting sort.");
sort(0,last_color);
printf("\nSort completed.");
printf("\nModifying extra colors [        ]");
for (i=0; i<256; i++)
     frequency[i] = i;
for (i=256; i<=last_color; i++)
{
     gotoxy(25,7);
     printf("%5d",i);
     d1 = 32768;
     for (j=0; j<256; j++)
     {
         Color.Red = (hues[i] << 1) & 0x3E;
         Color.Green = (hues[i] >> 4) & 0x3E;
         Color.Blue = (hues[i] >> 9) & 0x3E;
         Color2.Red = (hues[j] << 1) & 0x3E;
         Color2.Green = (hues[j] >> 4) & 0x3E;
         Color2.Blue = (hues[j] >> 9) & 0x3E;
         temp_d = (Color.Red - Color2.Red)*(Color.Red -
             Color2.Red) + (Color.Green -
             Color2.Green)*(Color.Green - Color2.Green) +
             (Color.Blue - Color2.Blue)*(Color.Blue -
             Color2.Blue);
         if (temp_d < d1)
         {
             d1 = temp_d;
             d2 = j;
         }
     }
     frequency[i] = d2;
}
for (j=0; j<256; j++)
{
     Color.Red = (hues[j] << 1) & 0x3E;
     Color.Green = (hues[j] >> 4) & 0x3E;
     Color.Blue = (hues[j] >> 9) & 0x3E;
     Pal_Array[j][0] = Color.Red;
     Pal_Array[j][1] = Color.Green;
```

```
            Pal_Array[j][2] = Color.Blue;
    }
    setMode(0x13);
    setVGApalette(&Pal_Array[0][0]);
    for (j=0; j<32768; j++)
        color_hist[j] = 0;
    for (j=0; j<=last_color; j++)
        color_hist[hues[j]] = frequency[j];
    rewind(file_1);
    x1 = 0;
    fread(&xres,sizeof(int),1,file_1);
    fread(&yres,sizeof(int),1,file_1);
    while (!feof(file_1))
    {
        fread(&scanline,sizeof(int),1,file_1);
        if (scanline >= xres)
        {
            printf("Faulty data file.\n");
            exit(1);
        }
        fread(&r[0],sizeof(char),yres+1,file_1);
        fread(&g[0],sizeof(char),yres+1,file_1);
        fread(&b[0],sizeof(char),yres+1,file_1);
        for (index=0;index<=yres;index++)
        {
            Color.Red  = (r[index] & 0x3e);
            Color.Green = (g[index] & 0x3e);
            Color.Blue = (b[index] & 0x3e);
            color_no = (Color.Red >> 1) | (Color.Green << 4) |
                (Color.Blue << 9);
            plot(x1,index,color_hist[color_no]);
        }
        x1 += 1;
    }
    getch();
    setMode(3);
    fclose(file_1);
}
```

```
/*
```

```
    setMode() = Sets video mode
```

```
*/
```

```c
void setMode(int mode)
{
    reg.h.ah = 0;
    reg.h.al = mode;
    int86 (0x10,&reg,&reg);
}
```

```
/*
```

```
    plot() = Function to plot point to VGA 256 color screen
```

```
*/
```

```c
void plot(int x, int y, int color)
{
    unsigned int offset;
    char far *address;
    offset = 320 * y + x;
    address = (char far *)(0xA0000000L + offset);
    *address = color;
}
```

```
/*
```

```
    setVGApalette() = Function to set all 256 color registers
```

```
*/
```

```c
void setVGApalette(unsigned char *buffer)
{
    reg.x.ax = 0x1012;
    segread(&inreg);
    inreg.es = inreg.ds;
    reg.x.bx = 0;
```

```
        reg.x.cx = 256;
        reg.x.dx = (int)&buffer[0];
        int86x(0x10,&reg,&reg,&inreg);
}
/*
```

┌───┐
│   │
│   sort() = Quicksort to sort colors by frequency   │
│   │
└───┘

```
*/

void sort(unsigned int start, unsigned int end)
{
    unsigned int pivot,temp2;
    unsigned char temp;

    if (start < (end - 1))
    {
        i = start;
        j = end;
        pivot = (frequency[i] + frequency[j] + frequency[(i+j)/2])/3;
        do
        {
            while (frequency[i] > pivot)
                i++;
            while (frequency[j] < pivot)
                j—;
            if (i < j)
            {
                temp = frequency[i];
                frequency[i] = frequency[j];
                frequency[j] = temp;
                temp2 = hues[i];
                hues[i++] = hues[j];
                hues[j—] = temp2;
            }
        }   while (i < j);
        if (j < end)
        {
            sort(start,j);
            sort(j+1,end);
```

```
            }
        }
        if (frequency[end] > frequency[start])
        {
            temp = frequency[start];
            frequency[start] = frequency[end];
            frequency[end] = temp;
            temp2 = hues[start];
            hues[start] = hues[end];
            hues[end] = temp2;
        }
    }
/*
```

```
    gotoxy() = Function to position cursor
```

```
*/

void gotoxy(int x, int y)
{
    reg.h.ah = 2;
    reg.h.bh = 0;
    reg.h.dh = y-1;
    reg.h.dl = x-1;
    int86(0x10, &reg, &reg);
}
```

Figure 11-3. Listing of *process.cpp* Program

Now, let's look at the program in detail. It begins by checking whether the program was called with a specified file name . If not, a message is printed out (with the display in text mode), which indicates that a file name must be included in running the program. The program then exits. If a file name was specified, an attempt is made to open the specified file. If the file cannot be opened, the program displays a message to this effect and then exits. If the file is successfully opened, the program next allocates memory for the array *color_hist*, which will be used to store the occurrences of colors. The array of information for the color registers, *Pal_Array*, and the *color_hist* array are then initialized to all zeroes. The first four bytes of the file, which are the

197

integer values for *xres*, the number of display pixels in the *x* direction and *yres*, the number of display pixels in the *y* direction, are then read. The heading and the resolution data are then displayed on the screen. Next, the program displays the line "Collecting color data [   ]" with a space for the line number. The program then starts a *while* loop which will continue until the end of the file is encountered. The loop begins by reading the number of the scan column from the file. If it is greater than the maximum line that was defined, there is an error and the program displays, "Faulty data file" and exits. If the scan column is acceptable, it is displayed at the proper place on the screen. Next, the program reads first a column of red data, then a column of green data, and then a column of blue data from the file. These are stored in *r*, *g*, and *b* arrays. A *for* loop is then begun which takes the red, green, and blue values for each pixel (not including the least significant bit, thereby accomplishing the division by two) and shifts and combines them into a unique color number. This value is then used as an index for the *color_hist* array and the contents of that address is incremented. Once the loop is complete, the program runs another *for* loop which scans the *color_hist* array and increments a variable, *last_color*, each time a color occurs at least once. The index for this color is placed in an array *hues* and the frequency with which it occurs in an array *frequency*. Each of these arrays is of size 8192, assuming that there will be no more than 8192 different colors in any particular picture. If there are more than 8192 colors, the program will probably bomb. The next thing that happens is that a line is displayed telling how many colors were in the picture, so if there are too many colors, you may get to see this before anything goes haywire. Assuming there weren't too many colors, the program displays "Starting sort", then runs the *sort* function, and then displays "Sort completed".

The frequency of occurrence data is no longer needed; instead we will fill the *frequency* array with a color number from 0 to 255 for each color. We begin by assigning the first 256 colors the numbers 0 to 255. Then the program displays "Modifying extra colors[   ]" with a space for the color number being processed. Next, the program enters a *for* loop which it iterates for each of the additional colors from 256 to the last_color number. Within this loop, first the number of the color being worked on is displayed. Next, another for loop is entered which is reiterated for each of the 256 initial colors. Within this loop, each color index for the current color being processed and the current one of the 256 initial colors is decomposed into the original red, green, and blue color data. The sum of the squares of the difference between red, green, and blue values is then computed. At each iteration, the smallest sum of squares is saved along with its color number. When the current color has been checked against all 256 initial colors, it is assigned the number of the color for which the sum of the squares of the differences was smallest. When the two loops are complete, all of the colors beyond the first 256 have been assigned color numbers that correspond to the color for which the sum of the squares of the differences was smallest. Next, the graphics mode is set for the 256 color display and *setVGApalette* is run to set the VGA color values for the first 256 colors. We then refill the *color_hist* array with the number of the color associated with each index value or with a zero if that index has no color. Next, we rewind the file. The file is then read all over again, beginning by reading the *xres* and *yres* values and then entering a *while* loop that reiterates until the end of file is encountered. For each iteration, the scan column number is read first and then the red, green, and blue data for a complete column. Then a *for* loop is run for each pixel of the line. The color data for that pixel is combined into an index number in the same manner as was done above. The color number for that index is taken from the *color_hist* array and the pixel is plotted in that color at the appropriate point on the screen. When both loops are complete, the full picture is being displayed. The program waits for a character to be entered at the keyboard. When this occurs, the screen is reset to the text mode, the file is closed, and the program terminates.

A Three-Dimensional Plasma Representation

In the previous chapter we described how the *plasma* program could save data files in a form that was suitable for processing to produce an unusually realistic mountain scene. A typical plasma three-dimensional mountain is shown in Plate 32. The *.zbf* data file is produced by running the plasma program until an attractive display occurs and then saving it with the *S* command. In this case, the desired plasma file was named *plasma01.zbf*. Table 11-1 shows the parameters that were entered into the *rend* program to produce the display shown in the color plate.

Light Phi	45
Light Theta	330
View Phi	55
Ambient Color	0.6, 0.3, 0.4
Diffuse Color	1.0, 0.8, 0.4
Specular Color	1.0, 0.8, 0.4
Background Color	0.6, 0.6, 1.0
Alternate Background Color	0.5, 0.2, 0.2
File Name	plasma01

Table 11-1. Parameters for Three-Dimensional Plasma Display

Three Dimensional Mandelbrot Sets

In chapter 6, one of the advantages of using the distance method for Mandelbrot sets was given as the fact that an interesting three-dimensional display could be created using the distance of any point from the Mandelbrot set as a height value. A program to do this and produce a *.zbf* file suitable for use with the *rend* program given above is listed in Figure 11-4. This is very similar to the program given in Chapter 6, except for the way in which the color (height) value is computed and for the fact that the height values are reversed in the *screen_save* function before being saved to the disk file. Table 11-2 shows the parameters that were used with the *rend* program to render this file and ultimately produce the picture shown in Plate 10. We need to point out that this display, although interesting, does not give a very accurate representation of the height values about the Mandelbrot set. This is probably a result of the fact that our simple method of obtaining the normal to the surface at every point is not a very good one. There is a technique by which a very accurate normal may be obtained for every point at the same time that the distance is being computed, using just a few additional steps. If you want to experiment with this, you can obtain the necessary information from the book, *The Science of Fractal Images* by Peitgen, et al. Note, however, that you will have to modify the way in which the data file is saved so that it includes not only a height for each pixel, but a normal also. Since each normal has three components, that will result in a very big file. The *rend* program would then need to be altered also, so that it would read normals from this enlarged data file, rather than calculating then internally.

```
/*

    dist3d = 3D Mandelbrot set with distance calculation

    By Roger T. Stevens  10-23-90

*/

#include <stdio.h>
#include <dos.h>
#include <complex.h>
#include <conio.h>
#include <math.h>
#include <stdlib.h>
#include "ftools.h"

void fractal(void);
double mdist(void);
void screen_save(void);
int readPixel(int x, int y);

#define Min(x,y) ((x)<(y) ? (x) : (y))
#define Max(x,y) ((x)>(y) ? (x) : (y))

double XMax, XMin, YMax, YMin, Pval, Qval, a, b, c, d, e, f, g, h,
    TXMax, TXMin, TYMax, TYMin, start_x, start_y;
int colors[15][3], max_iterations, color_option, CURSOR_X, CURSOR_Y;
unsigned char PALETTE[16]={0,1,2,3,4,5,20,7,56,57,58,59,60,61,62,63};

char *ptr;
const int maxcol = 319;
const int maxrow = 199;
double max_size = 1000.0;
int index,old_index;
double x,y,p,q,old_x,old_y;
double deltaP, deltaQ,threshold;
```

```
int i,j, row, col, scale_factor = 255;
char filename1[13],file_name[13];

main()
{
    max_iterations = 64;
    setMode(3);
    window(1,1,80,25);
    textbackground(0);
    clrscr();
    textbackground(1);
    window(9,9,62,19);
    clrscr();
    gotoxy(3,2);
    textcolor(15);
    cprintf("Enter parameters for display:\n");
    gotoxy(8,3);
    cprintf("X Max: ");
    cscanf("%lf",&XMax);
    gotoxy(8,4);
    cprintf("X Min: ");
    cscanf("%lf",&XMin);
    gotoxy(8,5);
    cprintf("Y Max: ");
    cscanf("%lf",&YMax);
    gotoxy(8,6);
    cprintf("Y Min: ");
    cscanf("%lf",&YMin);
    gotoxy(3,9);
    cprintf("Enter name of file for output data: ");
    cscanf("%s",filename1);
    ptr = strchr(filename1, '.');
    if (ptr == NULL)
    {
        strncpy(file_name,filename1,6);
        strcat(file_name,"00.PCX");
    }
    else
        strcpy(file_name,filename1);
    setMode(19);
```

```
        cls(7);
        fractal();
        screen_save();
        getch();
        getch();
        move_cursor(2,15,0,0);
        setMode(3);
}


/*
```

┌───┐
│ ┌───┐   │
│ │   fractal() = Computes, displays, and stores a Mandelbrot set │
│ └───┘   │
└───┘

```
*/

float delta;

void fractal(void)
{
        double distance, distance2, deltaD, temp;
        int k,end,color;

        deltaP = (XMax - XMin)/(maxcol+1);
        deltaQ = (YMax - YMin)/(maxrow+1);
        delta = (deltaP + deltaQ) / 4;
        delta = deltaQ / 2;
        for (col=0; col<= maxcol; col++)
        {
            p = XMin + col * deltaP;
            if (kbhit() != 0)
                exit(0);
            for (row=0; row<=maxrow; row++)
            {
                q = YMax - row * deltaQ;
                if ((distance = mdist()) < deltaQ)
                {
                    color = 0;
                    plot256(col,row,color);
                }
                else
```

```
            {
                end = Max(1,Min(20, (int)(distance/(2*deltaQ))));
                q = YMax - (row + end) * deltaQ;
                distance2 = mdist();
                deltaD = (distance - distance2) / end;
                for (k=0; k<=end; k++)
                {
                    color = (int)(distance / deltaQ);
                    if (color > 255)
                        color = 255;
                    else
                        if (color < 0)
                            color = 0;
                    plot256(col,row++,color);
                    if (row>maxrow)
                        break;
                    distance -= deltaD;
                }
                row—;
            }
        }
    }
}

/*
```

┌───┐
│ mdist() = Computes the distance from a point to the Mandelbrot set   │
└───┘

```
*/

double mdist()
{
    int i,flag,row_dist;
    static int old_index;
    double dist=0, temp, xsq, ysq, xprime,
    yprime,orbit_x[512],orbit_y[512],
        denom,old_x,old_y;

    i = 0;
    flag = 0;
```

```
xsq = 0;;
ysq = 0;
x = 0;
y = 0;
xprime = 0;
yprime = 0;
index = 0;
orbit_x[0] = 0;
orbit_y[0] = 0;
old_x = 0;
old_y = 0;
while ((index < max_iterations) && (xsq + ysq < max_size))
{
    index++;
    y = 2*x*y + q;
    orbit_y[index] = y;
    x = xsq -ysq + p;
    orbit_x[index] = x;
    xsq = x*x;
    ysq = y*y;
    if (old_index == max_iterations)
    {
        if ((index & 15) == 0)
        {
            old_x = x;
            old_y = y;
        }
        else
            if ((fabs(old_x - x) + fabs(old_y - x)) < delta)
                index = max_iterations-1;
    }
}
if (xsq + ysq > max_size)
{
    while ((i<index) && (!flag))
    {
        temp = 2 * (orbit_x[i] * xprime - orbit_y[i] * yprime) + 1;
        yprime = 2 * (orbit_y[i] * xprime + orbit_x[i] * yprime);
        xprime = temp;
        if (Max(fabs(xprime),fabs(yprime)) > 1e14)
```

```
                    flag = 1;
                i++;
            }
            if (!flag)
            {
                dist = log(xsq + ysq) * sqrt((xsq + ysq) /
                (xprime*xprime + yprime * yprime));
            }
        }

    return dist;
}

/*
```

┌───┐
│ ┌───┐ │
│ │ screen_save() = Save screen to disk file   │ │
│ └───┘ │
└───┘

```
*/

void screen_save(void)
{
    int row, col, color;
    FILE *fsave;

    sound (256);
    while (file_name[6] < 0x3A)
    {
        if ((fsave = fopen (file_name,"rb")) != NULL)
        {
            file_name[7]++;
            if (file_name[7] >= 0x3A)
            {
                file_name[7] = 0x30;
                file_name[6]++;
            }
            fclose(fsave);
        }
        else
```

```
        {
            fclose(fsave);
            fsave = fopen(file_name,"wb");
            fwrite(&maxcol,1,2,fsave);
            fwrite(&maxrow,1,2,fsave);
            fwrite(&scale_factor,1,2,fsave);
            for (col=0; col<=maxcol; col++)
            {
                for (row=0; row<=maxrow; row++)
                {
                    color = 255 - readPixel(col,row);
                    fwrite(&color,1,2,fsave);
                }
            }
            fclose(fsave);
            break;
        }
    }
    nosound();
}



/*

    readPixel() = Read a pixel from the screen

*/

int readPixel(int x, int y)
{

    union REGS reg;

    reg.h.ah = 0x0D;
    reg.x.cx = x;
    reg.x.dx = y;
        int86 (0x10,&reg,&reg);
    return (reg.h.al);
}
```

Light Phi	75
Light Theta	-35
View Phi	65
Ambient Color	0.0, 0.0, 0.0
Diffuse Color	0.6, 0.3, 0.6
Specular Color	0.6, 0.8, 0.8
Background Color	0.6, 0.6, 1.0
Alternate Background Color	0.1, 0.4, 0.4
File Name	mandis05

Table 11-2. Parameters for Three-Dimensional Mandelbrot Set Display

CHAPTER 12

L-Systems

In *Fractal Programming in C*, I devoted several chapters to describing fractals that are created using a recursive initiator/generator technique that results in complete self-similarity. This technique begins with an initiator, which may be any geometric figure made up of straight line segments. Each side of the initiator is then replaced by a generator, which is a pattern of straight line segments that replace the original line segment. This process is then repeated in a scaled-down fashion for all the new line segments, and so forth for as long as you want to repeat the process, or until the detail no longer is visible on a computer screen. The L-systems technique is really a language for describing the initiator and generator and their interactions. As with all languages, it is a convenient shorthand for describing reality, and it also turns out to be conveniently manipulated by a computer to create actual fractal drawings. The L-systems technique was first developed by Aristid Lindenmayer, who used it to describe the geometric structure of plants.

The Geometric Basis for L-Systems

The L-systems language is closely associated with the concept of turtle graphics, which was derived from the LOGO computer language. In LOGO, graphics are created by a *turtle*, that moves about the screen. Originally, the turtle is pointing straight up at the top of the screen. The turtle can take a step in the direction that it is pointing, in which case a line is usually drawn along the path taken by the turtle. The length of the step is determined by an independent variable. The turtle may also turn. In this case, nothing is drawn; the turtle simply changes its heading so that the next step that it takes will be in a different direction. We have already said that the turtle begins pointed toward the top of the screen. This is the direction *north* on all standard maps, and corresponds to zero degrees. In such a system, the direction angle

209

goes from north clockwise around the face of the compass, with east being 90 degrees, south, 180 degrees, and so forth. A system more natural to geometricians would have the turtle pointing in the x direction (toward the right), and having the x axis be zero degrees, with angles measured counter-clockwise. Finally, just to confuse things further, some LOGO systems have the turtle initially pointing north at zero degrees, but measure angles in the counter-clockwise direction. Since there is no real standard, we'll stick with the standard compass/mapping system, with the turtle starting pointed north and angles measured clockwise. In defining the L-systems language, one must remember that in this case also, there is presently no completely defined and recognized standard. We shall try to keep a certain amount of standardization with other versions of the language, but will also feel free to define our own additions to the language where necessary. We'll begin the L-systems language with a few simple words. The symbol D commands the turtle to take a step, drawing a line while doing so. (The step length must be predefined in the program.) The symbol d commands the turtle to take a step without drawing a line (the intervening space on the screen remains blank). The symbol + indicates that the turtle will turn in a clockwise direction by a predefined angle and the symbol - indicates that the turtle will turn in a counter-clockwise direction by the predefined angle. With just these few simple commands, we can begin drawing some fractal curves.

Overview of the L-Systems Program

The way that the L-systems technique is supposed to work is this. We begin with an initiator. Let's say that the initiator is just a straight line, D. We have a generator, which is used to replace the line. Suppose that the turn angle is 60 degrees and the divisor 3. We have a generator which is $D-D++D-D$. Now, we start at level zero, in which the string that we implement is just the initiator. So we draw a line one step long. On the next pass, we go to level 1. Now we replace D in the initiator with the generator string. We reduce the step length to one-third of the original, draw a line of that length, turn counter-clockwise 60 degrees, draw another line of step length, turn clockwise 120 degrees, draw another line, turn counterclockwise sixty degrees, and draw another line. Our geometry and step size has been arranged so that this new pattern of lines ends at exactly the end point of the original line that was drawn. On the next pass, we go to level 2. Every occurrence of D in the previous string is replaced by the entire generator string. We then implement this new string and find that each of the four line segments of the previous level is replaced by a smaller replica of the generator pattern. This process can continue for as long as we want it to.

More Complex Generator Schemes

The simple technique described above is adequate for drawing many fractal curves, but sometimes we want to get more complicated. Suppose that we want to have more than one possible generator and switch from one to another under certain circumstances. This is no problem. We simply define several different generators and specify in a generator string which one is to be used for replacement of each line segment. In this program, we have defined generators D, d, L, R, X, Y, and T. We've already defined the first two. The next ones, L and R are somewhat suggestive of cases where a right and left generator are used, but they really can be used for any purpose, as can X and Y. The generator T is a very special kind of generator. In many complex fractals, we have a generator pattern that we want to use in four different ways. We may want to use it directly to replace a line segment, as we have done above with D. However, we may also want to use it in reverse (if it is not symmetrical, starting at the end and drawing the pattern back to the beginning. We call this form of the generator t. Both these generators are oriented so that they perform as they should at the top of the line segment being replaced. But we may also want to use mirror images that do the same at the bottom of the line segment. These are called B and b respectively. (Please don't be confused by the small letters. In this case they mean reversed generators, whereas for the case of d the small letter means that the step is taken without drawing a line. However, this is just the way that each of these generators is defined.) What is unusual about T is that after you define it, the program automatically performs the necessary changes to create t, B, and b, so that you then have them available for use in your generator definitions without having to write down whole strings to make sure they are correct.

Recurrence in L-Systems

What happens if we actually carry out the procedure described above. For the first few levels, there is no problem. With each substitution of the generator for every step in the previous string, the overall string gets longer, but is still manageable. However, at higher levels, this soon gets out of hand. With a relatively simple generator, by the time we get to 16 levels we may well need over 16 megabytes of memory to store the entire string. This quickly exceeds the capabilities of a PC. Some L-Systems programs handle this problem by simply quitting when the string gets too large and reporting back, "Not enough memory". We are going to handle the problem by a recursion process that enables us to draw almost any fractal curve, no matter what level is selected. The technique works in this way: Instead of actually creating the entire string in advance, each time a step is called for, if the level is zero, we draw a line. But for a higher level, we call a generate program which substitutes the proper generator pattern and reduces the level by one. When the zero level is reached, all of the lines are drawn and then the function returns and deals with the next step. In this way, we only deal with a small part of the overall string at any one time, and thus the whole process becomes manageable.

Generating Simple Fractals with L-Systems

Before getting into the complexities of the L-systems program, let's see how it is used to generate some simple fractals. Figure 12-1 shows the data that will appear on your screen which will be used to generate the von Koch snowflake, one of the earliest fractal curves. The initiator for this curve is seen to be an equilateral triangle. Note that after each step in the initiator, the turtle turns by two angular increments, and that later in the display, this angle is defined to be 60 degrees. The starting angle is 90 degrees, so the turtle starts pointing in the x (horizontal to the left) direction. It takes a step, turns counter-clockwise 120 degrees, takes another step, turns counter-clockwise 120 degrees again, and takes a third step, thus creating the equilateral triangle. Now we proceed to the next level. At this level, we replace each line segment by the generator. Since the divisor is defined as 3.000000, each line segment in the generator is one-third of the length of the previous line segment. The turtle takes a step in the direction of the first level line segment, turns 60 degrees clockwise, takes another step, turns 120 degrees counter-clockwise, takes another step, turns 60 degrees clockwise (which puts it back on the original line and pointing in the direction of the original line) and takes another step (which brings it to the end of the original line. This substitution takes place for each of the three original line segments, resulting in the level 2 curve of Figure 12-3. The process is repeated for higher levels, giving the additional curves shown in Figure 12-3. The snowflake has a fractal dimension of 1.2618.

The next curve to be considered is the Gosper curve. The input data for this curve is shown in Figure 12-2. The Gosper curves for levels 2, 3, 4, and 5 are shown in Figure 12-4.

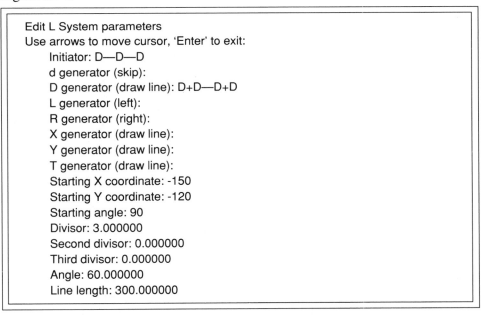

```
Edit L System parameters
Use arrows to move cursor, 'Enter' to exit:
     Initiator: D—D—D
     d generator (skip):
     D generator (draw line): D+D—D+D
     L generator (left):
     R generator (right):
     X generator (draw line):
     Y generator (draw line):
     T generator (draw line):
     Starting X coordinate: -150
     Starting Y coordinate: -120
     Starting angle: 90
     Divisor: 3.000000
     Second divisor: 0.000000
     Third divisor: 0.000000
     Angle: 60.000000
     Line length: 300.000000
```

Figure 12-1. Data for von Koch Snowflake Curve (snoflake.dat)

```
Edit L System parameters
Use arrows to move cursor, 'Enter' to exit:
      Initiator: D+++D+++D+++D+++D+++D
      d generator (skip):
      D generator (draw line): -D+++D—D+
      L generator (left):
      R generator (right):
      X generator (draw line):
      Y generator (draw line):
      T generator (draw line):
      Starting X coordinate: -150
      Starting Y coordinate: -100
      Starting angle: 0
      Divisor: 2.645751
      Second divisor: 0.000000
      Third divisor: 0.000000
      Angle: 20.000000
      Line length: 180.000000
```

Figure 12-2. Data for Gosper Curve (gosper.dat)

level = 2

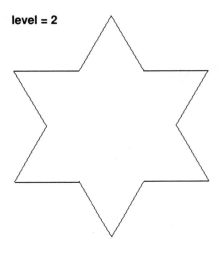

level = 3

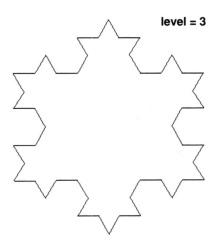

level = 4

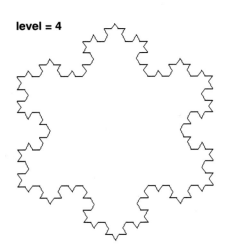

level = 5

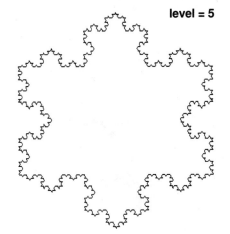

Figure 12-3. The von Koch Snowflake Curve

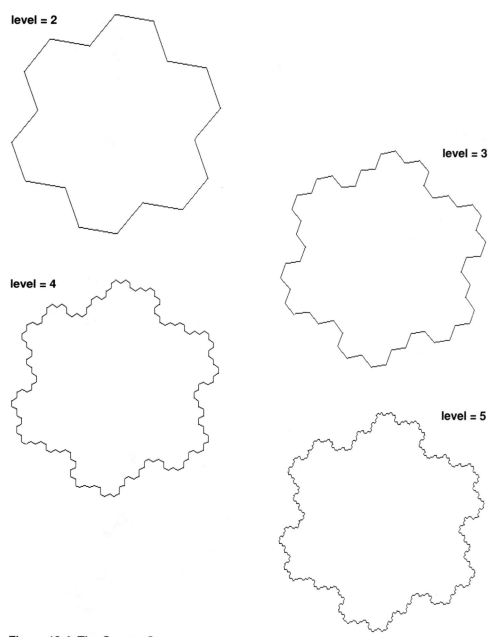

level = 2

level = 3

level = 4

level = 5

Figure 12-4. The Gosper Curve

Next, we will consider the 18 segment quadric von Koch curve. There is a whole family of these quadric curves, ranging from three segments up to about as many as you can fit into a picture. You will find some of them described in *Fractal Programming in C*. From the information given there, you should be able to transfer them to L-systems data files, or you can try creating them based upon the 18 segment model given here; They all begin with a square as an initiator. The input data for the 18 segment curve is given in Figure 12-5, and various levels of the curve are shown in Figure 12-6.

```
Edit L System parameters
Use arrows to move cursor, 'Enter' to exit:
      Initiator: D+D+D+D
      d generator (skip):
      D generator (draw line): D-DD+DD+D+D-D-DD+D+D-D-
      DD-DD+D
      L generator (left):
      R generator (right):
      X generator (draw line):
      Y generator (draw line):
      T generator (draw line):
      Starting X coordinate: -150
      Starting Y coordinate: -120
      Starting angle: 0
      Divisor: 6.000000
      Second divisor: 0.000000
      Third divisor: 0.000000
      Angle: 90.000000
      Line length: 200.000000
```

Figure 12-5. Data for 18 Segment Quadric von Koch Curve (koch18.dat)

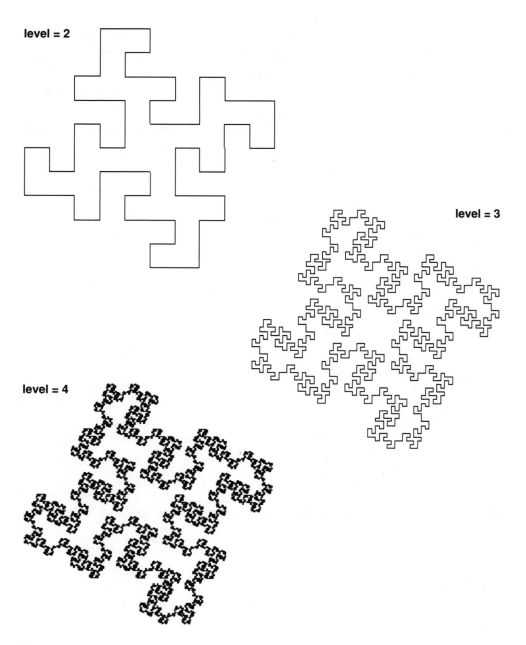

level = 2

level = 3

level = 4

Figure 12-6. The 18 Segment von Koch Quadric Curve

Figure 12-7 shows the input parameters for the Islands curve. This curve differs from the others in having parts that are completely isolated from the main curve. Several levels of the curve are shown in Figure 12-8.

```
Edit L System parameters
Use arrows to move cursor, 'Enter' to exit:
      Initiator: D+D+D+D
      d generator (skip): dddddd
      D generator (draw line): D+d-DD+D+DD+Dd+DD-d+DD-D-
      DD-Dd-DDD
      L generator (left):
      R generator (right):
      X generator (draw line):
      Y generator (draw line):
      T generator (draw line):
      Starting X coordinate: -150
      Starting Y coordinate: -120
      Starting angle: 0
      Divisor: 6.000000
      Second divisor: 0.000000
      Third divisor: 0.000000
      Angle: 90.000000
      Line length: 250.000000
```

Figure 12-7. Data for Islands Curve (islands.dat)

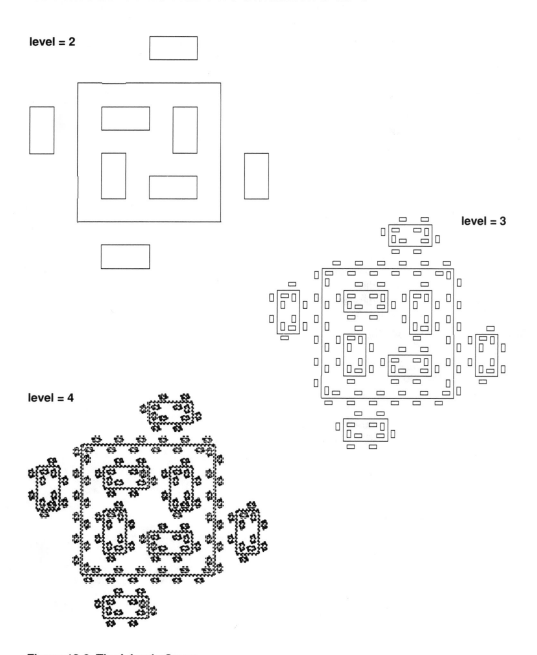

Figure 12-8. The Islands Curve

Next, we will look at the Peano curve. This curve has a fractal dimension of 2.0, so that it will fill an entire plane if carried to a high enough level. The input data for this curve is shown in Figure 12-9. As you look at the second level of this curve it my be a little difficult to visualize how the curve is traced out, but if you follow the turtle actions specified for the generator, you will see what is happening. Several levels of the Peano curve are shown in Figure 12-10.

```
Edit L System parameters
Use arrows to move cursor, 'Enter' to exit:
        Initiator: D
        d generator (skip):
        D generator (draw line): D-D+D+DD+D+D+DD
        L generator (left):
        R generator (right):
        X generator (draw line):
        Y generator (draw line):
        T generator (draw line):
        Starting X coordinate: 0
        Starting Y coordinate: -160
        Starting angle: 0
        Divisor: 3.000000
        Second divisor: 0.000000
        Third divisor: 0.000000
        Angle: 90.000000
        Line length: 300.000000
```

Figure 12-9. Data for Peano Curve (peano.dat)

level = 2

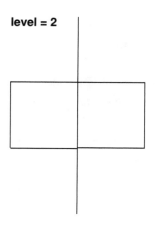

level = 3

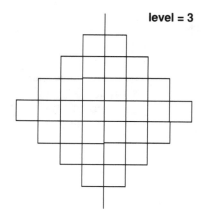

level = 4

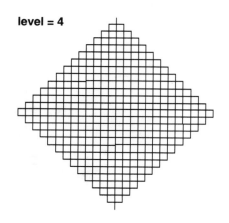

level = 5

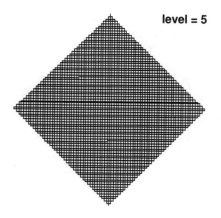

Figure 12-10. The Peano Curve

We've now looked at several fractal curves that can be created with only a simple generator. Next, we will start looking at ones that require two generators, sometimes specifying the right and left sides of a line segment. In *Fractal Programming in C*, various complicated ways of changing signs, etc. were used to draw these curves. With the L-systems approach, everything becomes much simpler. We'll start with the Cesaro curve. This is also a plane filling curve, having a fractal dimension of 2.0. The input data parameters for this curve are shown in Figure 12-11, and several levels of the curve are pictured in Figure 12-12. The initiator is an *R* step, so this generator is used to replace the line at the first level. From then on, every *R* is replaced by the R generator string and every *L* by the *L* generator string.

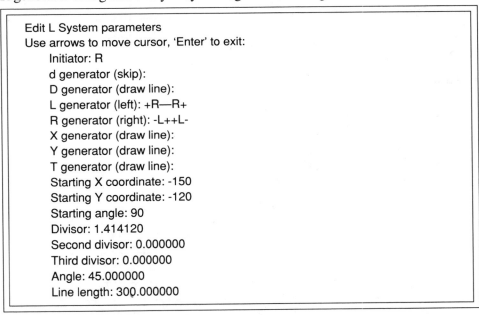

```
Edit L System parameters
Use arrows to move cursor, 'Enter' to exit:
    Initiator: R
    d generator (skip):
    D generator (draw line):
    L generator (left): +R—R+
    R generator (right): -L++L-
    X generator (draw line):
    Y generator (draw line):
    T generator (draw line):
    Starting X coordinate: -150
    Starting Y coordinate: -120
    Starting angle: 90
    Divisor: 1.414120
    Second divisor: 0.000000
    Third divisor: 0.000000
    Angle: 45.000000
    Line length: 300.000000
```

Figure 12-11. Data for Cesaro Curve (cesaro.dat)

223

level = 4

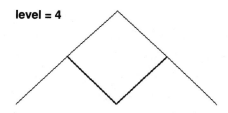

level = 7

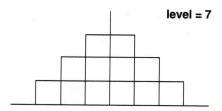

level = 10

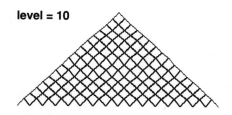

level = 11

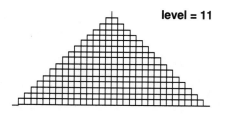

Figure 12-12. The Cesaro Curve

Another curve using two generators is the Harter-Heightway dragon curve, so-named because of its resemblance to a dragon at higher levels. The input parameters for this curve are shown in Figure 12-13 and several levels of the curve appear in Figure 12-14.

```
Edit L System parameters
Use arrows to move cursor, 'Enter' to exit:
    Initiator: R
    d generator (skip):
    D generator (draw line):
    L generator (left): +L—R+
    R generator (right): -L++R-
    X generator (draw line):
    Y generator (draw line):
    T generator (draw line):
    Starting X coordinate: -150
    Starting Y coordinate: -120
    Starting angle: 90
    Divisor: 1.414120
    Second divisor: 0.000000
    Third divisor: 0.000000
    Angle: 45.000000
    Line length: 300.000000
```

Figure 12-13. Data for Harter-Heightway Dragon Curve (dragon.dat)

level = 5

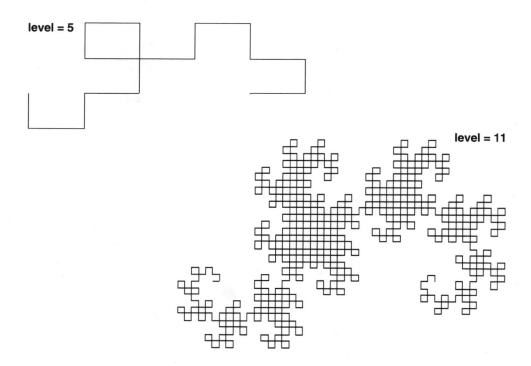

level = 11

level = 17

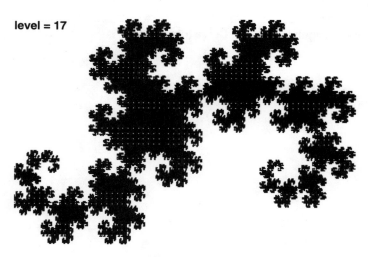

Figure 12-14. The Harter-Heightway Dragon Curve

The Peano-Gosper curve is another curve that makes use of two generators. It has the unusual characteristic that it exactly fits within the boundary of the Gosper curve. The input data for this curve is given in Figure 12-15 and several levels of the curve are shown in Figure 12-16.

```
Edit L System parameters
Use arrows to move cursor, 'Enter' to exit:
     Initiator: R
     d generator (skip):
     D generator (draw line):
     L generator (left): L+R+RR-L—L-R+
     R generator (right): -L+RR++R+L—L-R
     X generator (draw line):
     Y generator (draw line):
     T generator (draw line):
     Starting X coordinate: -120
     Starting Y coordinate: -100
     Starting angle: 90
     Divisor: 2.645800
     Second divisor: 0.000000
     Third divisor: 0.000000
     Angle: 60.000000
     Line length: 300.000000
```

Figure 12-15. Data for Peano-Gosper Curve (pgcurve.dat)

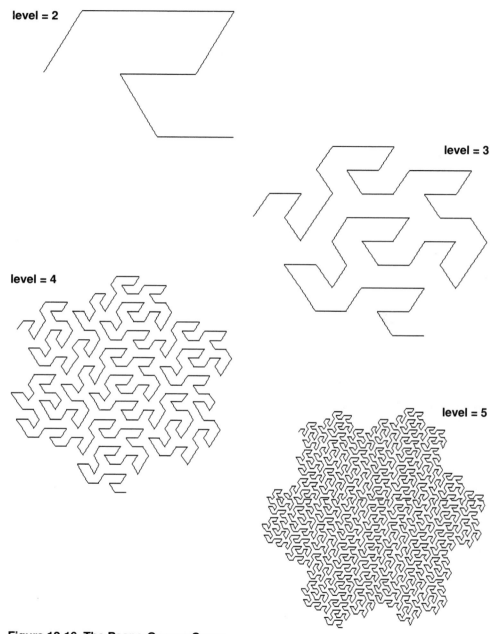

level = 2

level = 3

level = 4

level = 5

Figure 12-16. The Peano-Gosper Curve

The final curve to make use of two generators is the Sierpinski triangle. You have already encountered this in a different form in Chapter 9 and will see it again in another form in Chapter 13. It seems to turn up almost everywhere. The input data for this curve is shown in Figure 12-17, and several levels of the curve appear in Figure 12-18.

```
Edit L System parameters
Use arrows to move cursor, 'Enter' to exit:
    Initiator: R
    d generator (skip):
    D generator (draw line):
    L generator (left): +R-L-R+
    R generator (right): -L+R+L-
    X generator (draw line):
    Y generator (draw line):
    T generator (draw line):
    Starting X coordinate: -150
    Starting Y coordinate: -120
    Starting angle: 90
    Divisor: 2.000000
    Second divisor: 0.000000
    Third divisor: 0.000000
    Angle: 60.000000
    Line length: 300.000000
```

Figure 12-17. Data for Sierpinski Triangle (sierp.dat)

level = 5

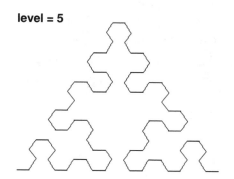

level = 7

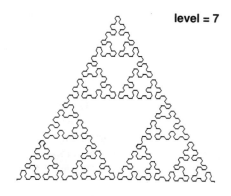

level = 8

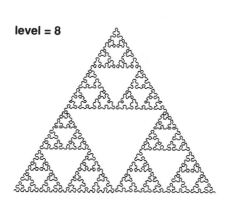

level = 10

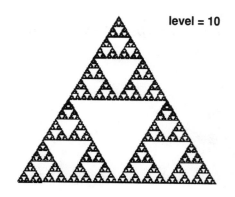

Figure 12-18. The Sierpinski Triangle

Now we come to the Hilbert curve, which is a very strange curve indeed. There are several unusual ways of drawing this curve, which seem to depend upon replacing existing line segments by the generator but also inserting some lines of the length of the previous level. Using L-systems, we can take a new look at the Hilbert curve. Note from the input data of Figure 12-19, that we make frequent use of the generator X which is actually empty. Now, you need to remember how all this works. When the X appears in a string, we draw a line segment of the current length. However, when we start substituting generators for line segments to go on another level, every X is replaced by nothing; i. e. it is just dropped from the new string. The result is the Hilbert curve, of which various levels are shown in Figure 12-20.

```
Edit L System parameters
Use arrows to move cursor, 'Enter' to exit:
    Initiator: T
    d generator (skip):
    D generator (draw line): DXX
    L generator (left):
    R generator (right):
    X generator (draw line):
    Y generator (draw line):
    T generator (draw line): +BDX-TDT-XDB+
    Starting X coordinate: -150
    Starting Y coordinate: -120
    Starting angle: 0
    Divisor: 2.333333
    Second divisor: 0.000000
    Third divisor: 0.000000
    Angle: 90.000000
    Line length: 200.000000
```

Figure 12-19. Data for Hilbert Curve (hilbert.dat)

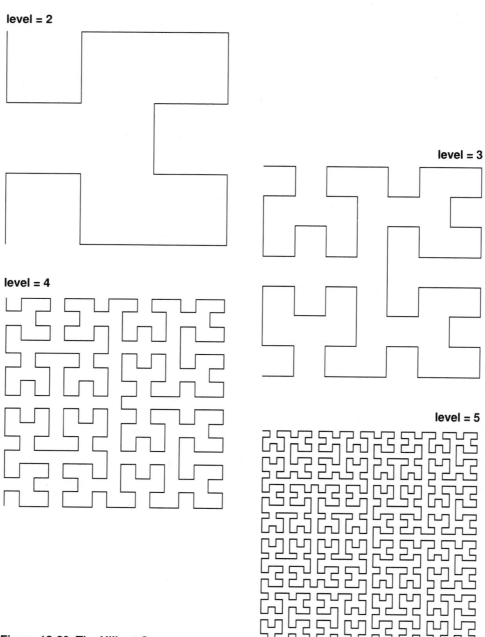

level = 2

level = 3

level = 4

level = 5

Figure 12-20. The Hilbert Curve

Complex Fractal Curves

We now come to three very interesting curves in which a part of the generator consists of smaller steps than the rest of it. To accommodate such complex curves, we have added *{}* and <> to the L-systems language. Everything between the curly brackets is divided by the second divisor instead of the usual divisor, and everything within <> is divided by the third divisor instead of the usual divisor. This permits having three different-sized line segments, although the most we've used is two. You may be able to create a new fractal that has three different-sized line segments. We'll begin with a curve that has all the same size line segments, but a very peculiar shape. It is the seven segment Peano snowflake curve. The input data for it appears in Figure 12-21 and several levels of the curve are shown in Figure 12-22. The shape of the generator is that of the figure where level = 2. The next curve is the thirteen segment Peano snowflake curve, which uses two different sized line segments. The input data for this curve appears in Figure 12-23 and several levels of the curve are shown in Figure 12-24. Again level = 2 represents the shape of the generator. Finally is the curve that Mandelbrot calls *Split Snowflake Halls*. The input data for this curve appear in Figure 12-25 and several levels of the curve (including level = 2, which is the generator) are shown in Figure 12-26.

Edit L System parameters
Use arrows to move cursor, 'Enter' to exit:
    Initiator: T
    d generator (skip):
    D generator (draw line):
    L generator (left):
    R generator (right):
    X generator (draw line):
    Y generator (draw line):
    T generator (draw line): - -Bt++t++t+++{b}- - - -Bt
    Starting X coordinate: -150
    Starting Y coordinate: -120
    Starting angle: 90
    Divisor: 3.000000
    Second divisor: 0.577350
    Third divisor: 0.000000
    Angle: 30.000000
    Line length: 300.000000

Figure 12-21. Data for Peano Seven Segment Snowflake (sevensg.dat)

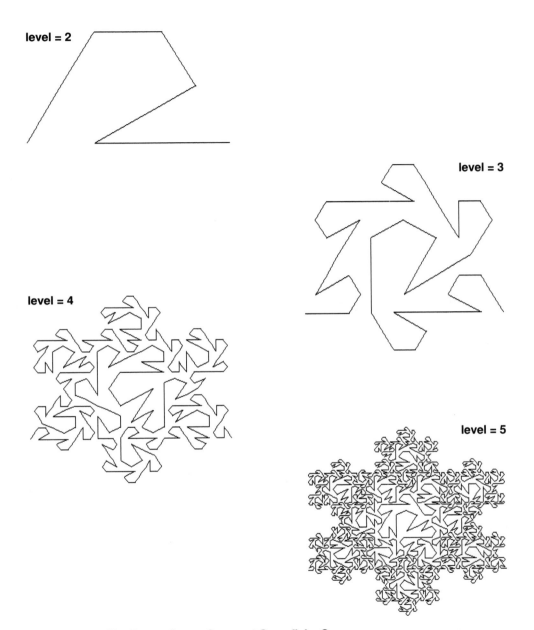

Figure 12-22. The Peano Seven Segment Snowflake Curve

Edit L System parameters
Use arrows to move cursor, 'Enter' to exit:
    Initiator: T
    d generator (skip):
    D generator (draw line):
    L generator (left):
    R generator (right):
    X generator (draw line):
    Y generator (draw line):
    T generator (draw line): - -BT++T++T+++++{TB- -B- -B- -
    }T{+++++TB}- - - -BT
    Starting X coordinate: -150
    Starting Y coordinate: -120
    Starting angle: 90
    Divisor: 3.000000
    Second divisor: 1.732051
    Third divisor: 0.000000
    Angle: 30.000000
    Line length: 300.000000

Figure 12-23. Data for Thirteen Segment Snowflake Curve (snow13.dat)

level = 2

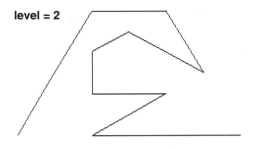

level = 3

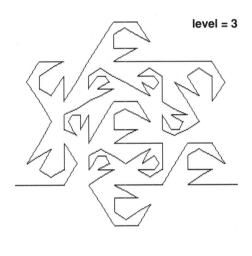

level = 4

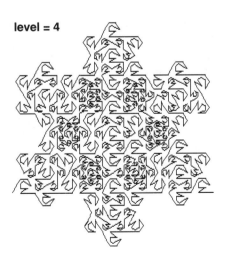

Figure 12-24. The Peano Thirteen Segment Snowflake Curve

Edit L System parameters
Use arrows to move cursor, 'Enter' to exit:
    Initiator: T
    d generator (skip): dddddd
    D generator (draw line):
    L generator (left):
    R generator (right):
    X generator (draw line):
    Y generator (draw line):
    T generator (draw line): - -Bt++T++t+++++{tB- -b- -bT}- - - -bT
    Starting X coordinate: -150
    Starting Y coordinate: -120
    Starting angle: 90
    Divisor: 3.000000
    Second divisor: 1.732051
    Third divisor: 0.000000
    Angle: 30.000000
    Line length: 300.000000

Figure 12-25. Data for Split Snowflake Halls Curve (snowhall.dat)

level = 2

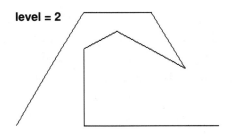

level = 3

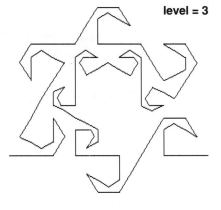

level = 4

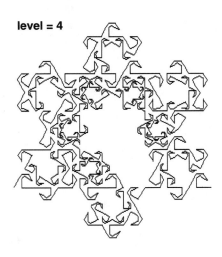

level = 5

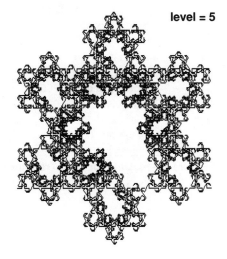

Figure 12-26. Split Snowflake Halls

239

Trees and Bushes

I mentioned earlier that the L-systems technique was first developed to represent the geometry of plants. You probably thought that was the last you'd hear of that subject. Not so. Here we are going to discuss trees and give you examples of six trees and one bush, whose input data and pictures at various levels are shown in Figures 12-27 to 12-40. The key to drawing trees, is having a mechanism that allows a branching point to be selected. At this point, the fractal continues on in the usual manner, but at some point the turtle returns to this selected point and draws another set of branches in a different direction. The L-systems language uses [] to perform this operation. At the beginning bracket, the turtle location and direction are stored; when the end bracket is encountered, the turtle is restored to the saved position and direction. The resulting trees appear in the figures.

```
Edit L System parameters
Use arrows to move cursor, 'Enter' to exit:
      Initiator: X
      d generator (skip):
      D generator (draw line): DD
      L generator (left):
      R generator (right):
      X generator (draw line): D[+X]D[-X]+X
      Y generator (draw line):
      T generator (draw line):
      Starting X coordinate: 0
      Starting Y coordinate: -160
      Starting angle: 0
      Divisor: 2.000000
      Second divisor: 0.000000
      Third divisor: 0.000000
      Angle: 22.500000
      Line length: 180.000000
```

Figure 12-14. Data for First Tree (tree1.dat)

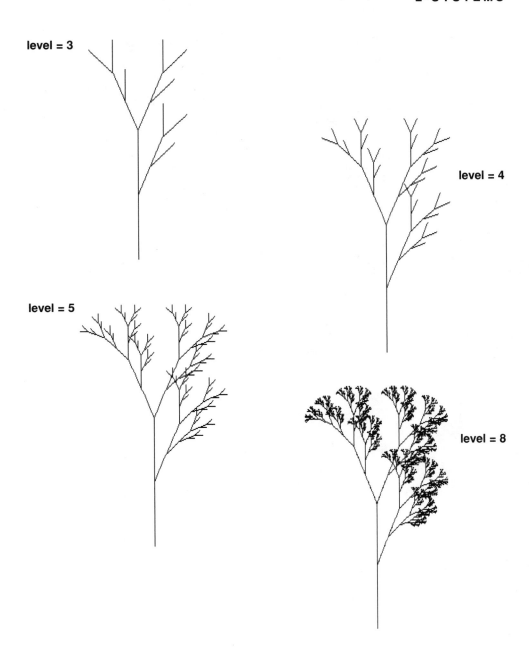

level = 3

level = 4

level = 5

level = 8

Figure 12-28. First Tree

Edit L System parameters
Use arrows to move cursor, 'Enter' to exit:
    Initiator: D
    d generator (skip):
    D generator (draw line): D[+D]D[-D]D
    L generator (left):
    R generator (right):
    X generator (draw line):
    Y generator (draw line):
    T generator (draw line):
    Starting X coordinate: 0
    Starting Y coordinate: -160
    Starting angle: 0
    Divisor: 2.700000
    Second divisor: 0.000000
    Third divisor: 0.000000
    Angle: 26.500000
    Line length: 200.000000

Figure 12-29. Data for Second Tree (tree2.dat)

level = 3

level = 4

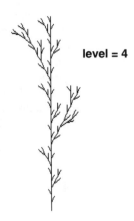

level = 5

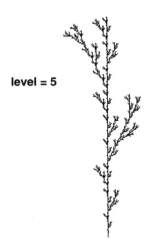

Figure 12-30. Second Tree

Edit L System parameters
Use arrows to move cursor, 'Enter' to exit:
    Initiator: X
    d generator (skip):
    D generator (draw line):
    L generator (left):
    R generator (right):
    X generator (draw line): D[+X][-X]DX
    Y generator (draw line):
    T generator (draw line):
    Starting X coordinate: 0
    Starting Y coordinate: -160
    Starting angle: 0
    Divisor: 2.000000
    Second divisor: 0.000000
    Third divisor: 0.000000
    Angle: 27.900000
    Line length: 200.000000

Figure 12-31. Data for Third Tree (tree3.dat)

level = 3

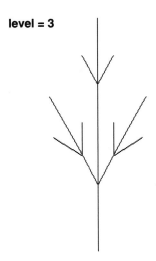

level = 5

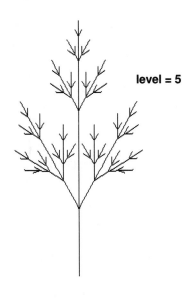

level = 6

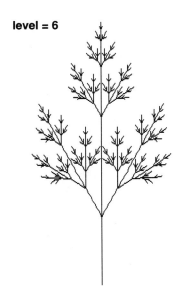

level = 8

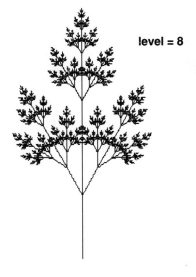

Figure 12-32. Third Tree

```
Edit L System parameters
Use arrows to move cursor, 'Enter' to exit:
      Initiator: D
      d generator (skip):
      D generator (draw line): DD-[-D+D+D]+[+D-D-D]
      L generator (left):
      R generator (right):
      X generator (draw line):
      Y generator (draw line):
      T generator (draw line):
      Starting X coordinate: 0
      Starting Y coordinate: -160
      Starting angle: 0
      Divisor: 2.000000
      Second divisor: 0.000000
      Third divisor: 0.000000
      Angle: 23.000000
      Line length: 110.000000
```

Figure 12-33. Data for Fourth Tree (tree4.dat)

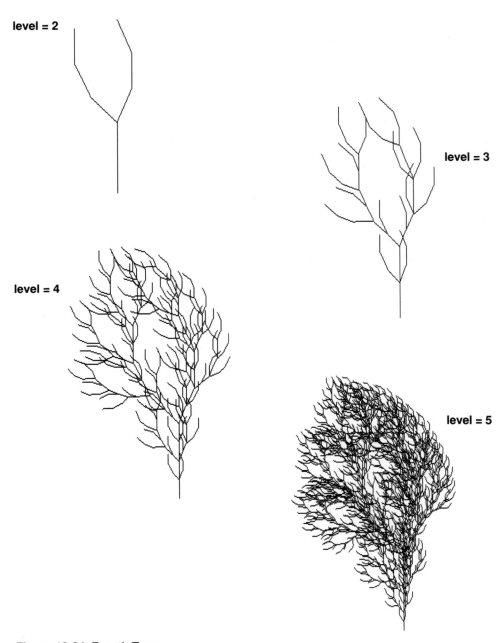

level = 2

level = 3

level = 4

level = 5

Figure 12-34. Fourth Tree

```
Edit L System parameters
Use arrows to move cursor, 'Enter' to exit:
      Initiator: X
      d generator (skip):
      D generator (draw line): DD
      L generator (left):
      R generator (right):
      X generator (draw line): D-[[X]+X]+D[+DX]-X
      Y generator (draw line):
      T generator (draw line):
      Starting X coordinate: 0
      Starting Y coordinate: -160
      Starting angle: 0
      Divisor: 2.000000
      Second divisor: 0.000000
      Third divisor: 0.000000
      Angle: 22.700000
      Line length: 150.000000
```

Figure 12-35. Data for Fifth Tree (tree5.dat)

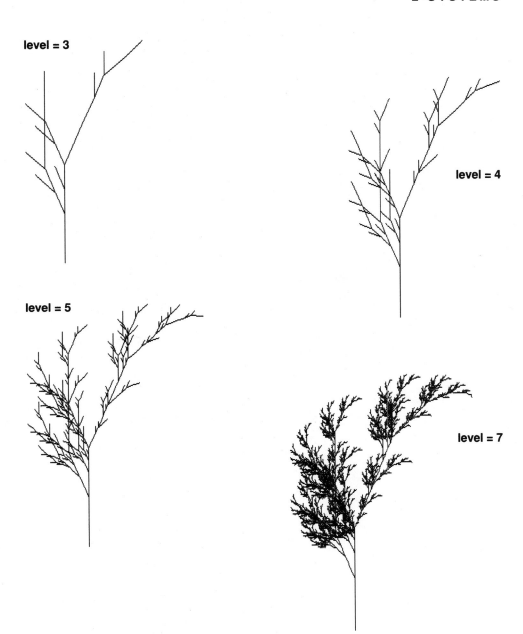

level = 3

level = 4

level = 5

level = 7

Figure 12-36. Fifth Tree

Edit L System parameters
Use arrows to move cursor, 'Enter' to exit:
    Initiator: D
    d generator (skip):
    D generator (draw line): D[+D]D[-D][D]
    L generator (left):
    R generator (right):
    X generator (draw line): D[+X][-X]DX
    Y generator (draw line):
    T generator (draw line):
    Starting X coordinate: 0
    Starting Y coordinate: -160
    Starting angle: 0
    Divisor: 2.000000
    Second divisor: 0.000000
    Third divisor: 0.000000
    Angle: 29.300000
    Line length: 200.000000

Figure 12-37. Data for Sixth Tree (tree6.dat)

level = 2

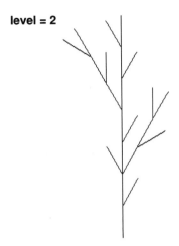

level = 3

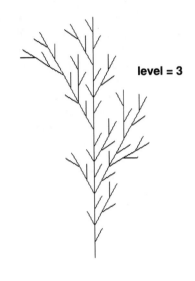

level = 4

level = 6

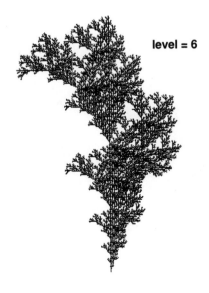

Figure 12-38. Sixth Tree

```
Edit L System parameters
Use arrows to move cursor, 'Enter' to exit:
    Initiator: RLDDD
    d generator (skip):
    D generator (draw line): D
    L generator (left): [-DDD][+DDD]D
    R generator (right): [+++X][—X]TR
    X generator (draw line): +Y[-X]L
    Y generator (draw line): -X[+Y]L
    T generator (draw line): TL
    Starting X coordinate: 0
    Starting Y coordinate: -150
    Starting angle: 0
    Divisor: 1.300000
    Second divisor: 0.000000
    Third divisor: 0.000000
    Angle: 18.000000
    Line length: 60.000000
```

Figure 12-39. Data for Bush (bush.dat)

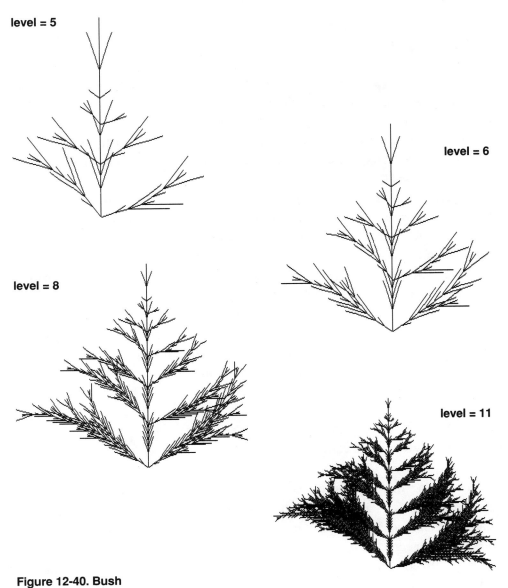

level = 5

level = 6

level = 8

level = 11

Figure 12-40. Bush

The *lsystems.c* Program

The *lsystems.c* program is a stand-alone program, so there may be some duplication of functions that are in the *ftools.cpp* package. However, there are also some subtle differences in some of the functions, that will be described when we get to them. This program is listed in Figure 12-1. The program begins with an infinite *for* loop. This loop never ends, so that there has to be some other way to terminate the program when that is desired. The program next sets up a full screen-sized window and then clears the screen by clearing this window. A smaller window is then set up, with a red background, and the legend, "Generate fractal curve (Y/N): ", is displayed. The program then waits for a keyboard entry. If an 'n' or 'N' is entered, the program terminates and returns to DOS. This is the only way to end the program, otherwise it loops forever, generating fractal curves. Next, the program opens a new window and clears it to a green background. The legend, "Enter file name: " is displayed. The program then reads the user entered filename from the keyboard. It then attempts to open this file (which contains the data for an L-systems display) and if successful, reads all of the file data into the file variables. (Note that if you enter the name of a non-existent file, the program will simply not read in any data. The various parameters will then contain whatever they held previously, and after editing, this data will ultimately be transferred to the new file.) The file is closed and a new window, with a blue background, is created. This window is headed:

Edit L System Parameters
Use arrows to move cursor, 'Enter' to exit:

Following this is a list of parameters as shown in Figure 12-1, and many succeeding figures. The very first string to be entered is the *initiator*, which is the starting geometry of the fractal. It may be a straight line, a triangle, a square, or some other simple geometric figure. Next come a series of generators, of which we have already defined D and d. Skipping down, we have the starting x and y coordinates. If you are creating a new fractal, these have to be found by trial and error to create a nicely centered fractal display. We are using a coordinate system in which the center of the screen is (0,0), x varies from -320 (at the left of the screen) to +319 (at the right of the screen) and y varies from -240 (at the bottom of the screen) to +239 (at the top). The *divisor* divides the step size to reduce it at each level in the recursion process, so that the new sets of steps will take up exactly the space of the old line segment. This depends upon what kind of fractal you are going to draw. If you replace an old line segment with a generator consisting of four line segments, each one third of the length of the original line segment, then your divisor is three. Next a second and third divisor are presented if they are needed for complicated fractals. The turn angle (in degrees) is then given. This is the angle that the turtle turns when you specify a + or - sign in a generator. Finally, the length of the line segment for the original step is specified.

The program then enters a *while* loop, which iterates until the Enter key is pressed. Within this loop, the arrow keys are recognized and used to move the cursor about the display. Any other character that is entered is displayed on the screen at the current cursor position. When the loop is terminated, every data item on the screen is read from its beginning to the first space. The resulting string is converted to an integer or floating point number, if necessary, and then stored in the proper memory location for the particular variable. The data file is then reopened for writing and these variables are all stored in it. Let us recapitulate what happens in this process. First, a file name is specified. An attempt is made to open this file. If successful, the file data is stored in the proper variables. Otherwise, the variables are unchanged. The variables are then displayed on the screen. The user may move the cursor around and change any variable as desired. The new information is then stored in the variable locations and saved to the file.

Once the input data has been edited and stored, the program creates the special generators B, t, and b. To create B (the bottom side generator), we interchange all of the angle signs and change all B's to T's and visa-versa and likewise interchange the b's and t's. Next we generate the backward generators by copying T and B into new generator arrays, and reversing them. We then have to reverse all of the *{}* and *<>* pairs so that they are in the right direction. Now we compute and store the length of each generator string. Then the program enters a *while* loop which it continues to iterate at each keystroke, as long as that keystroke is the Enter key. At the beginning of the loop, the screen is set to the graphics mode and cleared, the turtle is set to the beginning position, and the level is increased by one. The line length for the top level is set to the beginning line length, and the *generate* function is called to create the fractal. When the fractal is complete, the program awaits a keystroke. If the user hits the *Enter* key, the program iterates and generates a new fractal at the next higher level. If any other key is hit, the program terminates.

```
/*

    lsystems = Program to generate L system fractals

    By Roger T. Stevens 9-20-90

*/

#include <stdio.h>
#include <math.h>
#include <dos.h>
#include <conio.h>
#include <ctype.h>

#define UP_ARROW        328
#define DOWN_ARROW      336
#define LEFT_ARROW      331
#define RIGHT_ARROW     333
#define BACKSPACE       8

void cls(int color);
void drawLine(int x1, int y1, int x2, int y2, int color);
void generate (int type, float X1, float Y1, float X2, float Y2,
      float line_dim,      int level);
void plot(int x, int y, int color);
char read_char_from_screen(int x, int y);
void setMode(int mode);
void step (int type,int level, float turtle_r);
void turn(float angle);

char generator[11][128];

int LINEWIDTH = 1;
```

```
unsigned long int PATTERN=0xFFFFFFFF;
int attr, i, j, k, index=0, type, length[12];
int level,key, cursor_pos[16] = {16,25,30,25,26,30,30,30,28,28,21,
    14,21,20,12,18}, start_x, start_y, start_angle, cursor_x, cursor_y;
char filename[32], buffer[64],div_buf[64],ch;
float turtle_x,turtle_y, turtle_theta, angle, divisor, first_line,div2,
    div3,line_length[128], store_x[32], store_y[32], store_theta[32];
FILE *file;

main()
{
    for(;;)
    {
        level = 0;
        key = 0;
        setMode(3);
        window(0,0,79,24);
        textbackground(0);
        clrscr();
        textbackground(4);
        textcolor(15);
        window(15,5,60,8);
        clrscr();
        gotoxy(3,1);
        printf("Generate fractal curve (Y/N): ");
        ch = getch();
        if ((ch == 'N') || (ch == 'n'))
            exit(0);
        textbackground(2);
        textcolor(0);
        window(15,5,60,8);
        clrscr();
        gotoxy(3,1);
        printf("Enter file name: ");
        scanf("%s",&filename);
        file = fopen(filename,"rb");
        if (file != NULL)
        {
            i = 0;
            for (j=0; j<8; j++)
```

```
        {
                while ((generator[j][i++] = fgetc(file)) != NULL);
                i = 0;
        }
        fread(&start_x,1,2,file);
        fread(&start_y,1,2,file);
        fread(&start_angle,1,2,file);
        fread(&divisor,1,4,file);
        fread(&div2,1,4,file);
        fread(&div3,1,4,file);
        fread(&angle,1,4,file);
        fread(&first_line,1,4,file);
}
fclose(file);
textbackground(1);
textcolor(14);
window(3,5,78,22);
clrscr();
cursor_x = cursor_pos[0];
cursor_y = 3;
gotoxy(3,1);
printf("Edit L System parameters");
gotoxy(3,2);
printf("Use arrows to move cursor, 'Enter' to exit: ");
gotoxy(5,3);
printf("Initiator: %s",generator[0]);
gotoxy(5,4);
printf("d generator (skip): %s",generator[1]);
gotoxy(5,5);
printf("D generator (draw line): %s",generator[2]);
gotoxy(5,6);
printf("L generator (left): %s",generator[3]);
gotoxy(5,7);
printf("R generator (right): %s",generator[4]);
gotoxy(5,8);
printf("X generator (draw line): %s",generator[5]);
gotoxy(5,9);
printf("Y generator (draw line): %s",generator[6]);
gotoxy(5,10);
printf("T generator (draw line): %s",generator[7]);
```

```
gotoxy(5,11);
printf("Starting X coordinate: %d",start_x);
gotoxy(5,12);
printf("Starting Y coordinate: %d",start_y);
gotoxy(5,13);
printf("Starting angle: %d",start_angle);
gotoxy(5,14);
printf("Divisor: %f",divisor);
gotoxy(5,15);
printf("Second divisor: %f",div2);
gotoxy(5,16);
printf("Third divisor: %f",div3);
gotoxy(5,17);
printf("Angle: %f",angle);
gotoxy(5,18);
printf("Line length: %f",first_line);
k = 0;
while (key != 0x0D)
{
    gotoxy(cursor_x, cursor_y);
    key = getch();
    if (key == 0x00)
        key = getch() + 256;
    switch (key)
    {
        case UP_ARROW:
            k—;
            if (k<0)
                k = 15;
                cursor_x = cursor_pos[k];
                cursor_y = k + 3;
                break;
        case DOWN_ARROW:
            k++;
            if (k>15)
                k = 0;
                cursor_x = cursor_pos[k];
                cursor_y = k + 3;
                break;
        case LEFT_ARROW:
```

```
                    case BACKSPACE:
                        if (cursor_x > cursor_pos[k])
                            cursor_x—;
                        break;
                    case RIGHT_ARROW:
                        if (cursor_x < 78)
                            cursor_x++;
                        break;
                    default:
                        printf("%c",key);
                        cursor_x++;
            }
        }
        for (k=0; k<8; k++)
        {
            i = 0;
            cursor_x = cursor_pos[k];
            cursor_y = k + 3;
            while ((generator[k][i++] =
                read_char_from_screen(cursor_x++,
                cursor_y)) != ' ');
                generator[k][—i] = NULL;
        }
        i = 0;
        cursor_x = cursor_pos[8];
        while ((buffer[i++] = read_char_from_screen(cursor_x++,
            11)) != ' ');
        buffer[i] = NULL;
        start_x = atoi(buffer);
        i = 0;
        cursor_x = cursor_pos[9];
        while ((buffer[i++] = read_char_from_screen(cursor_x++,
            12)) != ' ');
        buffer[i] = NULL;
        start_y = atoi(buffer);
        i = 0;
        cursor_x = cursor_pos[10];
        while ((buffer[i++] = read_char_from_screen(cursor_x++,
            13)) != ' ');
        buffer[i] = NULL;
```

```
start_angle = atoi(buffer);
i = 0;
cursor_x = cursor_pos[11];
while ((buffer[i++] = read_char_from_screen(cursor_x++,
        14)) != ' ');
buffer[i] = NULL;
divisor = atof(buffer);
i = 0;
cursor_x = cursor_pos[12];
while ((buffer[i++] = read_char_from_screen(cursor_x++,
        15)) != ' ');
buffer[i] = NULL;
div2 = atof(buffer);
i = 0;
cursor_x = cursor_pos[13];
while ((buffer[i++] = read_char_from_screen(cursor_x++,
        16)) != ' ');
buffer[i] = NULL;
div3 = atof(buffer);
i = 0;
cursor_x = cursor_pos[14];
while ((buffer[i++] = read_char_from_screen(cursor_x++,
        17)) != ' ');
buffer[i] = NULL;
angle = atof(buffer);
i = 0;
cursor_x = cursor_pos[15];
while ((buffer[i++] = read_char_from_screen(cursor_x++,
        18)) != ' ');
buffer[i] = NULL;
first_line = atof(buffer);
file = fopen(filename,"wb");
if (file != NULL)
{
    for (j=0; j<8; j++)
    {
        i = 0;
        while (generator[j][i] != NULL)
            fputc (generator[j][i++],file);
        fputc (NULL,file);
```

```
            }
            fwrite(&start_x,1,2,file);
            fwrite(&start_y,1,2,file);
            fwrite(&start_angle,1,2,file);
            fwrite(&divisor,1,4,file);
            fwrite(&div2,1,4,file);
            fwrite(&div3,1,4,file);
            fwrite(&angle,1,4,file);
            fwrite(&first_line,1,4,file);
        }
        fclose(file);
        i = 0;
        while (generator[7][i] != NULL)
        {
            switch(generator[7][i])
            {
                case '+':
                    generator[8][i] = '-';
                    break;
                case '-':
                    generator[8][i] = '+';
                    break;
                case 'T':
                    generator[8][i] = 'B';
                    break;
                case 'B':
                    generator[8][i] = 'T';
                    break;
                case 't':
                    generator[8][i] = 'b';
                    break;
                case 'b':
                    generator[8][i] = 't';
                    break;
                default:
                    generator[8][i] = generator[7][i];
                    break;
            }
            i++;
        }
```

```
generator[8][i] = NULL;
strcpy(generator[9],generator[7]);
strrev(generator[9]);
strcpy(generator[10],generator[8]);
strrev(generator[10]);
i = 0;
while (generator[9][i] != NULL)
{
    switch(generator[9][i])
    {
        case '{':
            generator[9][i] = '}';
            break;
        case '}':
            generator[9][i] = '{';
            break;
        case '<':
            generator[9][i] = '>';
            break;
        case '>':
            generator[9][i] = '<';
            break;
    }
    switch(generator[10][i])
    {
        case '{':
            generator[10][i] = '}';
            break;
        case '}':
            generator[10][i] = '{';
            break;
        case '<':
            generator[10][i] = '>';
            break;
        case '>':
            generator[10][i] = '<';
            break;
    }
    i++;
}
```

```
for (i=0; i<11; i++)
    length[i] = strlen(generator[i]);
while (key == 0x0D)
{
    setMode(16);
    cls(0);
    turtle_x = start_x;
    turtle_y = start_y;
    level++;
    line_length[level] = first_line;
    generate (0, start_x,start_y,0,start_angle,
        first_line*divisor,level);
    key = getch();
}
}
}

/*
```

```
generate() = Generates a curve
```

```
*/

void generate (int type, float X1, float Y1, float X2, float Y2,
    float line_dim, int level)
{
    int j,k,line;
    float turtle_r;

    if (type == 0)
    {
        turtle_theta = Y2;
    }
    turtle_r = line_dim / divisor;
    turtle_x = X1;
    turtle_y = Y1;
    level—;
    for(j=0; j<length[type]; j++)
    {
        switch(generator[type][j])
```

```
{
    case 'd':
        step(1,level,turtle_r);
        break;
    case 'D':
        step(2,level,turtle_r);
        break;
    case 'T':
        step(7,level,turtle_r);
        break;
    case 'B':
        step(8,level,turtle_r);
        break;
    case 't':
        step(9,level,turtle_r);
        break;
    case 'b':
        step(10,level,turtle_r);
        break;
    case 'L':
        step(3,level,turtle_r);
        break;
    case 'H':
        step(11,level,turtle_r);
        break;
    case 'R':
        step(4,level,turtle_r);
        break;
    case 'X':
        step(5,level,turtle_r);
        break;
    case 'Y':
        step(6,level,turtle_r);
        break;
    case '+':
        turn(angle);
        break;
    case '-':
        turn(-angle);
        break;
```

```
        case '[':
            store_x[index] = turtle_x;
            store_y[index] = turtle_y;
            store_theta[index++] = turtle_theta;
            break;
        case ']':
            turtle_x = store_x[—index];
            turtle_y = store_y[index];
            turtle_theta = store_theta[index];
            break;
        case '{':
            turtle_r /= div2;
            break;
        case '}':
            turtle_r *= div2;
            break;
        case '<':
            turtle_r /= div3;
            break;
        case '>':
            turtle_r *= div3;
            break;
        }
    }
}


/*
```

┌──┐
│ ┌──┐ │
│ │ step() = Advances the turtle by step r in current direction   │ │
│ └──┘ │
└──┘

```
*/

void step (int type,int level, float turtle_r)
{
    float x1,y1;
    x1 = turtle_x;
    y1 = turtle_y;
    turtle_y += turtle_r*cos(turtle_theta*.017453292);
    turtle_x += turtle_r*sin(turtle_theta*.017453292);
```

```
        if ((level != 0) && (type != 11))
            generate (type, x1, y1, turtle_x, turtle_y, turtle_r, level);
        else
            if (type !=1)
                drawLine (x1,y1,turtle_x,turtle_y,15);
}
```

```
/*
```

┌───┐
│ ┌───┐ │
│ │   turn() = Changes turtle pointing direction   │ │
│ └───┘ │
└───┘

```
*/
```

```
void turn(float angle)
{
    turtle_theta += angle;
}
```

```
/*
```

┌───┐
│ ┌───┐ │
│ │   drawLine() = Draws a line from one set of coordinates to another │ │
│ │   in a designated color.   │ │
│ └───┘ │
└───┘

```
*/
```

```
void drawLine(int x1, int y1, int x2, int y2, int color)
{
    extern int LINEWIDTH;
    extern unsigned long int PATTERN;
    union REGS reg;

    #define sign(x) ((x) > 0 ? 1: ((x) == 0 ? 0: (-1)))

    int dx, dy, dxabs, dyabs, i, j, px, py, sdx, sdy, x, y;
    unsigned long int mask=0x80000000L;

    x1 += 320;
    y1 = 175 - ((y1*93) >> 7);
    x2 += 320;
```

```c
y2 = 175 - ((y2*93) >> 7);
dx = x2 - x1;
dy = y2 - y1;
sdx = sign(dx);
sdy = sign(dy);
dxabs = abs(dx);
dyabs = abs(dy);
x = 0;
y = 0;
px = x1;
py = y1;
if (dxabs >= dyabs)
{
     for (i=0; i<dxabs; i++)
     {
          mask = mask ? mask : 0x80000000L;
          y += dyabs;
          if (y>=dxabs)
          {
               y -= dxabs;
               py += sdy;
          }
          px += sdx;
          if (PATTERN & mask)
               {
               for (j=-LINEWIDTH/2; j<=LINEWIDTH/2; j++)
                    plot(px,py+j,color);
          }
          mask >>= 1;
     }
}
else
{
     for (i=0; i<dyabs; i++)
     {
          mask = mask ? mask : 0x80000000L;
          x += dxabs;
          if (x>=dyabs)
          {
               x -= dyabs;
```

```
                px += sdx;
                }
            py += sdy;
            if (PATTERN & mask)
            {
                for (j=-LINEWIDTH/2; j<=LINEWIDTH/2; j++)
                    plot(px+j,py,color);
            }
                mask >>= 1;
        }
    }
}

/*
```

```
plot() = Plots a point to the screen at designated system coordinates
                using a selected color.
```

```
*/

void plot(int x, int y, int color)     /* plot pixel at x, y */
{

    #include <dos.h>

    #define seq_out(index,val) {outp(0x3C4,index);\
                        outp(0x3C5,val);}
    #define graph_out(index,val) {outp(0x3CE,index);\
                        outp(0x3CF,val);}

    unsigned int offset;
    int dummy,mask,page;
    char far * mem_address;

    if ((x>= 0) && (x<640) && (y>=0) && (y<350))
    {
        offset = (long)y * 80L + ((long)x / 8L);
        mem_address = (char far *) 0xA0000000L + offset;
        mask = 0x80 >> (x % 8);
        graph_out(8,mask);
```

```
            seq_out(2,0x0F);
            dummy = *mem_address;
            *mem_address = 0;
            seq_out(2,color);
            *mem_address = 0xFF;
            seq_out(2,0x0F);
            graph_out(3,0);
            graph_out(8,0xFF);
        }
}

/*
```

┌───┐
│ ┌──┐   │
│ │ setMode() = Sets video mode   │   │
│ └──┘   │
└───┘

```
*/

void setMode(int mode)
{
    #include <dos.h>
    #include <stdio.h>
    union REGS reg;
    reg.h.ah = 0;
    reg.h.al = mode;
    int86 (0x10,&reg,&reg);
}

/*
```

┌───┐
│ ┌──┐   │
│ │ cls() Clears the screen   │   │
│ └──┘   │
└───┘

```
*/

void cls(int color)
{
    #include <dos.h>
    union REGS reg;
    reg.x.ax = 0x0600;
    reg.x.cx = 0;
    reg.x.dx = 0x184F;
```

```
        reg.h.bh = color;
        int86(0x10,&reg,&reg);
}

/*
```

```
    read_char_from_screen() = reads a character from the screen
```

```
*/

char read_char_from_screen(int x, int y)
{
        union REGS reg;

        char ch;

        gotoxy(x,y);
        reg.h.ah = 3;
        reg.h.bh = 0;
        int86(0x10,&reg,&reg);
        reg.h.ah = 8;
        int86(0x10,&reg,&reg);
        ch = reg.h.al;
        attr = reg.h.ah;
        return(ch);
}
```

Figure 12-41. Listing of the *lsystems.c* Program

The *generate* Function

If the type passed to the *generate* function is zero, the function sets the turtle direction to that passed in the parameter *Y2*. Otherwise the turtle pointing direction is not changed. The turtle step size is set to the length passed to the function, divided by the stated divisor. The turtle location is initialized to the coordinate position passed to the function in *X1* and *Y1*. The level is then reduced by one. Next the function starts a *switch* statement, which it performs for the generator string in the array specified by the *type* parameter for each character in the string associated with that generator. You can see that for every type of generator, the step function is called, with the generator type, level, and turtle step size passed to it. For angles, the *turn* function is called which changes the turtle-pointing direction. For the beginning square bracket, the turtle position and pointing angle are stored. For the closing square bracket, the turtle is returned to the stored position and aimed in the stored direction. For the beginning curly bracket, the turtle step size is divided by the second divisor, and for the ending curly bracket the step size is multiplied by the second divisor. The same actions take place for the carets, using the third divisor.

The *step* Function

The *step* function is the key to the recursive process. It stores the current turtle position and then moves the turtle to a new position determined by the step size and pointing direction. Then, if the level is higher than zero, it calls the *generate* function, which proceeds to process the proper generator string all over again, but at one level lower. When the level passed to is step, instead of calling the *generate* function, *step* draws a line from the old turtle position to the new one, except in the case of the *d* generator, where it just jumps without drawing the line.

Other Functions

The other functions used in the *lsystems* program have already been described in Chapter 3, except for the *drawLine* function. This function is a straightforward implementation of Bresenham's algorithm to draw a line between two points whose coordinates are specified in a specified color and with a specified width and line pattern. The function is used here only to draw solid white lines of one pixel width.

CHAPTER 13

Iterated Function Systems

Michael Barnsley, some of whose fractals are described in Chapter 9, has the distinction of discovering the technique of iterated function systems. Barnsley claims that any picture can be described using the IFS with compression ratios of up to 10,000. However, until recently, concrete details about how to do this sort of thing have been a closely guarded secret. Recently, however, work at the Naval Ocean Systems Center by Dr. Roger D. Boss, E. W. Jacobs, and Y. Fisher has demonstrated techniques for automatically determining the IFS coefficients which describe a desired picture. These people have also done interesting work in Recurrent Iterated Function Systems, about which more will be said later.

Affine Transforms

An affine transform is the combination of a set of rotations, scalings, and linear translations. For a two-dimensional system, the effect of such a transform on a point (x_n, y_n) can be described by the following equations:

$$x_{n+1} = a_i x_n + b_i y_n + e_i$$

$$y_{n+1} = c_i x_n + d_i y_n + f_i \qquad \text{(Equation 13-1)}$$

Barnsley proved the *collage* theorem, which shows that a picture can be accurately described by defining the affine transforms that are needed to produce smaller replicas of the picture positioned to tile the entire picture. The way this process is used is to start with a point and select from the group of affine transforms randomly in accordance with a probability table, where the probability of each transform occurring is usually proportional to the area of the picture that it will cover. This transform is applied to an initial point, another transform is selected and applied to the new point, and the process continues for as long as you want it to. The result is a picture that looks very much like the original.

A Gallery of Images

It is amazing that I have gotten this far in this book without mentioning *Fractint*. This program is in the public domain; you can get it for free on almost any bulletin board or from:

Timothy Wegner
4714 Rockwood
Houston, TX 77004

Tim is also writing a book on how to use Fractint, which should be in the bookstores very soon after you read this. The program has a host of contributing authors, principal among whom are Timothy Wegner, Bert Tyler, and Mark Peterson. The program is one of the best all round fractal programs that I have seen, with more fractals than any commercial program. It is fast (the basic Mandelbrot set is generated in less than 20 seconds), and robust, working with almost any IBM compatible computer and any display card that you can imagine. Don't wait! Get it as soon as you can.

The reason that I mention this program here is that it contains a lot of IFS files containing input data for new images that you haven't seen before. Unfortunately, the IFS part of Fractint generates only the traditional fern. No matter. The *image.c* program to be described below can be set up to read and display the IFS files from Fractint.

There is also a public domain program called *Fdesign*, which is often distributed with Fractint. It was written by Doug Nelson. This program enables you to design your own fractals to match a desired picture. I've looked at some of the fractals that are supplied with it and they are quite interesting. I haven't been able to design my own fractals yet, because Fdesign keeps insisting that I don't have a compatible mouse driver. The fractals designed by Fdesign can be stored in a file format compatible with that used by Fractint, so you should be able to read them with the *image.c* program.

274

The *image.c* Program

Figure 13-1 lists a program to display IFS images. The program is designed to read and display any Fractint *.ifs* file. However, the file contains a lot of information that is not necessary for this program. It should be a simple job to add to this program the capability to read a simpler type of information file and/or to write out such a file to the disk. If you will refer to the *L-systems* program in the previous chapter, you will see an approach to displaying data from the file onto the screen, modifying it, and then rewriting it to disk. You might want to adapt that to this program.

The program begins by entering an infinite *for* loop, which iterates until it is terminated in some way. Next, the program continues by setting the display to the text mode, setting up a full-screen window, clearing the screen to black, and creating a menu window with a blue background. The program then displays, "Hit 'Enter' for another fractal or any other key to exit...". It then reads a key from the keyboard; if that key is not the 'Enter' key, the *break* statement causes the program to leave the infinite loop and the program terminates and returns to DOS. If the 'Enter' key was hit, the program requests, "Enter file name: ". At this point, the user must enter the complete name (including extension) of the desired file. Note that if you make a mistake, you're done for and must restart the program. You can use the backspace to eliminate errors from the display, but the bad characters plus the backspace character will remain as part of the file name and the program will therefore be unable to find a matching file. If the file can't be found, the program prints out an error message and terminates. Otherwise, it asks the user first for a background color and then for a foreground color. These colors (0 to 15) are stored and used to draw the IFS picture. Next, the program begins the process of reading the pertinent data from the file using the function *get_string*.

```
/*

    image.c = Program to display iterated function system images
    By Roger T. Stevens 10-31-90

*/
```

```c
#include <stdio.h>
#include <math.h>
#include <dos.h>
#include <conio.h>
# include <stdlib.h>

void cls(int color);
void get_string(char string_buf[]);
void image_draw(int color);
void plots(int x, int y, int color);
void plot(int x, int y, int color);
void setMode(int mode);

int LINEWIDTH,OPERATOR,XCENTER,YCENTER,ANGLE;
unsigned long int PATTERN;
int adapt,mode,no_transformations,flag;
int j, k, temp, xoffset,yoffset,pr,p_cum[128];
long unsigned int i;
float a[128],b[128],c[128],d[128],e[128],f[128],p[128],p_sum,x,y,
      newx, xmax, xmin, ymax, ymin, xscale, yscale;
char ch, filename[13], buffer[64];
int color, background;
FILE *fin;

void main(void)
{
    for(;;)
    {
        setMode(3);
        window(1,1,80,24);
        textbackground(0);
        clrscr();
        window(10,8,60,15);
        textbackground(1);
        clrscr();
        textcolor(15);
        cprintf(" Hit 'Enter' for another fractal\n");
        gotoxy(6,2);
        cprintf("or any other key to exit...");
        cscanf("%c",&ch);
```

```
if (ch != 0x0d)
    break;
cprintf("\n Enter file name: ");
cscanf("%s",filename);
fin = fopen(filename,"rb");
if (fin == NULL)
{
    cprintf("\n File '%s' not found.", filename);
    getch();
    getch();
    break;
}
cprintf("\n Enter background color (0-15): ");
cscanf("%d",&background);
cprintf("\n Enter foreground color (0-15): ");
cscanf("%d",&color);
get_string(buffer);
no_transformations = atoi(buffer);
if ((strstr(filename,".ifs")) != NULL)
{
    for (i=0; i<6; i++)
        get_string(buffer);
}
for (i=0; i<no_transformations; i++)
{
    get_string(buffer);
    a[i] = atof(buffer);
    get_string(buffer);
    b[i] = atof(buffer);
    get_string(buffer);
    c[i] = atof(buffer);
    get_string(buffer);
    d[i] = atof(buffer);
    get_string(buffer);
    e[i] = atof(buffer);
    get_string(buffer);
    f[i] = atof(buffer);
    get_string(buffer);
    p[i] = atof(buffer);
    if ((strstr(filename,".ifs")) != NULL)
```

277

```
            {
                get_string(buffer);
                get_string(buffer);
            }
        }
        fclose(fin);
        setMode(16);
        p_sum = 0;
        for (i=0; i<no_transformations; i++)
        {
            p_sum += p[i];
            p_cum[i] = p_sum * 32767;
        }
        cls (background);
        image_draw(color);
        getch();
        getch();
    }
}
/*
```

```
image_draw() = Function to draw an IFS picture
```

```
*/
void image_draw(int color)
{

    int px,py;

    xmax = 0;
    ymax = 0;
    xmin = 0;
    ymin = 0;
    x = 0;
    y = 0;
    flag = 0;
    while (!kbhit())
    {
        for (i=0; i<256; i++)
        {
```

```
temp = rand();
for (k=0; k<no_transformations-1; k++)
{
    if (temp < p_cum[k])
        break;
}
newx = (a[k]* x + b[k] * y + e[k]);
y = (c[k] * x + d[k] * y + f[k]);
x = newx;
if ((flag == 0) && (i > 15))
{
    xmax = max(x,xmax);
    xmin = min(x,xmin);
    ymax = max(y,ymax);
    ymin = min(y,ymin);
}
else
{
    px = x*xscale + xoffset;
    py = (y*yscale + yoffset);
    if ((px>=0) && (px<639) && (py>=0) && (py<349))
        plot (px,349-py,color);
}
}
if (flag == 0)
{
    xscale = 418 / (xmax - xmin);
    yscale = min(315 / (ymax - ymin),xscale/1.38);
    if (yscale < xscale/1.38);
        xscale = 1.38 * yscale;
    xoffset = 320 - (xmax + xmin) * xscale / 2;
    yoffset = 175 - (ymax + ymin) * yscale / 2;
    flag = 1;
}
}
}
```

```
/*
```

```
cls() = Clears the screen
```

```
*/
```

```c
void cls(int color)
        {
        union REGS reg;

                reg.x.ax = 0x0600;
                reg.x.cx = 0;
                reg.x.dx = 0x184F;
                reg.h.bh = color;
                int86(0x10,&reg,&reg);
        }
```

```
/*
```

```
plot() = Plots a point on the screen at designated system coordinates
                         using a selected color.
```

```
*/
```

```c
void plot(int x, int y, int color)
{

    #include <dos.h>

    #define seq_out(index,val) {outp(0x3C4,index);\
                    outp(0x3C5,val);}
    #define graph_out(index,val) {outp(0x3CE,index);\
                    outp(0x3CF,val);}

    unsigned int offset;
    int dummy,mask,page;
    char far * mem_address;

    offset = (long)y * 80L + ((long)x / 8L);
    mem_address = (char far *) 0xA0000000L + offset;
```

```
        mask = 0x80 >> (x % 8);
        graph_out(8,mask);
        seq_out(2,0x0F);
        dummy = *mem_address;
        *mem_address = 0;
        seq_out(2,color);
        *mem_address = 0xFF;
        seq_out(2,0x0F);
        graph_out(3,0);
        graph_out(8,0xFF);

}


/*
    ┌─────────────────────────────────────────────────────┐
    │  setMode() = Sets video mode                          │
    └─────────────────────────────────────────────────────┘
*/

void setMode(int mode)
{
        union REGS reg;

        reg.h.ah = 0;
        reg.h.al = mode;
        int86 (0x10,&reg,&reg);
}

/*
    ┌─────────────────────────────────────────────────────┐
    │  get_string() = Reads a string of data from the input file │
    └─────────────────────────────────────────────────────┘
*/

void get_string(char string_buf[])
{
        char ch;
        int flag = 0,i,result,test;
```

```
        string_buf[0] = NULL;
        while (!feof(fin))
        {
            ch = toupper(fgetc(fin));
            if (flag == 0)
            {
                if ((isalnum(ch)) || (ch == '.') || (ch == '-') ||
                    (ch == ')'))
                {
                    string_buf[0] = ch;
                    break;
                }
                else
                {
                    if (ch == '#')
                        flag = 1;
                }
            }
            else
                if (ch == 0x0D)
                    flag = 0;
        }
        for (i=1; i<32; i++)
        {
            if (ch == ')')
            {
                string_buf[1] = NULL;
                break;
            }
            ch = toupper(fgetc(fin));
            if ((isalnum(ch)) || (ch == '_') || (ch == '.'))
                string_buf[i] = ch;
            else
            {
                string_buf[i] = NULL;
                break;
            }
        }
    }
}
```

Figure 13-1. Listing of image.c Program

This function reads through the file, discarding characters until it finds an alphanumeric or a minus sign or a decimal point. It then stores characters that are alphanumerics, decimal points, or minus signs or underscores in a string in a buffer, ending when the character read is not one of these. The function also has a flag that is set when a # is encountered. No more characters are then stored until a carriage return (0x0D) is encountered to turn the flag back off. The # is used in Fractint *.ifs* files to designate comments, which continue to the end of the line. The only information that is really needed by this program is the number of transforms and the values of *a, b, c, d, e, f,* and *p* for each transform. However the *.ifs* file has a lot more data. Any comments are automatically ignored, but we also have to ignore a number of unneeded numbers. To do this, at critical points the program checks to see whether an *.ifs* file was specified, and if it was, the additional values are read and dumped. My data files contain only the appropriate numbers. As long as they are separated, it doesn't matter what separation characters you use, as *get_string* is fully compatible. I have used the extension .img for my data files, but it doesn't matter. Anything other than an *.ifs* file will be read in the standard manner. The *get_string* function reads each string. It is then converted to an integer or floating point number as appropriate and stored in the proper variable location. When all needed parameters have been read, the file is closed and the screen set to the graphics mode. The *image_draw* function, which actually creates the picture, selects which transformation to use, based upon cumulative probabilities that are scaled in terms of a maximum of 32767. These probabilities are then computed from the standard probability numbers. The program then clears the screen to the desired background color, calls *image_draw* to draw the image, and then waits for a couple of keyboard entries. When these are received, the infinite loop iterates again to draw another fractal.

The *image_draw* Function

The *image_draw* function begins by zeroing the maximum and minimum coordinate values, the starting point, and the flag. It then enters a *while* loop which repeats until there is a keyboard entry. Thus you can watch the picture build and terminate it at any level of detail that you desire. Within the *while* loop is nested a *for* loop that reiterates 256 times. This loop speeds up operation by making sure that the test for a keyboard entry only occurs once for every 256 points plotted.

In previous programs to plot IFS images, one usually had to have a separate set of coordinate scaling factors and coordinate offsets for each fractal that was generated. These were usually found by trial and error and incorporated in the input data. This program determines the scaling and offset automatically. What it does is take the maximums and minimums from the first 256 points and use them to determine the proper scaling and offset to fill the screen and be nicely centered within it. (If a particular IFS has some points at the very extremes that it doesn't ever hit during the first 256 iterations, your scaling and offset will be a little off, but this is not usually a problem.) Once the first 256 iterations have been completed, the flag is set and after that all points are plotted to the screen with the computed scaling and offset. Using the first 256 points to automatically compute scaling and offset is a nice touch, but it also serves an additional purpose, in that the first few points of the IFS to be computed may not really have settled down. By the end of 256 points, these wild points are gone and only a good image appears. For all points, the new x and y coordinates are determined in the same way. First, the function selects a random number between 0 and 32767. It then enters a *for* loop which it leaves when the random number exceeds an entry in the cumulative probability table. The index value when the loop is exited is the index of the set of transformation parameters that are then applied to the old values of x and y to transform to the new coordinates. Figure 13-2 is a table of affine transformation data for six IFS images. You will find these on the disk that comes with this book as *.ifs* files. You will find many more in the Fractint program described earlier. Pictures from four of these are shown in Figures 13-3, 13-4, 13-5, and 13-6.

Recurrent Iterated Function Systems

Boss, Jacobs, and Fisher at the Naval Ocean Systems Center, have done some work on recurrent iterated function systems (RIFS) which make it possible to view these on a PC and gain some understanding of how they work. While the fern and Sierpinski triangle shown above are good examples of self-similar objects which can be ideally represented by the IFS technique, there are some pictures where application of the IFS technique becomes very difficult and the results are not too satisfactory.

The RIFS technique uses a process where affine transforms of only parts of the image are used to cover other parts. This gives considerably more flexibility.

Figure	a	b	c	d	e	f	e
Sierpinski	0.50000	0.0	0.0	0.50000	0.0	0.0	0.3333
Triangle	0.50000	0.0	0.0	0.50000	1.0000	0.0	0.3333
	0.50000	0.0	0.0	0.50000	0.5000	0.5000	0.3333
Fern	0.0	0.0	0.0	0.1600	0.0	0.0	0.0100
	0.20000	-0.2600	0.2300	0.2200	0.0	0.2000	0.0700
	-0.1500	0.28000	0.2600	0.2400	0.0	0.2000	0.0700
	0.85000	0.04000	-0.0400	0.8500	0.0	0.2000	0.8500
Tree	0.0	0.0	0.0	0.5000	0.0	0.0	0.0500
	0.10000	0.0	0.0	0.1000	0.0	0.2000	0.1500
	0.42000	-0.4200	0.4200	0.4200	0.0	0.2000	0.4000
	0.42000	0.4200	-0.4200	0.4200	0.0	0.2000	0.4000
Kantor	0.33333	0.0	0.0	0.3333	0.0	0.0	0.3333
Tree	0.33333	0.0	0.0	0.3333	1.0000	0.0	0.3333
	0.66667	0.0	0.0	0.6667	0.5000	0.5000	0.3334
Circle 2	0.15596	0.98776	-.98776	0.15596	-.0779	0.9124	0.9866
	0.04428	0.0	0.0	0.04116	0.0641	0.4829	0.0032
	0.05566	0.0	0.0	0.04527	0.0998	0.4779	0.0029
	0.11540	0.0	0.0	0.05094	0.1428	0.4761	0.0036
	0.27142	0.0	0.0	0.04932	0.2380	0.4781	0.0036
Maple	0.35173	0.35537	-.35537	0.35173	0.3545	0.5000	0.1773
Leaf	0.35338	-0.3537	0.35373	0.35338	0.2879	0.1528	0.3800
	0.50000	0.0	0.0	0.50000	0.2500	0.4620	0.1773
	0.50154	-0.0018	0.00157	0.58795	0.2501	0.1054	0.2091
	0.00364	0.0	0.0	0.57832	0.5016	0.0606	0.0562

Figure 13-2. Parameters for IFS Displays

Figure 13-3. Sierpinski Triangle

Figure 13-4. Fern

Figure 13-5. Circular Pattern

Figure 13-6. Maple Leaf

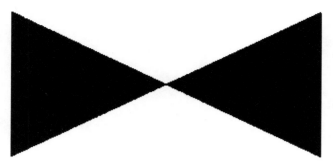

Figure 13-7. Bow Tie

Look at the bow tie of Figure 13-7. This figure is very difficult to produce using the IFS technique. Using the RIFS technique, we can accomplish the job using eight transforms. However, we must exercise the constraint that from transforms 1, 2, and 3 we can only go to transforms 1, 2, 3, or 4. Similarly, from transforms 5, 6, and 7, we can only go to transforms 5, 6, 7, and 8. From transform 4, we can go to transforms 5, 6, 7 and 8, and from transform 8, we can go to transforms 1, 2, 3, and 4. The program listed in Figure 13-8 shows how we accomplish these constraints. We have eliminated the functions that have not changed from the previous program, but they are still needed in order for the program to run. Otherwise, you will see much that is similar to the previous program. One difference is that all of the menu stuff is gone, as well as the code for reading the disk file. Instead a single set of information for the bow tie has been built in. The first major difference that you will note is that although there are eight transforms, there are only four probabilities. This is because there are only four places that the program can go to from any given transform. In some cases, we might have a matrix of probabilities to cover all cases, but in this situation, all of the probabilities are equal, which makes it easy.

```
/*

    rimage.c = Program to generate recurrent iterated function systems.
    By Roger T. Stevens 10-31-90

*/

#include <stdio.h>
```

```
#include <math.h>
#include <dos.h>
#include <conio.h>
# include <stdlib.h>

int LINEWIDTH,OPERATOR,XCENTER,YCENTER,ANGLE;
unsigned long int PATTERN;

void cls(int color);
void image_draw(int color);
void plots(int x, int y, int color);
void plot(int x, int y, int color);
void setMode(int mode);

int adapt,mode,no_transformations,flag;
int j, k, temp, xoffset,yoffset,pr,p_cum[128],plane_sel=0;
long unsigned int i;
float a[128],b[128],c[128],d[128],e[128],f[128],p[128],p_sum,x,y,
      newx, xmax, xmin, ymax, ymin, xscale, yscale;
char ch, filename[13], buffer[32];
int count,color, background;
FILE *fin;

void main(void)
{
    setMode(16);
    no_transformations = 8;
    a[0] =0.5; a[1] = 0.5; a[2] = 0.5; a[3] = 0.5;
    a[4] =0.5; a[5] = 0.5; a[6] = 0.5; a[7] = 0.5;
    b[0] = 0; b[1] = 0; b[2] = 0; b[3] = 0;
    b[4] = 0; b[5] = 0; b[6] = 0; b[7] = 0;
    c[0] = 0; c[1] = 0; c[2] =0; c[3] = 0;
    c[4] = 0; c[5] = 0; c[6] =0; c[7] = 0;
    d[0] = .5; d[1] = .5; d[2] = .5; d[3] = .5;
    d[4] = .5; d[5] = .5; d[6] = .5; d[7] = .5;
    e[0] = -0.5; e[1] = -0.5; e[2] = 0; e[3] = 1.0;
    e[4] = 0.5; e[5] = 0.5; e[6] = 0; e[7] = -1.0;
    f[0] = 0.25; f[1] = -0.25; f[2] = 0; f[3] = 0;
    f[4] = 0.25; f[5] = -0.25; f[6] = 0; f[7] = 0;
    p[0] = .25; p[1] = .25; p[2] = .25; p[3] = .25;
```

```
        background = 1;
        color = 14;
        cls (background);
        p_sum = 0;
        for (i=0; i<no_transformations; i++)
        {
            p_sum += p[i];
            p_cum[i] = p_sum * 32767;
        }
        image_draw(color);
        getch();
        getch();
}

void image_draw(int color)
{

        int px,py;

        xmax = 0;
        ymax = 0;
        xmin = 0;
        ymin = 0;
        x = 0;
        y = 0;
        flag = 0;
        while (!kbhit())
        {
            for (i=0; i<256; i++)
            {
                temp = rand();
                for (k=0; k<3; k++)
                {
                    if (temp < p_cum[k])
                        break;
                }
                if (plane_sel == 1)
                    k += 4;
                newx = (a[k]* x + b[k] * y + e[k]);
                y = (c[k] * x + d[k] * y + f[k]);
```

```
        x = newx;
        if (flag == 0)
        {
            xmax = max(x,xmax);
            xmin = min(x,xmin);
            ymax = max(y,ymax);
            ymin = min(y,ymin);
        }
        else
        {
            px = x*xscale + xoffset;
            py = (y*yscale + yoffset);
            if ((px>=0) && (px<639)
                && (py>=0) && (py<349))
                plot (px,349-py,color);
        }
        if (k==3)
            plane_sel = 1;
        if (k==7)
            plane_sel = 0;
    }
    if (flag == 0)
    {
        xscale = 418 / (xmax - xmin);
        yscale = min(315 / (ymax - ymin),xscale/1.38);
        if (yscale < xscale/1.38);
            xscale = 1.38 * yscale;
        xoffset = 320 - (xmax + xmin) * xscale / 2;
        yoffset = 175 - (ymax + ymin) * yscale / 2;
        flag = 1;
    }
  }
}
```

Figure 13-8. Program to Generate RIFS Bow Tie

The next thing to look at is the portion of *image_draw* which determines the transform index from the probability table. You will note that only numbers from 0 to 3 are available initially. One of these is selected, depending upon the random number that was read. Then, if the variable *plane_sel* has a value of one, 4 is added to the index, so that index values of only 4 to 7 are available. How do we get from one set to the other? If the index takes on a value of 3, we change *plane_sel* to 1, and if the index takes on a value of 7, we change *plane_sel* to 0. This is quite effective for this case, although some more sophisticated techniques might be in order if our RIFS gets more complicated.

Conclusion

We've given a lot of new fractal techniques in this book, and have included some already compiled programs on the disk, so that you can create a lot of fractals without worrying too much about the program details. But if you're interested in proceeding further into the frontier, the source code is there together with enough explanation so that you can branch off on your own and perhaps come up with some new discovery. The field of fractals is expanding rapidly; there is something new everyday. Perhaps you can be the one to make the next new discovery.

APPENDIX A

Format for .PCX Files

The ZSoft *.PCX* file format begins with a 128 byte header, the contents of which are shown below:

Byte	Size (Bytes)	Name	Description
0	1	Password	0AH designates ZSoft.PCX Files
1	1	Version	Versions of PC Paintbrush are:
			0 = vers. 2.5
			2 = vers. 2.8 with palette information.
			3 = vers. 2.8 without palette information.
			5 = vers. 3.0
2	1	Encoding	Encoding scheme used.
			1 = .PCX run length encoding.
3	1	Bits per pixel	No. of bits required to store data for 1 pixel from 1 plane.
			1 = EGA, VGA, or Hercules
			2 = CGA
4	8	Window Dimensions	4 integers (2 bytes each) giving top left and bottom right corners of display in order x1, y1, x2, y2.
12	2	Horizontal Resolution	Horizontal resolution of display device (columns)
			640 = EGA, VGA
			320 = CGA
			720 = Hercules

Byte	Size (Bytes)	Name	Description
14	2	Vertical Resolution	Vertical resolution of display divide (rows) 480 = VGA 350 = EGA 200 = CGA 348 = Hercules
16	48	Color Map	Information on color palette settings. See following figures for details.
64	1	Reserved	
65	1	Number of planes	Number of color planes in the original image 1 = CGA, Hercules 4 = EGA, VGA
66	2	Bytes per line	Number of bytes per scan line in the image
68	2	Palette description information	How to interpret the palette
70	8	Maximum X value	Special for fractal files
78	8	Minimum X value	Special for fractal files
86	8	Maximum Y value	Special for fractal files
94	8	Minimum Y value	Special for fractal files
102	8	P value	Special for fractal files
110	8	Q value	Special for fractal files
118	10	Not used	Fill to the end of the header block

Except for the color map, most of the header contents are self-evident. The items that are noted as being special for the fractal program are not part of the ZSoft format, but have been added to help handle fractal parameters.

The contents of a palette register for the EGA color system is shown as follows. Six bits are used, with two each for the primary colors red, green, and blue. The capital letters represent colors of 75% amplitude; the small letters colors of 25% amplitude. Thus for each of the primary colors, four levels are available: 0 (none of that color), 25% amplitude, 75% amplitude, and 100% amplitude (both capital and small letter bits are one). The color map in the file header contains 16 sets of triples, one for each EGA palette. For the first byte of a triple, the values of the capital and small letter position for red are extracted and combined to produce a number from one to three. This number is multiplied by 85 and stored in the header. The same procedure takes place for the second byte of the triple for green and the third byte for blue. The process is repeated sixteen times, once for each palette. Note that when we set the palette registers on the EGA we are setting a write-only register, so that we can never recover the contents if we want to know later what the setting was. Consequently, our *setEGApalette* function saves the palette register information in a global array *PALETTE [16]* . It is this data that we use to write the color map in the header when we are saving a screen.

The VGA is quite different in the way that it handles colors. With the VGA, each palette register contains the number of a color register. The color register contains six bits, permitting 64 shades of each color. With the VGA we can read the six bit value for each of red, green, and blue, information in the palette registers and in the color registers. To create the color map, we read each palette register and then go and read the color register pointed to by that palette register. We then multiply the red, green, and blue values by four and store the results in the triple associated with that palette. Note that when we restore a screen, we may not assign a color value to the same color register that it was obtained from originally, and that the palette registers may not select the same color registers. However, the net result is the same, because each palette register points to a color register that contains the same color information that was contained in the original screen. The VGA also has a color mode in which 256 different colors may be displayed simultaneously. To use it, we have special screen saving and restoring functions. The format is the same as used to display the 16 color palette, but due to the 256 colors, the palette information is much longer. It is appended at the end of the *.PCX* file. To access this information, you must first ascertain that the version number data in the header (byte 1) is 5 (version 3.0). Then read to the end of the file and count back 769 bytes. If the value in this byte position is '0CH' (12 decimal), the succeeding information is 256 color palette data.

Data is read from the screen, horizontally from left to right, starting at the pixel position for the upper left corner. For EGA and VGA, which have multiple memory planes, a line is read of the color red (to the end of the window boundary), then the green information for the same line is read, and finally the blue.

Data is run-length encoded in the following manner. If the byte is unlike the ones on either side of it, and if its two most significant bits are not 11, it is written to the file. Otherwise a count is made of the number of like bytes (up to 63) and this count is ANDed with *C0H* and the result written to the file, followed by the value of the byte. If there are more that 63 successive like bytes, the count for 63 and the byte are written and then the count begins all over again. (Note that the case for a singular byte having the two most significant bits 1 is handled by writing a count of one followed by the byte value.)

Byte	Palette	Color
16	0	Red
17	0	Green
18	0	Blue
19	1	Red
20	1	Green
21	1	Blue
22	2	Red
23	2	Green
24	2	Blue
25	3	Red
26	3	Green
27	3	Blue
28	4	Red
29	4	Green
30	4	Blue

Byte	Palette	Color
31	5	Red
32	5	Green
33	5	Blue
34	6	Red
35	6	Green
36	6	Blue
37	7	Red
38	7	Green
39	7	Blue
40	8	Red
41	8	Green
42	8	Blue
43	9	Red
44	9	Green
45	9	Blue

Contents of .PCX File Color Map

Byte	Palette	Color
46	10	Red
47	10	Green
48	10	Blue
49	11	Red
50	11	Green
51	11	Blue
52	12	Red
53	12	Green
54	12	Blue

Byte	Palette	Color
55	13	Red
56	13	Green
57	13	Blue
58	14	Red
59	14	Green
60	14	Blue
49	11	Red
50	11	Green
51	11	Blue

Contents of .PCX File Color Map

For the EGA, the values of color of each byte of each triple are: 00H to 54H = 0%, 55H to A9H = 25%, AAH to FEH = 75%. For the VGA, the value of each byte is the value of the six-bit color value from the color register pointed to by the appropriate palette register multiplied by four.

Byte 7	Byte 6	Byte 5	Byte 4	Byte 3	Byte 2	Byte 1	Byte 0
		R	G	B	r	g	b
		75%	75%	75%	25%	25%	25%

Contents of EGA Palette Register

Additions at the End of the .PCX File

The following are the additions to the end of the *.pcx* file for use by the fractal generating programs. They are not sanctioned by ZSoft.

Byte	Size (Bytes)	Name	Description
0	1	Code for additions	0CH designates additions to follow.
1	8	*a* equation parameter	
9	8	*b* equation parameter	
17	8	*c* equation parameter	
25	8	*d* equation parameter	
33	8	*e* equation parameter	
41	8	*f* equation parameter	
49	90	Colors	Color selection and range data.
139	2	maximum number of iterations	
141	2	Color option	Tells way in which colors were selected.
143	4	Starting X value	
147	4	Starting Y value	

Index

299

ADVANCED FRACTAL PROGRAMMING IN C

set_parameters function, 93, 106
seven segment Peano curve, 233
Sierpinski triangle, 9, 157, 229, 284
    data for, 229
    equation for, 157
    listing of function for, 157
    parameters for, 285
    picture(s) of, 286, 230
sine fractals, 128
    parameters for, 130
sine set, 128
    listing of, 129
sinh set, 133
    listing of, 135
sixth tree
    data for, 250
    pictures of, 251
snowflake, von Koch, 8, 212
    data for, 213
    pictures of, 215
sort function, 196
Split Snowflake Halls, 233
    curve, data for, 238
    curve, pictures of, 239
step function, 266
    description of, 272
subdivide function, 164, 169
subdividing the display, 169
subtracting complex numbers in C, 14

T

T Tchebychev
    fractal, listing of function for, 139
    polynomial, 139
    polynomial, coefficients for, 141
Taylor's series, 125
Tchebychev polynomial(s), 7, 138
    fractals, parameters for, 142

textbackground
    function, 19
    setting, 17
textcolor
    function, 19
    setting, 18
third Barnsley fractal
    equation for, 155
    listing of function for, 156
third tree
    data for, 244
    pictures of, 245
thirteen segment Peano curve, 233
three-dimensional
    geometry, 184
    techniques, 8
transcendental functions, 7, 125
transforms, affine, 273
tree(s), 8, 240
    fifth, data for, 248
    fifth, pictures of, 249
    first, data for, 240
    first, pictures of, 241
    fourth, data for, 246
    fourth, pictures of, 247
    parameters for, 285
    second, data for, 242
    second, pictures of, 243
    sixth, data for, 250
    sixth, pictures of, 251
    third, data for, 244
    third, pictures of, 245
Turbo C, 24
Turbo C++, 4, 11, 24, 52, 53, 115
turn function, 267
turtle, 209, 272
Tyler, Bert, 274

304

U
U Tchebychev polynomial, coefficients for, 141
unfinished display, completing, 74

V
VGA, 3, 4, 44, 161, 169, 173, 188, 189
    color register, setting, 44
    high resolution modes, 3
video mode, setting, 43
von Koch
    curve, quadric, 217
    snowflake, 8, 212
vprintf function, 19

W
Wegner, Timothy, 274
window function(s), 16
    for Microsoft C, 16
    for Zortech C++, 16

Z
z-buffering, 174
ZBF file, 174, 199, 200
Zortech C++, 4, 11, 24, 52, 115

A Library of
Technical References
from M&T Books

NetWare User's Guide
by Edward Liebing

Endorsed by Novell, this book informs NetWare users of the services and utilities available, and how to effectively put them to use. Contained is a complete task-oriented reference that introduces users to NetWare and guides them through the basics of NetWare menu-driven utilities and command line utilities. Each utility is illustrated, thus providing a visual frame of reference. You will find general information about the utilities, then specific procedures to perform the task in mind. Utilities discussed include NetWare v2.1 through v2.15. For advanced users, a workstation troubleshooting section is included, describing the errors that occur. Two appendixes, describing briefly the services available in each NetWare menu or command line utility are also included.

Book only	Item #071-0	$24.95

Blueprint of a LAN
by Craig Chaiken

Blueprint of a LAN provides a hands-on introduction to microcomputer networks. For programmers, numerous valuable programming techniques are detailed. Network administrators will learn how to build and install LAN communication cables, configure and troubleshoot network hardware and software, and provide continuing support to users. Included are a very inexpensive zero-slot, star topology network, remote printer and file sharing, remote command execution, electronic mail, parallel processing support, high-level language support, and more. Also contained is the complete Intel 8086 assembly language source code that will help you build an inexpensive to install, local area network. An optional disk containing all source code is available.

Book & Disk (MS-DOS)	Item #066-4	$39.95
Book only	Item #052-4	$29.95

Fractal Programming in C
by Roger T. Stevens

If you are a programmer wanting to learn more about fractals, this book is for you. Learn how to create pictures that have both beauty and an underlying mathematical meaning. Included are over 50 black and white pictures and 32 full color fractals. All source code to reproduce these pictures is provided on disk in MS-DOS format and requires an IBM PC or clone with an EGA or VGA card, a color monitor, and a Turbo C, Quick C, or Microsoft C compiler.

Book/Disk (MS-DOS)	Item #038-9	$36.95
Book only	Item #037-0	$26.95

Fractal Programming in Turbo Pascal
by Roger T. Stevens

This book equips Turbo pascal programmers with the tools needed to program dynamic fractal curves. It is a reference that gives full attention to developing the reader's understanding of various fractal curves. More than 100 black and white and 32 full color fractals are illustrated throughout the book. All source code to reproduce the fractals is available on disk in MS/PC-DOS format. Requires a PC or clone with EGA or VGA, color monitor, and Turbo Pascal 4.0 or better.

Book/Disk (MS-DOS)	Item #107-5	$39.95
Book	Item #106-7	$29.95

Programming the 8514/A
by Jake Richter and Bud Smith

Written for programmers who want to develop software for the 8514/A, this complete reference includes information on both the 8514/A register and adapter Interface. Topics include an introduction to the 8514/A and its architecture, a discussion on programming to the applications interface specification, a complete section on programming the hardware, and more. A sample source code and programs are available on the optional disk in MS-DOS format.

Book/Disk (MS-DOS)	Item #103-2	$39.95
Book only	Item #086-9	$29.95

1-800-533-4372 (in CA 1-800-356-2002)

ORDER FORM

To Order:

Return this form with your payment to M&T books, 501 Galveston Drive, Redwood City, CA 94063 or **call toll-free 1-800-533-4372 (in California, call 1-800-356-2002).**

ITEM #	DESCRIPTION	DISK	PRICE

Subtotal	
CA residents add sales tax ____%	
Add $3.50 per item for shipping and handling	
TOTAL	

Charge my:

❏ **Visa**
❏ **MasterCard**
❏ **AmExpress**

❏ **Check enclosed, payable to M&T Books.**

CARD NO. _____

SIGNATURE _____ EXP. DATE _____

NAME _____

ADDRESS _____

CITY _____

STATE _____ ZIP _____

M&T GUARANTEE: If your are not satisfied with your order for any reason, return it to us within 25 days of receipt for a full refund. Note: Refunds on disks apply only when returned with book within guarantee period. Disks damaged in transit or defective will be promptly replaced, but cannot be exchanged for a disk from a different title.